"The federal government has been dependent on the nonprofit sector to provide human service delivery for decades. This relationship or transactional activity has become a complicated proposition for policymakers, taxpayers, and service providers at the state and local levels, as the funding for health and human services continued to grow despite economic declines. This book lays out the challenges and opportunities to better understand how to assess human services delivery and judge the appropriate rate of return on public investment for good and services delivered. This text should be required in all fiscal management courses for human service professionals."

—David Rudder, Springfield College, USA

"Co-editors Robert Shick and Lawrence Martin have made a seminal contribution to the literature on human services contracting in terms of its history, current state, and future evolution. The range of innovative contracting policy and practice examples utilized by various chapter authors is national (e.g., Colorado, Kansas, Massachusetts, Michigan, New York, Ohio, Oklahoma, and Utah), as well as international (e.g., Canada and the Netherlands) in scope. Moreover, in-depth case examples of contracting for specialized human services such as child welfare, mental health, and work force development services, helps to make the challenges and rewards of contracting accessible, informative, and thought-provoking."

—Karun K. Singh, Rutgers University, USA

Human Services Contracting

In the last 35 years, governments around the globe have increasingly sought out and agreed to contracts with nonprofit and for-profit entities designed to provide a portion of the public sector's portfolio of goods and services. This trend can be traced to a variety of factors, including perceived or actual economic efficiencies in outsourcing goods and services, values concerning the role and size of government in society, and the financial and organizational constraints of many government entities. In the United States, child welfare services adopted a pro-contracting approach early, and a variety of other human services have followed suit, including mental health care, job training, homeless services and others. Although there is strong evidence to suggest that human service contracting is growing over time, scholarship continues to lag on topics related to human service contract management, policy implementation and innovation, performance-based contracting and evaluation.

This new volume in the Public Solutions Handbook series is the first volume-length treatment of human services contracting issues, integrating both policy and practice, and exploring a broad range of issues that includes the fields of history, growth, innovations, results and outcomes, best practices and the future of government human service contracting. Chapters examine specific human service contracts, both in the U.S. and abroad, geared to practitioners in the public sector—from local government service contractors to municipal employees—as well as MPA students and those enrolled in courses on intergovernmental relations and nonprofit management.

Robert A. Shick is an Adjunct Assistant Professor at John Jay College for Criminal Justice and an Affiliated Faculty member at Rutgers-Newark School of Public Affairs and Administration (SPAA). At SPAA, Dr. Shick was the Director of the Executive Master's in Public Administration Program. Dr. Shick has extensive experience as a senior manager in New York City government in the contracting of government services. He is the editor of *Government Contracting*, (Routledge, 2015), a volume that provides a foundation for all aspects of government contracting. Dr. Shick served on the Editorial Board of the *Journal for Health and Human Services Administration* for 15 years, until December 31, 2018.

Lawrence L. Martin is Professor of Public Affairs at the University of Central Florida, USA. Dr. Martin also taught at the Columbia University School of Social Work, where he directed the specialization in social work administration. He has published 42 books and major monographs and more than 100 professional articles and book chapters.

THE PUBLIC SOLUTIONS HANDBOOK SERIES

MARC HOLZER, SERIES EDITOR

MUNICIPAL SHARED SERVICES
A Public Solutions Handbook
Alexander C. Henderson, Editor

E-GOVERNMENT AND WEBSITES
A Public Solutions Handbook
Aroon Manoharan, Editor

MANAGING THE NEXT GENERATION OF PUBLIC WORKERS
A Public Solutions Handbook
Madinah F. Hamidullah

PARTNERSHIP GOVERNANCE IN PUBLIC MANAGEMENT
A Public Solutions Handbook
Seth A. Grossman and Marc Holzer

INNOVATIONS IN THE PUBLIC AND NONPROFIT SECTORS
A Public Solutions Handbook
Patria de Lancer Julnes and Ed Gibson, Editors

GOVERNMENT CONTRACTING
A Public Solutions Handbook
Robert A. Shick, Editor

PROBLEM SOLVING WITH THE PRIVATE SECTOR
A Public Solutions Handbook
Daniel Bromberg, Editor

HUMAN SERVICES CONTRACTING
A Public Solutions Handbook
Robert A. Shick and Lawrence L. Martin, Editors

THE PUBLIC SOLUTIONS HANDBOOK SERIES

MARC HOLZER, SERIES EDITOR

Human Services Contracting

A PUBLIC SOLUTIONS HANDBOOK

Edited by

Robert A. Shick and Lawrence L. Martin

Routledge
Taylor & Francis Group
NEW YORK AND LONDON

First published 2020
by Routledge
52 Vanderbilt Avenue, New York, NY 10017

and by Routledge
2 Park Square, Milton Park, Abingdon, Oxon, OX14 4RN

Routledge is an imprint of the Taylor & Francis Group, an informa business

Library of Congress Cataloging-in-Publication Data
A catalog record for this book has been requested

ISBN: 978-1-138-49801-3 (hbk)
ISBN: 978-1-138-49802-0 (pbk)
ISBN: 978-1-351-01723-7 (ebk)

Typeset in Times
by Apex CoVantage, LLC

Contents

Tables

Series Editor's Introduction

I am pleased to introduce the eighth volume in the *Public Solutions Handbook Series: Human Services Contracting*, edited by Robert A. Shick and Lawrence L. Martin. This volume addresses a particularly important area for provision of essential services. Human service partnerships encompass a broad range of services principally funded by state and local governments, including childcare, mental health, employment training, and similar investments in society's most important resources—people. Human service contracting has grown significantly over the years as government has identified an increasing number of services that vulnerable citizens cannot secure on their own due to inadequate financial resources, or has recognized unmet needs for services that meet broader societal goals.

Chapters in this volume cover the major issues in human services contracting: the type of contracts used; the move from reimbursement to pay-for-performance contracts; human service contracting in childcare, mental health, and employment training; a case study of human services contracting in New York City; human service contracting in the Netherlands and Canada; and the future of human service contracting.

The authors present particularly important information and insights. On a granular level, they provide analyses of the challenges that human service contracting presents in different service areas, the impact of using different contracting arrangements, and the relationship between government and its contractors. They offer insights into the future of such contracting. Contributing authors are both academicians and practitioners, and together they have contributed a balanced, significant and important blend of scholarly expertise and practical insights for the field.

Each volume in the series incorporates case-based research. Each volume draws helpful insights and guidelines from academe, government and foundation sources, focusing on an emerging opportunity or issue in the field. Each volume contributes to the literature, offers a clearly written resource for relevant coursework, and enables practitioners to access and apply evidence-based insights.

Marc Holzer

Introduction

Robert A. Shick and Lawrence L. Martin

To the best of our knowledge, this is the only book on human services contracting to be published in the United States in the last 20 years. This is somewhat surprising considering the importance of human service contracting. Contracting is the major mode of publicly funded human service delivery in the U.S. today and has been for several decades now. The dollar value of human service contracts today totals some $100 billion annually (Urban Institute, 2018).

Human services contracting policy and practice has changed and evolved over the last several decades. Changing times have led to different responses to policy questions. How does contracting fit into the overall human service system? How should human service contracting be structured, as a market model or a partnership model? Changing times have also led to different responses to practice questions. What procurement strategies are best suited to human service contracting? What types of contracts are most appropriate? Human service contracting has been, and continues to be, in a constant state of flux depending upon national trends, government policies and place sensitivity priorities. The goal of this book is to promote an understanding of where human services contracting has been, where it is now and where it might be headed.

Before proceeding further, it is necessary to define what we mean by "human service contracting." Federal departments and agencies utilize *contracts*, *grants* and *cooperative agreements* for both human services and non-human services (*Federal Grant & Cooperative Agreement Act of 1977* (Public Law 95–224). State and local governments make use of *grants* and *contracts* in human service contracting but often employ different terms to describe them (*contracting out*, *outsourcing*, *privatization*). Over the years, human service contracting has gone by a variety of names, including *purchase-of-service* and *purchase of service contracting (POSC)*. In other countries, human service contracting goes by still other names, such as *transfer payments* and *appropriations*. For the purposes of this book, we define "human service contracting" as any relationship where a government provides public funds to another government, nonprofit or for-profit to provide human services regardless of the terminology employed to describe the relationship.

CONTRIBUTORS TO THIS BOOK

In developing this book, a conscious attempt was made to involve individuals who would approach the subject matter of human services contracting from different perspectives. Human services contracting can be viewed through several different lenses: social work, social services, public administration, public procurement, the federal government, state and local government, academics and practitioners. These perspectives are all represented in this book. Just as human service contracting has been known by different names at different times and in different places, the chapter authors sometimes utilize different terms to describe human service contracting depending upon their own perspectives. As one might expect, a social worker may not view and describe human service contracting the same way that a local government procurement administrator does. Nonprofit contractors may also see human service contracting differently than state and local government administrators. The reader is asked to consider, are the authors of the chapters in this book saying different things or are they saying the same things differently?

FOUNDATION CHAPTERS

Chapters 1, 2 and 3 are foundation chapters. The major objective of these chapters is to ground the reader in the history of human service contracting including the identification of the national trends that helped shape its policies and practices. A secondary objective is to introduce and define the terms that the reader will encounter throughout the other chapters. Keeping in mind that this book was written not just for academics but for practitioners and students as well, each chapter concludes with a section entitled Key Points where the authors distill their research and findings into a few salient take away points.

Chapter 1—A Brief History of Human Service Contracting

This chapter by Robert Shick and Lawrence Martin chronicles the history of human service contracting from its modern inception in the 1960s up to the present day. The authors identify four major periods in the history and evolution of human service contracting and discuss how national trends and government priorities helped shape both the policy context and the contracting practices of each period.

Chapter 2—Performance-Based Contracting (PBC)

Chapter 2 by Lawrence Martin is a follow-on to Chapter 1. This chapter further develops the policies and practices of what Chapter 1 identifies as the "performance period" of human service contracting. The chapter identifies the origins of the performance measurement (output, quality and outcome) movement and how it affected human service contracting. The chapter chronicles how the linking of performance measures to contractor compensation resulted in a new approach (performance-based contracting [PBC]) to human services contracting.

Chapter 3—Pay-for-Success Contracting

Chapter 3 by Tamara Dimitrijevska-Markoski and Lawrence Martin is a follow-on to Chapter 2 and completes the foundation trilogy chapters. This chapter demonstrates how pay-for-success strategies have taken performance-based contracting (PBC) to the next level. Social impact bonds, the most complex of the pay-for-success strategies, are discussed at length and contrasted with PBC. With the discussion of social impact bonds, the history of human service contracting is brought up-to-date.

CONTRACTING FOR SPECIALIZED HUMAN SERVICES

Chapters 4, 5, 6 and 7 deal with contracting for specialized human services, including child welfare, mental health and workforce development. This set of chapters departs from discussing human service contracting in general and instead explores the history, the how and the why of contracting for these three specialized human services. The four chapters cover a cross section of human services and have the added advantage of representing a significant proportion of human service contracting.

Chapter 4—Contracting for Child Welfare Services

This chapter by Crystal Collins-Camargo and Bowen McBeath takes a comprehensive look at human service contracting for child welfare services. The authors provide a brief history of child welfare contracting and then proceed to identify lessons learned from their combined research efforts carried out over several years. The authors devote a considerable amount of attention to recommendations on how to improve the practice of human service contracting for child welfare services.

Chapter 5—Contracting for Mental Health Services

Chapter 5 by Melissa Hirschi and Sara S. Bachman covers a broad range of issues in mental health services contracting, from its history to lessons learned. The chapter reviews each of these issues in considerable detail, each of which is very well documented. The authors focus particular attention on the different types of financing and reimbursement systems that have been employed in mental health services contracting and how mental health services can be integrated with other human services. The authors point out that very little is known about the outcomes of the services provided to mental health clients and how to structure contracts to achieve desired outcomes.

Chapter 6—Contracting for Employment and Training Programs

In Chapter 6, Burt S. Barnow and Shayne Spaulding review arguments for and against contracting out employment and training services. The bulk of the chapter is an extensive review of each of the federal legislated programs from 1933 to the Workforce Innovation and Opportunity Act of 2014. The authors describe the philosophy and the elements underpinning each of these programs, their goals and the results achieved. In the lessons learned section, the authors integrate program and contracting observations and provide recommendations to guide the design of employment and training programs in the future.

Chapter 7—Contracting for Human Services in New York City

Contracting for specialized human services takes place within general government procurement policies and practices that are not service specific. This chapter by James Krauskopf looks at the multifaceted human service contracting history, policies and practices of New York City. With a total annual budget of around $6 billion, the city of New York has one of the largest human service contracting systems in the U.S. This chapter details how the city of New York manages its contracts for a variety of specialized human services within the broader context of the city's standardized procurement policies and procedures.

CONTRACTING FOR HUMAN SERVICES IN OTHER COUNTRIES

Two chapters comprise this section. Chapter 8 deals with human service contracting in Ontario, Canada. Chapter 9 provides an overview of human service contracting in the Netherlands. Whereas the two chapters deal with different human services systems and use different terminologies to describe them, they identify similar issues and challenges raised in the earlier chapters of this book that appear to transcend national borders.

Chapter 8—Contracting for Children and Youth Mental Health Services in Ontario, Canada, Using a Modified Lead Agency Approach

This chapter by Rosemary Vito takes an in-depth look at an unusual approach to implementing the "lead agency" approach to human service contracting. In the lead agency model, the government contracts with one prime contractor (the lead agency) to coordinate human services delivery in a defined geographical area. The lead agency then sub-contracts with other human service agencies to provide direct services. In the case of Ontario, Canada, the government designated several lead agencies but maintained contract administration responsibilities. This "modified" lead agency approach represents an interesting experiment with implications for human service delivery in the U.S. Can lead agencies succeed in coordinating human service delivery when they lack contracting authority?

Chapter 9—Results-Based Funding for Youth Care in the Netherlands: From Conditions and Challenges to the Outlines of a System

This chapter by M. S. de Vries looks at human service contracting in the Netherlands. The Netherlands made significant changes to its human service delivery system by decentralizing contracting from the national government to regional governments while simultaneously changing to a pay-for-performance approach. The author draws several conclusions about these changes and makes observations and recommendations that have implications for human service contracting in the U.S.

THE FUTURE OF HUMAN SERVICE CONTRACTING

This concluding chapter takes a look at how human service contracting has developed over the last 50 years and speculates how it might develop in the future.

Chapter 10—Where Has Human Services Contracting Been and Where Is It Going?

This chapter by Robert A. Shick and Lawrence Martin provides a summary of the previous chapters within a framework of discussing where human service contracting has been and where it might be going. The authors speculate about how human service contracting may evolve and change going forward.

REFERENCE

Urban Institute. (2018). *Human service government non-profit contracting*. Retrieved from www.urban.org/policy-centers/center-nonprofits-and-philanthropy/projects/human-service-nonprofit-government-contracting

Part 1

Foundation Chapters

1

A Brief History of Human Service Contracting

Robert A. Shick and Lawrence L. Martin

INTRODUCTION

This chapter briefly chronicles the history of human service contracting. The frame of reference used is that of the federally designated state human service agencies. These 50 state agencies originally administered the "social services titles" of the *Social Security Act* and today administer the federal *Social Services Block Grant*. Adopting this frame of reference makes it possible to place human service contracting in its historical context and to identify how it has changed and evolved over time. Any attempt to put dates on historical events must necessarily be somewhat arbitrary. The events and the timeframes discussed herein are not representative of all human service contracting at any point in time. The intent of this chapter is to identify the major themes that played out broadly on the national scene.

Human service contracting has been around for a long time. Its origins can be traced back to the Colonial era (Kamerman & Kahn, 1998). Paupers, both children and adults, were frequently "farmed out" by governments to local individuals who were paid an agreed upon sum of money for their care. If the pauper was able bodied, the agreement (the contract) frequently called for the pauper to be instructed in a useful trade (Kahn, 1978; Gibelman & Demone, 1989).

The modern era of human service contracting dates from the 1960s. Four periods can be identified: (1) the *formative period* from the mid-1960s to the end of the 1970s, (2) the *maturation period* comprising the decade of the 1980s; (3) the *performance period* from the 1990s to roughly 2005 and (4) the *pay-for-results period* that stretches from 2005 to the present day. In the sections that follow, the human service policy context of each period is discussed and how the policy context shaped human service contracting.

THE FORMATIVE PERIOD (1960S–1979)

Prior to the 1960s, two separate human service systems existed, one public and one private. Little interaction took place between the two systems. Governments raised revenue from taxes and other sources and directly provided human services to *public* clients. Private nonprofit organizations raised revenues from donations and other sources and provided human services to their *private* clients (Martin & Frahm, 2010). Federal policy initiatives beginning in the 1960s merged these two previously independent systems into one interdependent public/private human service system where government provided the funding and the private sector, primarily the nonprofit sector, provided the service. Much of the literature (e.g., Wedel, 1973, 1976; Kahn, 1978; Fisk, Kiesling, & Muller, 1978; Mueller, 1978; Kettner & Martin, 1983) during this formative period used the terms "purchase of service" and "purchase of service contracting" rather than human service contracting.

Policy Context

Several major federal policy changes during the 1960s contributed to uniting the public and private human service systems through the mechanism of contracting.

The *Demonstration (Model Cities) Act of 1966*, the *Economic Opportunity Act of 1964*, the *Community Mental Health Centers Act of 1963* Act and the 1962 and 1967 amendments to the social service titles of the *Social Security Act* allowed state human service agencies for the first time to use federal funds when contracting with nonprofit organizations and for-profit businesses. Prior to these changes, state human service agencies could only use federal funds in contracts with other government agencies.

The amendments to the social services titles of the *Social Security Act* mandated that states provide child day and other supportive services to welfare recipients enrolled in the work incentive (WIN) program. States had the option of either directly providing these services or contracting for them. The amendments included provisions for "open-ended" federal appropriations. Consequently, the amount of federal funding available to states for human services was essentially unlimited! The amendments did contain cost-sharing requirements. State human service agencies were required to cover 25% of the cost of providing human services; the federal government would pay the remaining 75%. However, the amendments allowed state human service agencies to use "donated funds" to satisfy the 25% cost sharing requirements. The donated funds could come from other state agencies, local governments and in some instances private sources (e.g., the United Way).

The expansion of contracting options combined with "open-ended" federal funding and the ability to use donated funds to satisfy federal matching requirements enabled state human service agencies to significantly increase the types and amounts of human services they provided, frequently at *no cost* to themselves. The increasing importance that contracting played during this period was acknowledged by the convening of the first "National Institute on Purchase of Service Contracting" held in 1978 (Wedel, Katz, & Weick, 1978).

Contracting Context

In the 1960s, most state human service agencies, as well as their contractors, had little experience with contract service delivery (Demone & Gibelman, 1989). Consequently, financial accountability was the primary concern of state human service agencies (Elkin, 1985). Cost reimbursement contracting was the preferred method. State human service agencies and their contractors mutually agreed to detailed budgets. Only those expenditures in keeping with the mutually agreed upon budgets were allowable. State human service agencies conducted frequent audits of their contractors to ensure the proper use of federal funds.

Human service contract administration was in its infancy during this period. Contract service requirements were basic. Contract monitoring was sporadic at best (Gurin & Friedman, 1980; Kettner & Martin, 1985). Programmatic concerns (efficiency, quality, effectiveness, equity, etc.) were of secondary importance (Austin, 2002). The American Public Welfare Association (APWA) noted at the time that the focus on financial accountability resulted in a "relatively weaker focus on quality, adequacy and effects of services" (Slack, 1979, p. 30).

Summary

To summarize, during the formative period:

- Contracting resulted in two previously separate human service systems (one public, one private) being combined into one interdependent public/private human service system.
- Contracting and the use of donated funds enabled state human service agencies to increase the types and amounts of services provided.
- Contract administration was primarily concerned with financial accountability.
- Cost reimbursement was the preferred method of contracting.

THE MATURATION PERIOD (1980–1990)

By the beginning of the 1980s, contracting was ***the*** major mode of human service delivery nationally (Benton, Field, & Millar, 1978). A consequence of creating one interdependent public/private human service system was that contractors had become dependent on government contracts to fund their basic operations and state human service agencies had become dependent on their contractors for the delivery of mandated human services.

The creation of an interdependent public/private human service delivery system left many policy and administrative questions unanswered. One of the more pressing unanswered questions involved the exact nature of the human service contracting relationship. Many state human service agencies saw their contractors as interchangeable *vendors* or *suppliers* (Hatry & Durman, 1985). Most contractors saw themselves as *partners*, preferably in long-term relationships with state human service agencies (Gibelman & Demone, 1983). The maturation period of human service contracting began a process of attempting to sort out these and other issues.

The sorting out process included dealing with the two dueling paradigms of human service contracting that had been around since the 1960s, the *market model* and the *partnership model* (Kettner & Martin, 1990). The market model posited that competition between contractors should be encouraged as a method of improving human services while driving down costs. The partnerships model posited that the strengths of government and the private sector should be combined in long term stable contracting relationships that lead to better human services (Hatry & Durman, 1985; Gibelman & Demone, 1983; Kettner & Martin,1989, 1990).

Policy Context

Much of the human service literature of the 1980s focused on "privatization." This literature was primarily negative. Privatization, applied to human service contracting, was admonished for eroding the administrative state and for the de-institutionalization of social welfare among other concerns. A great deal of this criticism was unwarranted because contracting had become the major mode of human service delivery before privatization existed as a defined public policy (Martin, 2004). In other respects, some criticism was warranted owing to the fact contracting was initiated and expanded primarily for creative financing purposes and not as a method of improving the efficiency, quality and effectiveness of human services.

The original social service titles of the *Social Security Act* were replaced in the later part of the 1970s by the *Title XX program.* The Title XX program also brought an end to "open-ended" federal funding for human services. During the 1980s, the Title XX program was itself replaced by the *Social Services Block Grant* (SSBG). The SSBG became the major federal funding source for human services. As a block grant, the SSBG gave increased flexibility to state human service agencies, but also reduced overall federal funding (Carter, 1983).

Contracting Context

By the decade of the 1980s, state human service agencies had created major contracting human service programs. Now they had to manage them. Federal funding for human service program was no longer expanding. State human service agencies had to consider such programmatic issues as the efficiency and quality of their contracted services (Kettner & Martin, 1989). State human service agencies began developing standard operating procedures for contracting. The use of requests for proposals (RFPs) became the procurement tool of choice. Standardized contract formats and procedures became the norm (e.g., University of Texas, 1986; Kettner & Martin, 1987). Human service contracting began to function more like mainstream public procurement.

Efficiency Considerations

Efficiency considerations initially took the form of "unit-of-service" contracting. A unit of service is a measure of the amount of service or product provided by a human service program (Table 1.1).

Table 1.1

Units of Service

Counseling	One hour
Information and referral	One referral
Transportation	One trip
Home delivered meals	One meal
Job placement	One

Unit-of-service contracting enabled state human service agencies to "purchase" specific amounts of services at predetermined prices. State human service agencies expended considerable time and effort searching for the best units of service (Bowers & Bowers, 1976) and the best methodologies for computing unit-of-service costs (e.g., Elkin, 1985).

Quality Considerations

The 1980s was the decade of "quality management" (Deming, 1986; Crosby, 1985). Concerns about the quality of contract human services were raised, particularly the quality of human services provided by for-profit contractors. By the mid-1980s, for-profit contractors were the recipients of nearly a quarter of all state human service contracts (Table 1.2).

The more use made of for-profit contractors, the more the human service literature raised quality concerns (Gurin & Friedman, 1980). Hatry and Durman (1985) summarized the sentiment of the time:

> The greatest obstacle to use of for-profit firms is the fear that thy will not deliver the appropriate quality of service and that in order to make a profit, they will not give adequate service, especially to more difficult and needy clients.
>
> (p. 11)

A study of state human service agency administrators conducted in 1986 addressed the issue of contract quality. Administrators evaluated the quality of services provided by their government, nonprofit and for-profit contractors (Table 1.3). The study reported that for-profit contractors scored slightly higher then government contractors, but lower than nonprofit contractors. However, differences in the scores were not statistically significant.

Outcome Considerations

Gurin and Friedman (1980) suggested another reason for the concern with the quality of human service contract delivery, the difficulty in developing outcome measures.

Table 1.2

Percentage of All Human Service Contractors by Type (1986)

Government	20.0%
Nonprofit	57.1%
For profit	22.9%

Source: Adapted from: Martin (1986)

Table 1.3

Quality Scores for Contracted Human Services by Type of Contractor*

	All states	Top sevens states using for-profits	Other states
Government	4.45 (n = 40)	4.50 (n = 6)	4.41 (n = 34)
Nonprofit	4.61 (n = 41)	4.83 (n = 6)	4.54 (n = 35)
For profit	4.53 (n = 40)	4.57 (n = 7)	4.52 (n = 33)

(n) = the number of states reporting

* scores = means on a five-point scale

Source: Kettner and Martin (1988)

Outcome measures and their potential use in contracting began receiving increased attention in the late 1970s (Millar, Hatry, & Koss, 1977a, 1977b; Schainblatt, 1977). Some state human service agencies began experimenting with requiring contractors to report client outcome data (Carter, 1983; Millar & Millar, 1981). However, the widespread use of outcomes in human service contracting is a phenomenon that had to wait until 1990s.

Summary

To summarize, during the maturation period of human service contracting (1980s):

- Improving the management of the human service contracting became a priority.
- The use of requests for proposals (RFPs) and standardized contracts became the norm.
- Many state human service agencies adopted unit-of-service contracting.
- Financial accountability was supplemented with concerns about programmatic accountability (efficiency, quality and effectiveness), where.

THE PERFORMANCE PERIOD (1990–2005)

A study of state human service agencies in 1990 provides a snapshot of the status of human service contracting at the time. The study looked at the contracting priorities of ten state human service agencies across five human service areas (residential treatment, alcohol-drug-mental health services, employment and training, child day care and specialized transportation) (Kettner & Martin, 1993). The study reported that "funding and fiscal considerations" continued to be the most important factor in contracting decisions. However, the second most important factor was "client outcome" considerations. Human service contracting from the 1990s to the present day is a history of the increasing important of "performance" and a focus on the use of efficiency (output) and effectiveness (outcome) measures.

Policy Context

Several factors account for the increasing important of effectiveness (outcome) considerations in government programs and in human service contracting during this period. The year 1993 proved to be a watershed moment. Osborn and Gaebler (1993) published their highly influence book *Reinventing Government.* Osborn and Gaebler argued persuasively, "what gets measured gets done" (p. 146). In the same year, 1993, two government actions mirrored Osborn and Gaebler's recommendations. The federal *Government Performance & Results Act of 1993* (GPRA, 1993), passed by Congress, required all federal departments and agencies to annual report on the performance of their programs with a special emphasis on "outcomes." Likewise, in 1993, the Governmental Accounting Standards Board (GASB, 1993) issued guidance on its "service efforts and accomplishment" (SEA) reporting initiative. SEA reporting encouraged state and local governments to collect and report data on the outputs, quality and outcomes of their programs.

Contracting Context

The combination of Osborn and Gaebler, GPRA and GASB's SEA reporting initiative resulted in state human service agencies rethinking how they contracted. A 1994 study looked at the contract performance expectations of state human service agencies (Table 1.4).

The study found that financial considerations continued to be important with 67.3% of respondents stating that "staying within budget" was an important contract expectation. However, a shift in perspective towards performance considerations was discernable. Nearly two-thirds of respondents identified output and quality as important contracting expectations and over 40% identified the achievement of client outcomes.

Along with the importance of performance as a contracting expectation came a contractor complaint that state human service agencies were not paying the full cost of care (Kettner & Martin, 1996). Contractors, long used to recovering all their costs under cost

Table 1.4

Human Service Contracting Expectations

	% of response
- Stay within budget	67.3
- Provide units of service (outputs)	71.3
- Provide quality services	73.3
- Achieve client outcomes	44.6

Source: Adapted from Kettner and Martin (1994)

reimbursement contracts, were beginning to discover a different reality when payment was tied to performance, no performance no payment. Studies conducted in the later part of the 1990s indicated that many state human service agencies were using various approaches to performance contracting. For example, the General Accounting Office (GAO, 1997) identified 15 states that were experimenting with performance contracting for child support enforcement services. The Child Welfare League of American estimated that as many as 25 states were experimenting with performance contracting in child welfare (cited in Eggers, 1997).

Summary

To summarize, during the performance period of human service contracting:

- The policy context for government in general shifted towards performance and performance measurement.
- Human service contracting maintained its financial focus but also began requiring contractors to report performance in terms of efficiency (output), quality and effectiveness (outcome).
- Some experimentation began with replacing cost reimbursement contracts with performance-based contracts.

THE PAY-FOR-RESULTS PERIOD (2005–PRESENT DAY)

Human service contracting today remains as popular and important as it was in the 1960s. Government contracts are a major source of revenue for most nonprofit human service agencies. According to a recent Urban Institute study, nonprofit organizations nationally are recipients of some 200,000 government contracts and grants annually (Pettijohn & Boris, 2013).

In the human services, the achievement of client outcomes has become a primary policy objective (Magnabosco & Manderscheid, 2011). In human service contracting, performance and tying contractor payments to performance achievement, particularly outcomes is a major focus. This approach to human service contracting goes by many names including: performance-based contracting, pay-for-performance, pay-for-success, outcome funding, results based funding and social impact bonds. These contemporary approaches to human service contacting are deserving of more in-depth explorations. The following two chapters discuss performance-based contracting (PBC) and pay-for-success approaches.

KEY POINTS

- Human service contracting began as a pragmatic response by states to federal policy and funding encouragement.
- The widespread use of contracting has resulted in the creation of an inter-dependent public/private human service system.
- The history of human service contracting can be described as an ongoing attempt to sort out the relationships between state human service agencies and their contractors.
- Accountability in human service contracting has evolved from primarily a financial focus to more of a combined financial/performance focus.
- Human service contracting today is increasingly characterized by performance approaches (e.g., performance-based contracting, pay-for-success and others) that tie contractor compensation to performance.

REFERENCES

Austin, D. (2002). *Accountability in his human services management* (pp. 396–422). New York: Columbia University Press.

Benton, B., Field, T., & Millar, R. (1978). *Social services—federal legislation versus state implementation*. Washington, DC: Urban Institute.

Bowers, C., & Bowers, M. (1976). *The elusive unit of service*. Washington, DC: Project SHARE, Office of the Secretary, U. S. Department of Health, Education and Welfare.

Carter, R. (1983). *The accountable agency*. Newbury Park, CA: Sage Publications.

Crosby, P. (1985). *Quality without tears: The art of hassle free management*. New York: Plum.

Deming, W. (1986). *Out of the crisis*. Cambridge, MA: MIT Center for Advanced Engineering Studies.

Demone, H., & Gibelman, M. (1989). *Services for sale: Purchasing health and human services*. New Brunswick, NJ: Rutgers University Press.

Eggers, W. (1997). *Performance-based contracting: How to guide no 17*. Los Angeles, CA: The Reason Foundation.

Elkin, R. (1985). Paying the piper and calling the tune: Accountability in the human services. *Administration in Social Work, 9*, 1–13.

Fisk, D., Kiesling, H., & Muller, T. (1978). *Private provision of public services: An overview*. Washington, DC: Urban Institute.

General Accounting Office (GAO). (1997). *Child support enforcement: Results on comparability of privatized and public offices*. Washington, DC: GAO.

Gibelman, M., & Demone, H. (1983). Purchase of service: Forging public-private partnerships in human services. *Urban & Social Change Review, 16*, 21–26.
Gibelman, M., & Demone, H. (1989). The evolving contract state. In H. Demone & M. Gibelman (Eds.), *Services for sale: Purchasing health and human services* (pp. 17–57). New Brunswick, NJ: Rutgers University Press.
Government Performance & Results Act (GPRA). (1993). Public Law No 103–62.
Governmental Accounting Standards Board (GASB). (1993). *Proposed statement of the governmental accounting standards board on concepts related to service efforts and accomplishments reporting.* Norwalk, CT: Author.
Gurin, A., & Friedman, B. (1980). *Contracting for services as a mechanism for delivery of human services.* Waltham, MA: Florence Heller Graduate School for Advanced Studies in Social Welfare, Brandeis University.
Hatry, H., & Durman, E. (1985). *Issues in competitive contracting for social services.* Falls Church, VA: National Institute of Governmental Purchasing.
Kahn, A. (1978). The impact of purchase of service contracting on social service delivery. In K. Wedel, A. Katz, & A. Wick (Eds.), *Proceedings of the national institute on purchase of service contracting* (pp. 11–16). Lawrence: Social Work, University of Kansas.
Kamerman, S., & Kahn, A. (1998). *Privatization, contracting & reform of child and family social services.* Washington, DC: The Finance Project.
Kettner, P., & Martin, L. L. (1983). *Purchase of service contracting.* Newbury Park, CA: Sage Publications.
Kettner, P., & Martin, L. L. (1985). Issues in the development of monitoring systems for purchase of service contracting. *Administration in Social Work, 9*, 69–82.
Kettner, P., & Martin, L. L. (1987). *Purchase of service contracting.* Newbury Park, CA: Sage Publications.
Kettner, P., & Martin, L. L. (1988). Purchase of service contracting with for-profit organizations. *Administration in Social Work, 12*, 47–60.
Kettner, P., & Martin, L. L. (1989). Making decisions about purchase of service contracting. In H. Demone & M. Gibelman (Eds.), *Services for sale* (pp. 187–199). New Brunswick, NJ: Rutgers University Press.
Kettner, P., & Martin, L. L. (1990). Purchase of service contracting: Two models. *Administration in Social Work, 14*(1), 15–30.
Kettner, P., & Martin, L. L. (1993). Purchase of service contracting in the 1990s: Have expectations been met? *Journal of Sociology & Social Welfare, 20*, 89–103.
Kettner, P., & Martin, L. L. (1994, Summer). Purchase of service at 20: Are we using it well? *Public Welfare*, 14–20.
Kettner, P., & Martin, L. L. (1996). The impact of declining resources and purchase of service contracting on private non-profit agencies. *Administration in Social Work, 20*, 21–38.
Magnabosco, J., & Manderscheid, R. (2011). *Outcomes measurement in the human services* (2nd ed.). Washington, DC: National Association of Social Workers.
Martin, L. L. (1986). *Purchase of service contracting for human services: An analysis of state decision making* (Dissertation), Arizona State University.
Martin, L. L. (2004). The privatization of human services: Myths, civil society & social capital. *Journal of Health & Human Services Administration, 27*(2), 175–193.
Martin, L. L., & Frahm, K. (2010). The changing nature of accountability in administrative practices. *Journal of Sociology & Social Welfare, 27*(1), 137–148.
Millar, A., Hatry, H., & Koss, M. (1977a). *Monitoring the outcomes of social services, volume I: Preliminary suggestions.* Washington, DC: Urban Institute.
Millar, A., Hatry, H., & Koss, M. (1977b). *Monitoring the outcomes of social services, volume II: A review of past research and attest activities.* Washington, DC: Urban Institute.

Millar, R., & Millar, A. (1981). *Developing client outcome monitoring systems*. Washington, DC: Urban Institute.

Mueller, C. (1978). Purchase of service from the viewpoint of the provider. In K. Wedel (Ed.), *Proceedings of the national institute on purchase of service contracting*. Lawrence: University of Kansas, School of Social Work.

Osborn, D., & Gaebler, T. (1993). *Reinventing government*. Reading, MA: Addison-Wesley Publishing Company.

Pettijohn, S., & Boris, E. (2013). *Contracts and grants between nonprofits and governments*. Washington, DC: Urban Institute. Retrieved from www.urban.org/research/publication/contracts-and-grants-between-nonprofits-and-government

Schainblatt, A. (1977). *Monitoring the outcomes of state mental health treatment programs: Some initial suggestions*. Washington, DC: Urban Institute.

Slack, I. J. (1979). *Title XX at the crossroads*. Washington, DC: American Public Welfare Association.

University of Texas, Lyndon B. John School of Public Affairs. (1986). *Contracting selected state government functions: Issues and next steps*. Austin, TX: Author.

Wedel, K. (1973). *Government contracting for social services: Purchase of service in state's public assistance programs* (Dissertation), University of Pittsburg.

Wedel, K. (1976). Government contacting for purchase of service. *Social Work*, *21*, 101–105.

Wedel, K., Katz, A., & Weick, A. (1978). *Proceedings of the national institute on purchase of service contracting*. Lawrence: University of Kansas, School of Social Welfare.

2

Performance-Based Contracting (PBC)

Lawrence L. Martin

INTRODUCTION

As Chapter 1 pointed out, from the beginnings of human service contracting, government agencies were primarily concerned with financial issues. Holding contractors financially accountable was a priority. Financial accountability continues to be an overriding concern today, but programmatic issues (efficiency, quality and effectiveness) have become increasingly important. Using the "expanded systems model" as a conceptual framework (Kettner, Moroney, & Martin, 1990, 2017), Table 2.1 graphically illustrates the evolution of accountability in human service contracting from inputs and process to outputs, quality and outcomes.

In the language of public procurement, governments attempt to ensure contractor accountability through two types of contract specifications: *design specifications* and *performance specifications* (NASPO, 2015). Design specifications deal with the inputs and process of human service delivery. Performance specifications deal with efficiency (output), quality and effectiveness (outcome). Design specifications tell contractors how to provide a human service. Performance specifications tell contractors the expectations of a human service, while giving them more flexibility over how the service is designed (inputs) and delivered (process). Performance-based contracting (PBC) derives its name from the focus and use of performance specifications.

DEFINITION OF PERFORMANCE-BASED CONTRACTING (PBC)

No universally agreed upon definition of performance-based contracting (PBC) exits. However, the National Institute of Governmental Purchasing (NIGP, 2012) provides a definition frequently used in human service contracting:

> A performance—based contract is a results oriented contracting method that focuses on the outputs, quality and outcomes of service provision and may tie a portion or all of a contractor's compensation as well as contact extension or renewals to their accomplishment.

Table 2.1

The Systems Model and Human Service Contracting

Inputs →	Process →	Outputs →	Quality →	Outcomes
- Clients - Funding - Staff - Facilities - Other	- Service Delivery & Professional Standards	- Units of Service - Measures of Service Volume	- Timeliness - Reliability - Empathy - Accessibility	- Results - Accomplishments - Impacts
[. . . *Design Specifications* . . .]		[. . . *Performance Specifications* . . .]		

Table 2.2

Performance Measures Used in PBC for Job Training

Arizona Works Program PBC	
Performance measures	Type of measures
Job placements	Output
Highest and most appropriate jobs	Quality
Job placement for at least 890 days	Outcome

Oklahoma Performance-Based Milestone Contracting for Supportive Services

Design and performance measures	Type of measures	Fee ($450)
Determination of need	Process	10%
Vocational preparation	Process	10%
Job placement	Output	10%
Job training	Process	10%
Job retention	Process	15%
Job stabilization	Quality/outcome	20%
Case closed	Outcome	25%

Sources: Adapted from Martin (2002)

PBC is an "umbrella" term that covers a variety of contracting approaches. PBC works by including *performance measures* in human service contracts and tying contractor compensation to their accomplishment. The earliest uses of PBC were in job training programs under the federal *Job Training Partnerships Act of 1982*. Job training programs have generally accepted output (e.g., completion of training), quality (e.g., salary level, provision of health benefits) and outcome (e.g., placement in a job) performance measures. An example of some early PBC performance measures utilized in job training programs in the states of Arizona and Oklahoma are shown in Table 2.2.

The Arizona (Arizona DES, 2001) example uses relatively simple output, quality and outcome performance measures. The Oklahoma example is more complex. The Oklahoma example uses a mix of output, quality and outcome performance measures combined with some input and process measures. Compensation is tied to the accomplishment of both design and performance specifications. The Oklahoma example demonstrates the tying of contractor compensation (partially) to performance in keeping with the NIGP definition of PBC.

Today, PBC is used by many government human service agencies. PBC is the federal government's preferred method when contracting for services, including human services. The *Federal Acquisition Regulation* (FAR, 2017), which governs federal contracting, requires the use of PBC when contracting for services to the "maximum extent possible."

PBC VERSUS TRADITIONAL HUMAN SERVICE CONTRACTING

Table 2.3 highlights the differences between PBC and more traditional approaches to human service contracting.

Traditional human service contracting focuses on the design (inputs) and delivery (process) of human services by using design specifications. PBC focuses on the effects of human service delivery by using output, quality and outcome performance measures. In the absence of performance measures, traditional human service contracting uses cost reimbursement payment mechanisms. When output, quality and performance specifications are included in human service contracts, it becomes possible to tie contractor compensation to their accomplishment using unit-cost, fixed-cost and incentive payment mechanisms. Combining compensation and performance results in a performance-based (PBC) approach to accountability.

Table 2.3

PBC Versus Traditional Human Service Contracting

	Traditional human service contracting	Performance-based contracting (PBC)
Focus	The design and delivery of human services	The effects of human services delivery
System elements	Inputs and Process	Outputs, quality and outcome
Types of specifications	*Design*	*Performance*
Payment mechanism	Cost reimbursement	Unit-cost, fixed-cost and incentive
Accountability perspective	Financial	Performance
Principal-agent relationship	Unaligned	Aligned

Traditional human service contracting and PBC also differ in how they deal with the "principal-agent" problem. The principal-agent problem exists whenever an agent carries out a function or activity for a principal, such as when a contractor (the agent) provides a human service for a government agency (the principal). The principal-agent challenge is how to ensure that agents act in the best interests of the principals and not in their own best interests. In traditional human service contracting, the performance and financial expectations of the principal and the agent are unaligned. The financial and performance expectations of the government human service agency may not be the same as that of the contractor. For example, the government may be more concerned with efficiency (providing the greatest amount of service possible at the lowest possible cost). The contractor, may be more concerned with performance (providing better client outcomes), but at a higher cost. In PBC, tying compensation to performance attempts to ensure that the financial and performance expectations of both parties align. Both parties agree upfront on both the performance to be achieved and the costs of that performance operationalized as prices per unit of output, quality and outcome.

APPROACHES TO PERFORMANCE-BASED CONTRACTING (PBC)

There are numerous approaches to PBC. Three approaches frequently used in the human services are (1) the unit of service approach, (2) the milestone approach and (3) bonus approaches.

Unit of Service Approach to PBC

This approach ties contractor compensation (prices) to the accomplishment of specific output performance measures. Table 2.4 identifies some units of service commonly used in PBC. A performance-based contract might state that the contractor is to be paid a specific price for each meal provided (home delivered meals), each trip provided (specialized transportation service), each hour of service provided by a visiting nurse, each referral made by an information and

Table 2.4

Examples of Outputs Used in PBC

Type of human service	Output performance measure
Home delivered meals	One meal
Specialized transportation	One trip
Visiting nurse service	One visit
Counseling	One hour
Case management	One hour
Information and referral	One referral

The unit of service approach to PBC works best when readily understandable units of service are employed. For example, one hour, one visit and one referral are readily understandable, observable, easy to use and account for, monitor and invoice.

Milestone Approach to PBC

The milestone approach to PBC works by tying contractor compensation to specific activities (milestones). The milestone approach is essentially project management applied to human service contracting. In project management, there is a start date, progress benchmarks (milestones) and a completion date. Applied to human services contracting, the milestone approach to PBC assumes that participants enter a human service program, make progress towards some desired end state and eventually exit service. Contractor compensation is tied to the accomplishment of the identified milestones. The Oklahoma example shown in Table 3.1 is a milestone approach. In the Oklahoma PBC example, a participant begins (enters) a job training program, receives an assortment of job training and preparation services based on a determination of needs, and is placed in a job (exit). The contractor has agreed upfront to a price of $450 per participant served. The contractor earns a predetermined percentage of the $450 fee each time it accomplishes a specific milestone with a specific client (Oklahoma DRS, 2001).

Bonus Approaches to PBC

Bonus approaches to PBC work by rewarding human service contractors for superior performance over and above some predetermined level. Three examples of bonus approaches to PBC are: award fee, award term and benchmarking

Award Fee

Award fee approaches to PBC involve lump-sum monetary payment that human service contractors receive for exceeding agreed upon performance levels. Performance levels are specified up-front in the contracts and involve output, quality or outcome performance measures or any combination. Award fees are usually paid at the end of a contract when performance is documented.

Award Term

Award term approaches to PBC reward contractors for the achievement of specific levels of performance by extending existing contracts or awarding new contracts. The required levels of performance are specified in the original contracts. In the language of public procurement, award term approaches to PBC reward contractors for "past performance." Award term contracts enable human service agencies to continue serving as contractors without the necessity of going through additional procurement cycles with their inherent costs and uncertainty.

Benchmarking

Benchmarking approaches to PBC involving comparing a human service contractor's performance to some benchmark. The benchmark can be (1) the performance of another contractor providing the same or a similar human service, (2) the average performance of all contractors providing the same or similar services, (3) the performance of direct government delivery, (4) the performance of a contractor compared to its own past performance, or (5) some other benchmark. Contractor compensation can take the form of a lump-sum payment for exceeding the predetermined benchmark(s) or a proportional approach that relates compensation to increments (5%, 10%, . . .) of performance above the benchmark.

DOES PERFORMANCE-BASED CONTRACTING (PBC) PERFORM?

How does the performance of PBC compare to the performance of the traditional approach to human service contracting? Numerous studies and evaluations of PBC have been carried out over the years comparing PBC to the traditional approach for a variety of different human services across multiple localities (e.g., Florida, Minnesota, Pennsylvania, Oklahoma, Kansas, others). Most of these studies have found that tying compensation to performance does result in changing the behavior of contractors to focus more on performance (Martin, 2005).

A study of job placement services in Minnesota over three years reported an increase of some 240% after adopting PBC (Minnesota DHS, 2000). A study of PBC in Florida reported that 80% of contractors met or exceed all output, quality and outcome performance measures (Florida DCF, 2000). The Illinois Department of Children and Families increased its child permanency placements from 2,220 to 7,000 over a two-year period after adopting PBC (Martin, 2005). More recently, Desai, Garabedian and Snyder 2012) reported that New York City's welfare-to-work program reduced caseloads from a high of 121,00 in 2000 to a low of 75,438 in 2010 owing to the use of PBC. Likewise, a study of Indiana's vocational rehabilitation program reported that employment results increased and time to employment was reduced because of PBC (Lu, 2015).

PBC AND CONTRACTOR FINANCIAL RISK

When human service contractors fail to achieve agreed upon levels of performance, there is a negative effect on revenue. The traditional approach to human service contracting (cost reimbursement payment mechanisms) essentially holds contractors financially harmless for failure to perform. With PBC, no performance means no payment. Different approaches to PBC carry different levels of contractor financial risk (Martin, 2007). For example, PBC approaches that tie contractor compensation to outcome performance measures carry greater financial risk to human service contractors than PBC approaches that do not. An evaluation of an early PBC experiment in the state of Kansas carried out by the state legislature found that human service contractors experienced severe financial problems that pushed some to the brink of bankruptcy (State of Kansas, 2000). Many of the human service contractors in Kansas lacked the necessary cost accounting systems to determine the full costs of their services. Consequently, these contractors tended to underprice their services (Scott, 2002). A recent study finds that the cost of complying with and documenting the performance requirements of PBC has a significant financial effect on small human service agencies (Never & de Leon, 2017).

Several other financial risk issues arise when compensation is tied to performance.

First, human service contractors that rely on others (either the government or third parties) for participant eligibility determinations and referrals place themselves at significant financial risk. The performance of the human service contractor then becomes dependent upon the performance of the organization conducting the eligibility determinations and making the referrals. If this organization fails to satisfactorily perform it duties, then participant referrals may be insufficient to generate the revenues that the human service contractor needs to cover tis operating costs.

Second, the time lag between when contractors provide services and incur expenses and when they receive payments increases with PBC. This situation in particularly problematic when outcome performance measures are used. Some human service outcomes can take weeks, even months to accomplish. In these situations, the time lag can be extensive between when human service contractors incur costs and when they finally receive government payments.

Third, when contractor payments are tied to performance, the performance itself becomes auditable. Human service contractors must be able to document that billings submitted under performance-based contracts can be tied back to actual services provided to eligible participants. When performance cannot be verified by auditors, human service contractors may encounter audit exceptions, questioned costs and demands for repayment of monies (Martin, 2003).

FROM PBC TO PAY-FOR-SUCCESS

According to a recent Brookings Institute study, somewhere between 9% and 28% of human service contracts today are performance-based depending upon the level of government funding involved (Gustafsson-Wright, 2017). The increased use of PBC may explain, at least partially, why so-called pay-for-success contracting has become so popular in the human services today. Chapter 4 covers "pay-for-success" contracting.

KEY POINTS

- Performance-based contracting (PBC) is an umbrella term that include numerous approaches.
- PBC involves the use of output, quality or outcome performance measures.
- Unit of service contracting is the most common form of PBC.
- Because compensation is tied to performance in PBC, the performance itself becomes auditable.

REFERENCES

Arizona Department of Economic Security (Arizona DES). (2001). *Arizona works contract with amendments 1–6*. Phoenix: Arizona DES.

Desai, S., Garabedian, L., & Snyder, K. (2012). *Performance-based contracts in New York City*. Albany, NY: The Nelson a Rockefeller Institute of Government, University of Albany.

Federal Acquisition Regulation (FAR). (2017). *Part 37—service contracting*. Retrieved from www.gsa.gov/policy-regulations/regulations/federal-acquisition-regulation-far

Florida Department of Children & Families (2000). (Florida DCF). *Status report on compliance with annual performance outcome standards fy 1990–2000: Substance abuse & mental health programs*. Tallahassee, FL: Author.

Gustafsson-Wright, E. (2017). Performance-based contracting can provide flexibility, drive, efficiency and focus resources on what works in social services. In V. Bartlett, et al. (Eds.), *What matters—investing in results to build strong vibrant communities* (pp. 56–68). San Francisco, CA: Federal Reserve Bank of San Francisco and the Nonprofit Finance Fund.

Kettner, P., Moroney, R., & Martin, L. L. (1990, 2017). *Designing and managing programs: An effectiveness—based approach*. Thousand Oaks, CA: Sage Publications.

Lu, J. (2015). The performance of performance-based contracting in human services: A quasi-experiment. *Journal of Public Administration Research and Theory*, *26*, 277–293.

Martin, L. L. (2002). *Making performance-based contracting perform: What the federal government can learn from state and local governments*. Washington, DC: IBM Center for the Business of Government. Retrieved from www.businessofgovernment.org/sites/default/files/PerformanceBasedContracting.pdf

Martin, L. L. (2003). *Performance-based contracting (PBC) for human services: A review of the literature*. Orlando, FL: University of Central Florida, Center for Community Partnerships.

Martin, L. L. (2005). Performance-based contracting for human services: Does it work? *Administration in Social Work*, *29*(1), 63–77.

Martin, L. L. (2007). Performance-based contracting for human services: A proposed model. *Public Administration Quarterly*, *31*(2), 130–158.

Minnesota Department of Human Services (Minnesota DHS). (2000). *Request for Proposals to Provide Social Services to Refugees in the State of Minnesota*. St. Paul: Author.

National Association of State Purchasing Officials (NASPO). (2015). *State and local government procurement: A practical guide*. Lexington, KY: NASPO.

National Institute of Governmental Purchasing (NIGP). (2012). *Public procurement practice: Performance-based contracting*. Herndon, VA: NIGP. Retrieved from www.nigp/docs/default-source/New-Site/global-best-practices/performancebased.pdf?sfvrsn=2

Never, B., & de Leon, E. (2017). The cost of accountability for small human service contractors. *Human Service Organizations: Management, Leadership & Governance*, *4*, 403–415.

Oklahoma Department of Rehabilitative Services (Oklahoma DRS). (2001). *Milestone payment system*. Oklahoma: Oklahoma DRS.

Scott, J. (2002, February 6–8). *Successful contracting for child services*. Presentation at the Third National Summit on Partnerships, Contracts & Grants for Social Services, San Diego.

State of Kansas. (2000, September 26). Minutes of the joint meeting with the SRS Oversight Committee and Children's Issues Committee of the Kansas State Legislature.

3

Pay-for-Success Contracting

Tamara Dimitrijevska-Markoski and Lawrence L. Martin

INTRODUCTION

In recent years, a number of new approaches to human service contracting have appeared on the scene referred to collectively as "pay-for-success." These pay-for-success approaches go by various names including, pay-for-performance, payment-for-results, outcome funding, results- based funding, social impact bonds and other appellations (Bartlett et al., 2017; Eldridge & TeKolste, 2016; GAO, 2015). The best-known example of the pay-for-success approach is the social impact bond (SIB). This chapter uses social impact bonds (SIBs) as the major representative of the pay-for-success approach.

THE GROWTH OF SOCIAL IMPACT BONDS (SIBS)

SIBs are a relatively recent phenomenon. The SIB at HMP (Her Majesty's Prison) Peterborough in the United Kingdom started in 2010 was the first SIB project (Jackson, 2013; Dimitrijevska-Markoski, 2016). SIBs quickly spread to other countries. Today, some 108 SIB projects are operating in 24 countries, including Australia, Belgium, Canada, Germany, Israel, India and others. In the United States, 18 states have passed legislation authorizing the use of SIBs (Gustafsson-Wright, 2017) and some 12 SIB projects are currently underway. SIBs are being used in several different areas, workforce development, homelessness, preschool programs and others (Katz, Brisbois, Zerger, & Hwang, 2018; *Social Finance*, 2018; Dear et al., 2016).

WHAT ARE SOCIAL IMPACT BONDS?

In some respects, SIBs are similar to performance-based contracting (PBC); in other respects, they are different and break new ground. Comparing and contrasting SIBs with PBC is a useful way of describing what SIBs are and how they operate (Table 3.1).

Table 3.1

Comparing and Contrasting SIBs and PBC

	Performance-based contracting (PBC)	Social impact bonds (SIBs)
Types of human services	All	Prevention type
Focus	Human service delivery	Promoting evidence-based learning
Parties involved	Government and contractor	Government, contractor, private investor, independent outside evaluator (sometimes an Intermediary)
Financing	*Ex-anti* contractor	*Ex-anti* private investor
Funding	*Ex-post* government to contractor	*Ex-post* government to private investor or intermediary
Value base	Efficiency, quality and effectiveness	Effectiveness
Performance measures	Outputs, quality and outcomes	Outcomes
Standard of performance	Achievement of performance measures	Documentation of cause and effect relationship
Government procurement policies and procedures	Conforming	Non-conforming
Contractor financial risk	Moderate to high	Low to non-existent
Compensation–Performance nexus	Present	Absent

Types of Human Services

Most human services lend themselves to performance-based contracting (PBC). Social impact bonds (SIBs) target "prevention" type services.

Focus

The focus of PBC is on human service delivery. The focus of SIBs is on evidence-based learning.

Parties Involved

There are two parties in PBC, a government human service contracting agency and a contractor. SIBs require additional parties, a private investor who finances the SIB project and an independent outside evaluator. Some SIBs include an intermediary. The intermediary is involved in the development of the SIB project, securing investors and managing service delivery (Fraser et al., 2018).

Financing

Financing deals with the *ex-anti* (upfront) working capital needed to cover the expenses incurred during the delivery of a contracted human service. In PBC, the contractor provides its own *ex-anti* financing. With SIBs, a private investor provides the *ex-anti financing*, either directly to the contractor or indirectly through the intermediary.

Funding

Funding is different from financing. Funding is the *ex-post* (after-the-fact) payment made for a contracted human service. In PBC, the government contracting agency directly funds (pays) the contractor. With SIBs, the government pays the private investor, either directly or indirectly through the intermediary. The source of funding for SIBs comes from the cost savings, either actual or estimated, achieved by a government agency by reducing future human service delivery costs. The cost savings focus is why SIBs focus on prevention type services.

Value Base

The value base of PBC is the delivery of efficient, effective and quality human services. The SIB value base is determining the effectiveness of human service programs (interventions).

Performance Measures

PBC uses output, quality and outcome performance measure or any combination thereof. SIBs use outcome performance measures.

Standard of Performance

The standard of performance in PBC is the achievement of output, quality and outcome performance measures. In SIBs, the standard of performance is the documentation of a cause and effect relationship between a human service program and the outcomes reportedly achieved. The difference is important. In PBC demonstrating and documenting the achievement of output, quality and outcome performance measures is a *necessary sufficient condition* for a human service contractor to be paid. With SIBs, demonstrating and documenting the outcomes achieved is a *necessary, but insufficient condition* for a human service contractor to be paid. The independent outside evaluator must determine and document, utilizing social science techniques, that the outcomes are attributable to (caused by) the human service program and not external factors.

Government Procurement and Contracting Policies and Procedures

PBC is a recognized form of government contracting. PBC conforms to government procurement and contracting policies and procedures. SIBs, because they involve multiple parties, do not conform and thus require special treatment.

Contractor Financial Risk

With PBC, human service contractors are at moderate to high financial risk for performance failure. Failure to achieve the mutually agreed upon performance measures means that a contractor receives either no compensation or reduced compensation. With SIBs, the contractor is held harmless financially for performance failure. In the case of performance failure, the private investor suffers any loses, whereas the contractor is financially unaffected.

Compensation—Performance Nexus

PBC has a nexus between contractor compensation and performance; contractor compensation and performance are directly lined. No performance, no compensation. With SIBs, no compensation-performance nexus exists. The contractor gets compensated regardless of its performance. It is the investor that suffers the economic consequences of the contractor's nonperformance.

THE BENEFITS OF SIBs

SIBs have several potential benefits according to proponents:

- SIBs are means of securing financing for human services when governments are either unable or unwilling.
- SIBs shift the financial risk for performance failure from government human service agencies and contractors to private investors.
- SIBs bring market discipline to the human services by financing only programs that work.
- SIBs reduce the financial risk to governments associated with human service delivery experimentation (Edmiston & Nicholls, 2018; Saltman, 2016).

FINANCING AND FUNDING OF SIBs IN THE UNITED STATES

The federal government's Corporation for National and Community Service has created the "Pay-for-Success Initiative" as part of the organization's Social Innovation Fund. The "Pay-for-Success Initiative" has provided some $20 million to more than 40 governments and service providers nationwide (Dear et al., 2016). The U.S. Department of the Treasury administers the *Social Impact Partnerships to Pay for Results Act* (SIPPRA) that provides $92 million to support SIB projects nationwide (The U.S. Impact Investing Alliance, 2018). Other federal government programs, *Every Student Succeeds Act* and *Workforce Innovation & Opportunity Act*, include provisions for the use of SIBs (Dear et al., 2016; Saltman, 2016).

Eleven states (Alaska, California, Colorado, Idaho, Maine, Maryland, Massachusetts, New Jersey, Oklahoma, Texas and Utah) have enacted legislation supporting the use of SIBs (NCSL, 2016). This legislation covers a variety of public sector programs such as health, early childhood education and criminal justice in addition to human service programs (NCSL, 2016).

By some estimates, financing and funding for SIBs in the U.S. may exceed $400 billion by 2020 (Saltman, 2016). The number of organizations, both government and private, promoting SIBs as well as financing and funding them suggest that they are rapidly becoming a part of the human service contracting landscape.

CASE EXAMPLES OF SOCIAL IMPACT BONDS (SIBS)

HMP Peterborough (United Kingdom) SIB

The first SIB was implemented in 2010 at HMP Peterborough in the United Kingdom (UK). The Peterborough SIB project started in 2010 and addressed reducing prison recidivism by providing a prevention program called "One Service" (Jackson, 2013; Dimitrijevska-Markoski, 2016). In 2010, the estimated cost for each prisoner returning to incarceration was $50,000 per year (Jackson, 2013). The UK Ministry of Justice established a recidivism reduction target of 7.5%. The Peterborough SIB project was evaluated by several organizations including the RAND Corporation (Disley, Giacomantonio, Kruithof, & Sin, 2015). In July 2017, seven years after its start, *Social Finance* (2017) announced that the project had achieved an overall recidivism rate decrease of 9% and that the private investors will be repaid their original investments plus a profit of 3% per annum.

Rikers Island—Adolescent Behavioral Learning Experience (ABLE) SIB

The first U.S. SIB project addressed juvenile recidivism at New York City's Rikers Island jail complex (Dimitrijevska-Markoski, 2016). This SIB project implemented a program called Adolescents Behavioral Learning Experience (ABLE) program that provided "moral recognition therapy" to youth 16 to 18 years of age. The goal of the SIB project was to decrease juvenile recidivism (Parsons, Weiss, & Wei, 2016).

In 2010 prior to start of the ABLE program, 47% of juveniles released from Rikers returned within one year (Parsons et al., 2016). The ABLE SIB project specified a decrease of 10% in the recidivism rate in order for investors to recover their principle (break-even point). For investors to earn a profit, recidivism had to decrease by more than 10%. If the targeted 10% reduction was achieved, the city would avoid the costs of incarceration and would use the sayings to repay the investors (Dimitrijevska-Markoski, 2016; Parsons et al., 2016).

MDRC, a nonpartisan social policy research organization, served as the ABLE SIB project intermediary. MDRC worked with New York City, oversaw implementation and contracted with both the service delivery agencies and the investors. The investment firm of Goldman Sachs was the major investor contributing some $9.6 million in financing, backstopped by a $7.2 commitment from Bloomberg Philanthropies. The Osborne Association and the Friends of Island Academy were the contractors. The Vera Institute of Justice served as the independent outside evaluator (Parsons et al., 2016).

The Vera Institute of Justice utilized a quasi-experimental design to evaluate the ABEL SIB project. The targeted outcome was bed days (how many days ABLE juveniles spent at Rikers within 12 months following their release). Their outcomes were compared with bed days from a historical cohort released from Rikers prior to 2013 and who not receive the ABLE SIB project intervention (Parsons et al., 2016; Dimitrijevska-Markoski, 2016). The Vera Institute of Justice evaluation concluded that the ABLE SIB project did not decrease recidivism among the juvenile subjects (Parsons et al., 2016). The final report stated that, "while the ABLE program reached the majority of adolescents, aged 16 to 18, who entered Rikers in 2013 and stayed for seven days or longer, it did not reduce recidivism and therefore did not meet the predefined threshold for success" (Parsons et al., 2016, p. 7). The ABLE SIB project was discontinued (MDRC, 2015).

Cuyahoga County Partnering for Family Success SIB

The Cuyahoga County (Cleveland, Ohio, area) SIB project addresses homelessness and child welfare. Children in homeless families are more likely to spend time in out-of-home foster care than children in stable housing situation. The Cuyahoga SIB, started in December 2014, will provide case management and links to affordable housing to 135 homeless caregivers through therapy known as "critical time intervention." A proof of concept pilot demonstration project was funded by a $780,000 grant from the Laura and John Arnold Foundation (Blum et al., 2015; Third Sector Capital Partners, 2018).

Financing for implementation of the Cuyahoga SIB project is provided by a number of organizations: the Reinvestment Fund, the George Gund Foundation, the Nonprofit Finance Fund, the Cleveland Foundation and others. The contractor is Frontline Services, Inc. Enterprise Community Partners, Inc. serves as the intermediary, the project manager and the fiscal agent.

Funding for the Cuyahoga SIB project will be provided by the Cuyahoga County Division of Children and Family Services. The Division will make payments of $75 per day for each child not requiring foster care. The evaluator for the Cuyahoga SIB project is the Center for Poverty and Community Development at the Mandel School of Applies

Social Sciences at Case Western University. The evaluator will conduct a randomized controlled trial evaluation (Blum et al., 2015: Third Sector Capital Partners, 2018).

UTAH High Quality Preschool SIB

The Utah High Quality Preschool Program SIB project started in 2013 (Williamson, 2015). The objectives of this SIB project are twofold: (1) to increase school reediness and academic performance and (2) to reduce the need for future special education services (Nonprofit Finance Fund, 2017; Williamson, 2015). The SIB project (intervention) is a high-quality pre-kindergarten program for three- and four-year-olds (Williamson, 2015). The premise of this prevention type service is that the government will reduce the future costs of special needs education for the participating children. The cost savings will fund the contractors (Williamson, 2015; Nonprofit Finance Fund, 2017).

The Utah SIB project encountered a major problem. The procurement and contracting policies and procedures of the state of Utah did not allow payments to investors. Consequently, the Utah's SIB was implemented in two phases. Phase 1 was designed to demonstrate "proof of concept." Implementation would occur in Phase 2 to take place from 2014 to 2018. In Phase 1, the United Way of Salt Lake and Salt Lake County contributed a combined $1.3 million to pay the investors. In 2014, Utah created the School Readiness Board and authorized it to engage in pay-for-success contracts and to utilize state funding to compensation investors (Goldman Sachs, 2015).

The United Way of Salt Lake served as the intermediary for the Utah SIB project. The investors were Goldman Sachs and the J. & M. K. Pritzker Family Foundation. Goldman Sachs invested $4.6 million (Williamson, 2015) and the Pritzker Family foundation contributed $2.4 million (Nonprofit Finance Fund, 2017). Multiple contractors were involved in the Utah SIB project: Granite School District, Park City School District, Guadalupe School, YMCA of Northern Utah, Children's Express and Lit'l Scholars (Goldman Sachs, 2015). The independent outside evaluator was Utah State University.

The Utah High Quality Preschool Program is the first U.S. SIB project to make full payments to investors (Williamson, 2015).The Utah SIB project helped 109 at risk kindergarteners to increase their school achievement and to avoid special education (Popper, 2015; NCSL, 2016). The Utah SIB had a 99% success rate in avoiding future special education classes compared to similar programs that achieved reductions of between 10% and 20%. Critics suggest that the Utah SIB project used questionable assumptions about the numbers of children who would require special education services in the future. This questionable assumption is said to account for the unusually high success rate of the Utah SIB project (Popper, 2015).

OVERALL, HOW WELL ARE SOCIAL IMPACT BONDS (SIBS) PERFORMING?

The overall results of SIB projects to date have been unequivocal. Ten SIBs have made full payments to investors and eight SIBs are making payments (*Social Finance*, 2018, np). Only one SIB, the Rikers Island ABLE project, resulted in investors losing their investments (Katz et al., 2018). To date, however, little evidence exists to suggest that SIBs achieve better outcomes than either PBC or other pay-for-success approaches to human service contracting (Edmiston & Nicholls, 2018).

KEY POINTS

- Pay-for-success approaches are a popular approach to human service contracting.
- The Social Impact Bond (SIB) is the most popular of the pay-for-success approaches.
- The Social Impact Bond is more complex than most approaches to human service contracting.
- The Social Impact Bond breaks new ground by utilizing private sector financing for human services.
- The Social Impact Bonds does not appear to outperform performance-based contracting (PBC).

REFERENCES

Bartlett, V., Bugg-Levine, A., Erickson, D., Galloway, I., Gesler, J., & Talansky, J. (Eds.). (2017). *What matters: Investing in results to build vibrant communities*. San Francisco, CA: The Federal Reserve Bank of San Francisco and Nonprofit Finance Fund.

Blum, J., Ciurea, M., Levin, M., Moazed, T., Porowski, A., & Sparks, A. (2015). *State of the pay for success field: Opportunities, trends, and recommendations*. Washington, DC: Corporation for National and Community Service. Retrieved from www.nationalservice.gov/sites/default/files/documents/CNCS%20PFS%20State%20of%20the%20Field%20Document%20Final%204-17-15%20sxf.pdf

Dear, A., Helbitz, A., Khare, R., Lotan, R., Newman, J., Sims, G. C., & Zaroulis, A. (2016). *Social impact bonds: The early years*. Retrieved from http://socialfinance.org/content/uploads/2016/07/SIBs-Early-Years_Social-Finance_2016_Final.pdf

Dimitrijevska-Markoski, T. (2016). Social impact bonds: A new tool for governance of social program-evidence from UK, USA and Australia. *International Journal of Public Policy*, *12*(3–5), 261–275.

Disley, D., Giacomantonio, C., Kruithof, K., & Sin, M. (2015). *The payment by results social impact bond at HMP Peterborough: Final process evaluation report*. London: Ministry of Justice. Retrieved from https://assets.publishing.service.gov.uk/government/uploads/system/uploads/attachment_data/file/486512/social-impact-bond-pilot-peterborough report.pdf

Edmiston, D., & Nicholls, A. (2018). Social impact bonds: The role of private capital in outcome-based commissioning. *Journal of Social Policy*, *47*(1), 57–76.

Eldridge, M., & TeKolste, R. (2016). *Results-based financing approaches*. Washington, DC: Urban Institute.

Fraser, A., Tan, S., Lagarde, M., & Mays, N. (2018). Narratives of promise, narratives of caution: A review of the literature on social impact bonds. *Social Policy & Administration*, *52*(1), 4–28.

Goldman Sachs. (2015). *First social impact bond for early childhood education*. Retrieved from www.goldmansachs.com/what-we-do/investing-and-lending/impact-investing/case-studies/impact-bond-slc-multimedia/fact-sheet-pdf.pdf

Government Accountability Office (GAO). (2015). *Pay for success: Collaboration among federal agencies would be helpful as governments explore new financing mechanisms*. GAO-15-646. Washington, DC: Author.

Gustafsson-Wright, E. (2017). Performance-based contracting can provide flexibility, drive, efficiency, and focus resources on what works in social services. In V. Bartlett, A. Bugg-Levine, D. Erickson, I. Galloway, J. Gesler, & J. Talansky (Eds.), *What matters: Investing in results to build vibrant communities* (pp. 56–67). San Francisco, CA: The Federal Reserve Bank of San Francisco & Nonprofit Finance Fund.

Jackson, E. (2013). Evaluating social impact bonds: Questions, challenges, innovations, and possibilities in measuring outcomes in impact investing. *Community Development: Journal of the Community Development Society*, *44*, 608–616.

Katz, A., Brisbois, B., Zerger, S., & Hwang, S. (2018). Social impact bonds as a funding method for health and social programs: Potential areas of concern. *American Journal of Public Health*, *108*, 210–215.

MDRC. (2015). *MDRC statement on the Vera institute's study of the adolescent behavioral learning experience (ABLE) program at Rikers Island*. Retrieved from www.mdrc.org/news/announcement/mdrc-statement-vera-institute-s-study-adolescent-behavioral-learning-experience

National Conference of State Legislatures (NCSL). (2016). *Social impact bonds*. Retrieved from www.ncsl.org/research/labor-and-employment/social-impact-bonds.aspx

Nonprofit Finance Fund. (2017). *Utah high quality preschool program*. Retrieved from www.payforsuccess.org/project/utah-high-quality-preschool-program

Parsons, J., Weiss, C., & Wei, Q. (2016). *Impact evaluation of the adolescent behavioral learning experience (ABLE) program*. Vera Institute of Justice. Retrieved from https://storage.googleapis.com/vera-web-assets/downloads/Publications/rikers-adolescentbehavioral-learning-experience-evaluation/legacy_downloads/rikers-adolescent-behavioral-learning-experience-evaluation.pdf

Popper, N. (2015). Success metrics questioned in school program funded by Goldman. *New York Times*. Retrieved from www.nytimes.com/2015/11/04/business/dealbook /did-goldman-make-the-grade.html

Saltman, K. (2016). The promise and realities of pay for success/social impact bonds. *Education Policy Analysis Archives*, *25*(59), 1–21.

Social Finance. (2017). *World's first social impact bond shown to cut reoffending and to make impact investors a return*. Retrieved from www.socialfinance.org.uk/sites/default/files/news/final-press-release-pb-july-2017.pdf

Social Finance. (2018). *Social impact bonds reach global mass: 108 projects launched in 24 countries*. Press Release.

Third Sector Capital Partners. (2018). *The Cuyahoga partnering for family success program*. Retrieved from www.thirdsectorcap.org/portfolio/cuyahoga-county-partnering-for-family-success-program/

The U.S. Impact Investing Alliance. (2018). *Congress passes the social impact partnerships to pay for results act (SIPPRA)*. Retrieved from http://impinvalliance.org/news-updates/2018/2/9/congress-passes-the-social-impact-partnerships-to-pay-for-results-act-sippra

Williamson, R. (2015). Goldman Sachs social impact bond pays off in Utah. *Bond Buyer*, p. 1. Retrieved from www.cdfa.net/cdfa/cdfaweb.nsf/pages/27016/$file/Goldman%20Sachs%%20Impact%20Bond%20Pays%20Off%20in%20Utah%20_%20The%20Bond%20Buyer.pdf

Part 2

Contracting for Specialized Human Services

4

Contracting for Child Welfare Services

Crystal Collins-Camargo and Bowen McBeath

INTRODUCTION

Services to child welfare-involved children and their families have historically been organized, particularly in systems with large numbers of private agencies, through contracts between public fiduciary agencies and private service providers. This process of contracting out public services to the private sector has grown in recent decades as jurisdictions have experimented with privatization to achieve desired system outcomes amidst cost containment pressures (Collins-Camargo, McBeath, & Ensign, 2011; Smith, 2012). Although some state and local governments have contracted with private agencies for some child welfare services since the 1800s (Rosenthal, 2000), the configuration of public versus private agency service delivery in this field has shifted back and forth over time.

At the turn of the twenty-first century, studies of child welfare contracting (McCullough & Schmitt, 1999, 2003) found that states had been engaged in outsourcing to the private sector in pursuit of three objectives: (1) to achieve better outcomes for children and families; (2) to pursue broad, systemic performance goals such as service array enhancement, flexibility and community engagement; and (3) to align fiscal and program concerns by shifting financial risk and seeking cost containment. Historically, per diem and fee-for-service or case-rate based approaches have been primarily used. However, with increased emphasis on accountability and through the mandated outcomes of safety, permanency and well-being measured through the Child and Family Service Reviews (Administration for Children and Families, n.d.), some jurisdictions have initiated strategies that move beyond traditional structures to enlist contractual partners in contributing to the quest for outcome achievement and compliance with established service delivery standards (Collins-Camargo et al., 2011).

A consequence of this diffusion of innovation across state child welfare systems has been the development and implementation of a wide variety of market-based models that yoke contracting, child welfare financing and service delivery. Whereas purchase of service contracts have grown in their explication of expected performance, they have traditionally specified type and quantity rather than the impact of services, but for the past couple of decades this has been changing. Some of these models, notably performance-based contracting, link agency payment to service delivery and child and family outcomes, such that private agency reimbursement is contingent on meeting and/or exceeding contractually specified objectives set by the public child welfare agency. Other structural adaptations of contracting, including network-based systems in which an administrative service organization serves as a lead contractor (Bunger, Cao, Girth, Hoffman, & Robertson, 2017), and organize private agency service delivery through networks of sub-contractual relationships with other local service providers.

Some public agencies have selected this "lead agency approach," to outsource more than just direct service provision, especially in early child welfare privatization initiatives such Florida's which still uses this model (McCullough & Schmitt, 2003). In this approach, the public agency contracts with an intermediary private agency, which in turn subcontracts with other community-based private agencies to provide direct services. The lead agency manages many of the contract administration processes, such as bidding, facilitating communication with the provider network and contract monitoring, which would otherwise remain with the public agency. In some cases, the lead agency also is a service provider, typically for a limited portion of the cases to be served. In some versions of this approach, the lead agency also may provide needed infrastructure to the network of providers such as training and provision of technical assistance and quality improvement. The lead agency approach enables a public agency to manage only one contract, but distances it from service providers and the work being contracted, which could inhibit informed decision-making in the future.

As is the case in all contracting, risk sharing involves the private sector taking on a portion of the risk traditionally born by the public agency in exchange for organizational independence and the possibility of financial gain. In child welfare, in which public agencies have little control over the number of families needing to be served or the ultimate cost of meeting the needs of children with complex needs, the balance of risk when services are contracted is a significant variant. From an economic perspective, private providers are asked to shoulder the risk of overspending when the needs of some children exceed the average rate of payment in exchange for autonomy in service delivery. Alternately, private providers may stop short of spending what some children and families need in order to stay within budget allocations. In some states, the public agency agrees to maintain some degree of the risk in order to keep private providers solvent.

The promise of these models therefore rests on their ability to reduce inefficiency by imposing a budget constraint and to motivate agency performance and innovation (Garstka, Collins-Camargo, Hall, Neal, & Ensign, 2012; Lynch-Cerullo & Cooney, 2011; Smith, 2012). Arguments emphasizing these potential benefits are used to support the growth of public-private partnerships in child welfare systems. In contrast, a theoretical literature drawn from public and nonprofit management as well as an emerging child welfare research base suggests that these models can promote goal displacement by private agencies and can be difficult for most child welfare agencies to implement and manage properly—particularly in light of technical uncertainty related to how to achieve optimal outcomes for children and families (Meezan & McBeath, 2008; Courtney, 2000). These arguments suggest a more cautious approach and attention to the scientifically grounded development, testing and refinement of market-based models in child welfare.

A BRIEF HISTORY OF CONTRACTING FOR CHILD WELFARE SERVICES

The provision of public services to children and families in the United States has, to varying degrees, occurred through a purchase of service contracting partnership between the public and nonprofit sectors, in which public agencies contract with the private sector and monitor these agencies to ensure compliance (Agranoff & McGuire, 2001a; Kettner & Martin, 1990; Salamon, 1995; Smith & Lipsky, 1993; U.S. GAO, 1999). In 1998, it was suggested that at least half of all child welfare services were provided by nonprofit organizations (Kahn & Kamerman, 1999), and there is little evidence to suggest this has changed substantially.

From the perspective of the historical development of the American welfare state, the role of the private sector in the broad field of child welfare was grounded in the work of charitable agencies. During the Gilded Age and the Progressive Era, immigrant communities in the largest U.S. cities depended upon private associations, charities, churches and sectarian agencies for social services (Monkkonen, 1988). Private social service agencies developed independently of the larger public social service sector (Abbott, 1968; Katz, 2001), typically through association with and services to specific religious communities (Jansson, 2001).

The establishment of the Children's Bureau in 1912, and its subsequent foray into promoting government services to address social policy concerns regarding primarily poor children and families, began a decades-long debate regarding the contrasting roles of the two sectors. The Social Security Act of 1935 enabled expansion of public child welfare; and over the next several years, states passed legislation establishing public social service agencies. With the amendment of the Social Security Act in 1958, federally assisted child welfare programs were extended to all states (Rosenthal, 2000).

Thus, privately provided services became publicly subsidized over time through direct mechanisms such as state and local contracts, grants and lump sum appropriations. Whereas many private agencies originated in response to community needs that were not being met through existing public programs, state and local governments quickly began to support the service efforts of such agencies, with the result that many agencies grew reliant upon government funding and patronage (Katz, 2001; Rosenthal, 2000; Salamon, 1995). This was not without controversy, as critics decried the loss of independence. For example, the Child Welfare League of America (1958) published a position paper emphasizing the importance of private agencies being funded primarily through philanthropy, thereby maintaining their autonomy.

During the early years of the Reagan presidency, the increased use of block grants was combined with significant reductions in federal aid to states. Non-defense discretionary program areas such as community development, employment and training, housing and social services, as well as means-tested entitlements such as Aid to Families with Dependent Children (AFDC) and Food Stamps, sustained reductions in federal outlays between 25% and 70% within the *Omnibus Budget Reconciliation Act of 1981* (Conlan, 1988). Devolution paved the way for experimentation with market models (Katz, 2001) from federal expectations for local governments and the private sector to "pick up the slack" (Salamon, 1995, p. 194) resulting from reduced government capacity to provide services. However, this also resulted in the nonprofit sector focusing less on charitable services to the poor and focusing more on fee-for-service programing (Salamon, 1995).

Faced with increasing numbers of abused and neglected children entering out-of-home care in the mid- to late-1990s (U.S. Department of Health and Human Services, National Clearinghouse on Child Abuse and Neglect Information, 2002), states responded to these increases in federal child welfare funding by increasing their own outlays on existing child welfare programs and, in some states, by requesting waivers of compliance with the statutorily mandated requirements of federal Title IV-E of the Social Security Act. Specifically, the federal Title IV-E waiver approach involves states requesting the opportunity to develop innovative programs by accessing federally matched funds in accordance with federal and state statutes (Bess, Andrews, Jantz, Russell, & Geen, 2002). A number of states took advantage of these waivers to contract out more of their child welfare functions to the nonprofit sector (Pecora, Whittaker, Maluccio, & Barth, 2000).

In the current day, child welfare occurs across a continuum of public-private partnership, as in all states public agencies contract to varying degrees with the private sector to provide services. In some states, this is restricted to specialized services to particular populations, such as individual and family counseling (Embry, Buddenhagan, & Bolles, 2000; Smith, 1989). Yet in others, core child welfare services including case management have been outsourced (Collins-Camargo, Ensign, & Flaherty, 2008; McCullough & Schmitt, 2000). In a few states, large-scale privatization of statutorily mandated services has occurred (e.g., Kansas and Florida) (Collins-Camargo et al., 2011).

Policymakers and researchers have not yet determined the impact of increased private sector contracting on the overall cost of child welfare services. Anecdotally, some states with large portions of the service array report increased cost. Others assert that contracting results in a more adequately funded child welfare system. However, the overall cost of contracting for child welfare services is unknown, either as defined in individual jurisdictions or at the federal level. There is no centralized reporting of direct contracting costs. Federal Child and Family Service Reviews conducted by the Administration for Children and Families do not collect these data when they are assessing state compliance with statutory requirements. In addition, many costs of providing services are hidden within the infrastructure of large public bureaucracies so it can be difficult to compare what it costs a private agency to provide a service with accurate public agency cost.

Lessons Learned: Contracting Amidst the Organizational Realities of Child Welfare Services

In summary, child welfare occurs through the combined efforts of the public and private sectors in many jurisdictions in the U.S. (Wells, Jolles, Chuang, McBeath, & Collins-Camargo, 2014). The role of private providers varies by service arena, organizational scope and the extent to which case management decisions are devolved to them (Collins-Camargo et al., 2008, 2011). Although core child welfare services are the mandated responsibility of public agencies, they turn to varying degrees to their private partners to provide an array of discrete services critical for the care of children and families implied by those statutory mandates.

Thus, the private agency role has evolved into an essential part of public child welfare service delivery, programmatically and systematically. Yet until recently, little was known about the population of private providers serving the child welfare population. The first national survey of private child and family serving agencies found that these agencies are often large, mature, freestanding entities that are significantly reliant on governmental contracts (McBeath, Collins-Camargo, & Chuang, 2012). Many provide an array of core child welfare services as well as behavioral health and other human services. This broader expertise holds promise for assisting public agencies in pursuing those elusive well-being outcomes. Despite the previously mentioned emphasis on performance in child welfare systems, over three-quarters of these agencies reported having no performance-based contracts. Whereas 42% of responding directors reported contractual performance was appropriately evaluated by public agencies, 35% did not perceive that their agency collected adequate data to assess their performance (McBeath et al., 2012).

"Partnership" and Provider Pool Challenges Within the Context of Contractual Relationships

Part of what is particularly challenging about this cross-sector relationship in child welfare contracting is that whereas the phrase "public-private partnership" is often used in system design to support the development of contracting regimes, there is an inherent power imbalance in the contractual relationship that sits at odds with a vision of collaboration among co-equal and historical partners. There is often a "taken-for-grantedness" imparted by the scholarly literature when describing the process of managing private agencies through contracting. There can also be a basic belief that service delivery and overall accountability are enhanced through competition for contracts (Romzek & Johnston, 2005), which can be taken to imply that individual private providers are replaceable.

The enterprise of organizing and financing child welfare services through contracts depends on the existence of a strong pool of providers with access to relevant administrative infrastructural supports, best practice models and facility with performance management techniques (Collins-Camargo, Chuang, McBeath, & Bunger, 2014). At the local child welfare system level, an inadequate private provider pool can hamstring this process, particularly if the public agency has difficulty enforcing contract compliance with performance expectations (Van Slyke, 2003). Given the difficulty of building a competitive marketplace for child welfare services, the contract monitoring and evaluation process on the part of the public agency may be of most importance (Lamothe & Lamothe, 2008). This is particularly of concern in child welfare, where public scrutiny is high, and the evidence base is relatively weak. Additionally, policy requirements may be vague and may shift over time in response to internal and external pressures, whereas funding to support legislatively mandated services is typically perceived as inadequate.

Challenges to Child Welfare Contracting Through a Principal-Agent Theoretical Lens

These dynamics illustrate the theoretical challenge that emerges when public child welfare agencies contract with private providers for service delivery. Principal-agent theory (PAT) was developed in part to explain the emergence of management structures in situations where ownership and service delivery are separated, such as through contracting. PAT presumes that there exist differences between the goals of owners (principals) and managers who are tasked with executing their goals (agents), termed moral hazard. The theory presumes principals have limited resources and the costs associated with gathering more information and engaging in more direct oversight of agents is substantial. As a result, the risk of agents pursuing self-interest rather than carrying out their contractually obligated responsibilities is of concern.

As seen through a PAT lens, public-private relationships can benefit public agencies through the careful development and implementation of contracts in alignment with the careful selection of service providers. Public agencies may be more confident of overall accountability when they develop contracts that contain clear roadmaps for private providers that delineate expected objectives, methods to achieve them and financial penalties and/or incentives to support goal attainment; and when they select providers that are able to follow these roadmaps to meet contractually specified goals. In principle, if these two conditions were met, then private providers would be required to follow contract parameters to attain financial incentives (or avoid penalties) and reduce the threat of future contract loss. Public agencies would be able to assume a more passive role of monitoring contracts and evaluating performance (Kettl, 2002).

Part of the poor fit we observe in applying PAT to child welfare contracting may result from the fact that PAT's simple assumption of moral hazard in which the private contractor is expected to willfully pursue goals that are independent of the public agency doesn't fit. This theory does not reflect credibly on either the motivations of private agencies (whose mission is to promote the well-being of children and families) or the long history of privately provided child and family services. One case study of New York State's contracting of child welfare agencies, illustrates nonprofit providers sometimes must subsidize service provision through private contributions when government funding is inadequate. This arrangement may be at their own peril and yet agencies remain committed to this work (Marwell & Calabrese, 2016).

Scholars have recently sought to enlarge the model to encompass other types of agency relationships in which the motivations are other-oriented (e.g., affine and fiduciary agency relationships), and agency autonomy and asymmetry of information are less of a problem (e.g., non-hierarchical agency relationships). In many respects, PAT's focus on extrinsic motivations seems misplaced when considering the historical reliance of public child welfare agencies on the intrinsic motivations of private agencies.

Van Slyke (2007) suggests that under these conditions, fiduciary agency theory or stewardship theory may better capture the complex motives of public and private agencies. Stewardship theory "defines situations in which managers are not motivated by individual goals, but rather are stewards whose motives are aligned with the objectives of their principals" (Davis, Schoorman, & Donaldson, 1997, p. 21). This alternative way of conceptualizing the agency relationship, which is associated with traditional purchase-of-service and fee-for-service arrangements, relies on some degree of shared mission and goals and an evolving relationship that may over time focus less on enforcement and more on shared decision-making characterized by trust and reciprocity, understanding that this relationship is subject to fluctuation given internal and external pressures. The characteristics of public goods to be produced must be collectively defined especially in circumstances when these goods are complex in nature, such as global economic security (Brousseau, Dedeurwaerdere, & Siebenhuner, 2012; Brown, Potoski, & Van Slyke, 2010) or, in our case, child permanency and well-being.

Network models reflecting a stewardship theory-based approach to contracting hold promise for child welfare systems. These models still direct attention to how public managers monitor and shape contractor behavior (Provan & Kenis, 2008). But they also consider non-hierarchical and relational approaches that promote collaborative decision-making and problem solving between public and private agencies (Tilbury, 2007). Dubnick and Fredrickson (2010) found that whereas hierarchical controls can promote accountability, lateral and trust-based relational contracting models do so as well even in federally funded and mandated human service programs. Network effectiveness goes beyond outcomes that could be achieved by independent participants to network-level outcomes, the governance of such being an important focus of the public agency particularly in goal-directed networks (Provan & Kenis, 2008).

Classical agency theory assumes that the private sector relentlessly seeks autonomy and high payment, jeopardizing governmental accountability and efficiency (Kramer & Grossman, 1987). However, contractual components cannot in themselves ensure efficiency, equity or outcome achievement. The social, economic, cultural and political environments play an important role (Miraftab, 2004). If the complexity of contracting for child and family well-being can be managed, and, if Van Slyke (2007) is correct in suggesting that over time fiduciary agency (principal-steward) relationships have been recognized as relevant in human service contracting, perhaps the concept of relational contracting and an approach that pursues collective impact across the service system deserves further consideration and study.

Insufficient Technical Knowledge Is a Barrier in Child Welfare Contracting

In sum, public child welfare agencies wishing to "steer but not row" might try to spur outcome achievement by (1) relying on private providers with excellent track records (preferring high-performing providers); (2) identifying appropriately powerful economic incentives and penalties to motivate desired provider behavior (a sticks-and-carrots based approach); and (3) engaging in the structuring and evaluation of contracts to clearly specify the objectives to be achieved and the expected service mechanisms and timeframe for their achievement.

However, in the human services and child welfare in particular, these conditions are difficult to meet for a variety of reasons. First, there may exist legitimate conflict between what public and private agencies deem to be the appropriate child welfare outcomes. This challenge may reflect the narrower focus of the public agency as compared with the scope of community-based agencies. Whereas private contracting agencies may seek to meet a broader array of community needs through the provision of services, the public agency, due to statutory mandate, limited resources and public scrutiny, may lean toward narrower focus in contracted services. This dynamic plays out in public child welfare's emphasis on child safety and permanency, while resisting and to some degree faltering related to more recently imposed goals related to the social and emotional well-being of children and youth. The public agency's emphasis has traditionally been focused on keeping children safe, bearing the brunt of media backlash. Private agencies, often with a history of behavioral health service provision, traditionally are more focused on voluntary services to improve well-being or functioning.

Second, the causal maps needed to link organizational and managerial strategies with the downstream child welfare outcomes of permanency and well-being have yet to be fully drawn. Research has not determined with certainty how child welfare agencies and systems should calibrate service provision to children, parents and other groups (e.g., relatives, foster parents) to achieve these outcomes (Hasenfeld, 2010; McBeath & Meezan, 2010). However, organizational capacity for using information technology to demonstrate these connections through analysis of data in their management information systems is growing. It would seem that harnessing processes that promote evidence-informed decision-making, including the use of data dashboards to track performance, and providing administrators and the frontline with relevant information on the relationships between specific practices and desired outcomes, can only benefit the field. The technology is available to do so. However, affordability as well as technical capacity are issues for public and private agencies alike.

More broadly, questions remain as to the external validity and feasibility of the most prevalent EBPs available for implementation by child welfare agencies. Child welfare client populations are diverse within and across agencies, and this diversity can be understood to influence the needs of clients and how they respond to mandated as well as discretionary services. Few EBPs have been determined to be effective across diverse child welfare client populations; and fewer of these interventions have robust implementation protocols that allow for their use in real-world agency settings characterized by staff turnover, poor worker training and limited resources to support new service approaches (Chaffin, Hecht, Bard, Silovsky, & Beasley, 2012). These considerations highlight the great differences in scale between intervention testing for the purpose of identifying causal pathways promoting permanency and well-being and implementing interventions in real-world settings with diverse clients and agencies.

In a field where the safety and well-being of children, and custody issues of their families, predominate, there has been a call for more rigorous, data-driven approaches to outcome monitoring, program evaluation and quality improvement (Lindsey & Shlonsky, 2008; Testa & Poertner, 2010; Weigensberg, 2009). Some agencies have responded to this dilemma of insufficient technical knowledge by investing in learning organizational approaches promoting data-driven experimentation at the frontline and programmatic level (Austin, 2008), but the proportion of these agencies is likely small due to the significant investment needed. Additionally, although some agencies have invested in performance measurement and management, questions concerning the selection of performance indicators, what programmatic data reported and how agencies can use performance management to monitor and enact frontline and programmatic changes to "move the needle" around child welfare outcomes remain (Carnochan, Samples, Myers, & Austin, 2014; Jolles, Collins-Camargo, McBeath, Bunger, & Chuang, 2017). More agency-university research partnerships are needed to move the field forward in understanding the efficacy of core child welfare practices.

These interrelated problems limit the potential benefits and increase the potential challenges associated with contracting in child welfare. The condition of insufficient technical knowledge plagues both the public and private agencies serving this population. Without sufficient a priori knowledge concerning what services should be provided to reach child and family outcomes, public agencies cannot develop complete contracts that identify proven service pathways for outcome achievement. As a result, public child welfare agencies have generally sought to avoid prescribing service delivery strategies for private providers and have increasingly relied on performance-based contracts to motivate goal attainment.

A difficulty with these approaches, however, is that they devolve decision-making for public services down to private providers, who may not be able to identify desirable treatment modalities or implement best practices for delivering services effectively. This condition can result in neither public nor private agencies knowing exactly how to structure frontline care to child welfare populations, while private agencies accept greater financial risk for this care. If statutorily mandated services are devolved to the private sector, we must ascertain how to encourage the collaboration of public and private child welfare agencies and comparative effectiveness research in ways that promote positive outcomes for children and families within the context of the on-the-ground contractual relationship between public and private agencies. There are examples around the country in which networks of providers and public agencies transparently share and discuss practice and outcome data, so that agencies can learn from each other to enhance system improvement.

Motivating Performance Through Contracting: Child Welfare Evidence

Because the contract is the formal, legal linchpin at the nexus of the public-private partnership, one strategy that jurisdictions have used to "steer but not row" is by using performance-based approaches to contracting. Outside the child welfare arena, performance-based contracting has increased in an effort to incentivize compliance and outcome achievement (Martin, 2003), and has been associated with increased efficiency (Faith et al., 2010) and outcome productivity (Martin, 2005). In child welfare, however, the field is still experimenting with the first generation of incentive-driven performance models, and there remain many unresolved questions regarding how best to develop, implement, evaluate and improve these models (McBeath, 2016). There is also evidence that private providers experience numerous barriers in the areas of staffing, training, financial management and information technology when moving to performance-based contracting environments (Meezan & McBeath, 2011). Thus, whereas performance contracting has been demonstrated on a limited basis to have the potential to promote desired outcomes (Garstka et al., 2012), this market-based approach is far from a panacea for child welfare's production problems at the current stage of development.

Meezan and McBeath (2008) and Taylor and Shaver (2010) each found that children served within a performance contracting environment were more likely to be adopted or placed in long-term relative care than to experience other permanency outcomes when compared to a prior per-diem reimbursement structure (Taylor & Shaver, 2010) and a concurrent control group that was served under the traditional fee-for-service structure (Meezan & McBeath, 2008). Taylor and Shaver (2010) concluded that the utility of performance contracting cannot be generalized beyond the desired outcomes of adoption and kinship guardianship; whereas Meezan and McBeath (2008) cautioned that performance contracting has the potential to incentivize the pursuit of more expedient permanency goals rather than the goal that seems most appropriate to the child when faced with the significant complexities of family needs, intervention efficacy and limited resources to serve a large, diverse population.

These studies suggest agencies should incentivize other outcomes rather than permanency achievement, but the best formula for motivating effective services through contractual components remains unclear. The selection of distal outcomes such as permanency and well-being as incentivized contractual indicators adds additional complexity to this process. If the performance contracting system seeks to yield the most appropriate outcome for each child as opposed to driving service delivery narrowly to the most cost-effective outcomes, research-supported metrics must include well-being measures that support the permanency goal sought.

Encouraging this orientation toward permanence or well-being delegates greater discretion to the private sector and presents the opportunity to be innovative in service delivery, which is sometimes touted as a strength of service delivery in the private sector (Noonan, Sabel, & Simon, 2009; Flaherty, Collins-Camargo, & Lee, 2008; Hood, 2000). Such outcomes, however, also involve a complex array of contributors outside the control of the private agency, such as judicial decisions. Alternatively, some performance-based contracts incentivize proximal outcomes, such as stepping youth down from residential to community-based placements (Kearney, Bloom-Ellis, & Thompson, 2012) or practice-level indicators such as quality supervisory review (Elder, DeStefano, Blazevski, & Schuler, 2012). If the intention, however, is to yield broader child outcomes, it would be important for public agencies to assess the statistical validity of the selected practice indicators by examining the extent to which proximal outcomes are actually associated with the desired ultimate outcomes of safety, permanence and well-being.

FUTURE DIRECTIONS FOR PRACTICE, PROGRAM AND POLICY IMPROVEMENT: ORGANIZING CONTRACTING IN CHILD WELFARE TO ENHANCE SYSTEM AND CLIENT OUTCOMES

Contracting for child welfare services needs to be closely connected to the goals of policymakers and the efforts of public managers to avoid creating a disconnect between high-level policy design, mid-level policy implementation and frontline-level program delivery (Bertelli & Smith, 2010). Successful contracting is partially dependent on the quality and continuity of long-term relationships present between public and private agencies, as well as skill in contract negotiation and monitoring (Austin, 2003). Managerial competency in leading these contractual processes as well as interagency networks varies (Collins-Camargo et al., 2011). Available research has suggested that when the right leadership is engaged, processes are delineated, and there is content clarity, collaborative governance can be effective in mediating the power imbalances that often characterize service contracting (Purdy, 2012).

These thoughts are contingent on the development of a coordinated and networked approach to contracting in which public and private organizations engage in collaborative problem solving to achieve objectives and ultimately outcomes that is more purposive than the "invisible hand" that is assumed to guide market transactions toward collectively beneficial results. Within networked forms of contracting, formal control and authority remain but are supplemented by informal forms of mutual accountability, which evolve through organizational interactions grounded in bounded solidarity and enforceable trust and communal sharing (Rhodes, 1996). Recent human services research has suggested these informal forms of accountability may be at least as important in knowledge transfer and identification of best practices as more formal mechanisms such as contractual requirements (Romzek, LeRoux, & Blackmar, 2012). With the evolution of public-private partnerships, there is a need to overcome challenges to promote accountability and performance measurement, which requires shared goals and trust as well as the adoption of agreed upon performance management structures (Alexander, Brudney, & Yang, 2010). Collaborative approaches based in relational contracting and performance management and accountability structures need not be mutually exclusive. Such an approach could potentially move the field toward collaborative performance measurement (Amirkhanyan, 2009) and more of a systemic approach to assessing collective impact system-wide (Hanleybrown, Kania, & Kramer, 2012), which has been identified by the Children's Bureau as a goal for the future of child welfare (Mitchell et al., 2012).

How, then, do we get there? Clearly more rigorous public and private sector experimentation with the use of different contracting approaches is needed. Such study may help to enhance our understanding of the relational and other institutional factors that may promote performance achievement within the context of a joint, public-private endeavor in child welfare (McBeath et al., 2014).

Additionally, Behn and Kant (1999) identified the following practical management-and-policy-focused strategies for avoiding the pitfalls of performance contracting. Although their analysis reflected first-generation state human service contracting initiatives, their eight concepts continue to be relevant.

1. Understand the relationship and difference between the mission and the measures.
2. Create contracts based on outputs that are (a) linked to the mission; (b) easy to measure, understand and reproduce; and (c) facilitate benchmarking.
3. Start simple and ratchet up.
4. Monitor frequently lots of indicators of performance.
5. Be prepared to learn, change, improve, and learn some more.
6. Work collaboratively—not adversarially—with contractors.
7. Pay vendors not just for the final output but also for significant, well-defined progress.
8. Favor contractors with a track record. (pp. 479–483)

In tandem with these concepts, a number of strategies suggested by the literature are worthy of consideration by policymakers, public and private agency directors and researchers, and are described in the following paragraphs.

Alignment of contracts within a shared vision of family continuity and child well-being, and mutual understanding of the purpose of the partnership, is clearly consistent with a fiduciary agency and stewardship model. Reducing goal asymmetry is also a requirement of a relational contracting approach. If the purpose of delegating services to the private sector is reframed as an attempt to build on sector-based strengths to improve the well-being of children and their families, collaborative planning can ensue to maximize relevant input into the best configuration of services, not to mention the selection and use of performance indicators most likely to promote vision achievement within the contract itself. Outside of child welfare, development of shared commitment and understanding has been associated with successful collaborative governance among public and private agencies (Ansell & Gash, 2008). Child well-being as an outcome depends on the monitoring of a counterbalanced set of indicators, which reflects the interrelated nature of child welfare outcomes (Webster, Usher, Needell, & Wildfire, 2008). For example, safety is a necessary yet insufficient component of well-being. Accountability may in fact be greater, when desired results are not narrowly defined, and this may underlie the potential for child well-being to serve as a unifying outcome for child welfare networks (Testa & Poertner, 2010). When we move beyond procedural compliance to a shared goal of well-being, relational contracting processes within the context of cross-sector partnership may reach their true potential.

Linking incentive-based contracts with performance measurement systems to move the system forward represents another factor that must be empirically examined more thoroughly. Child welfare performance measures often focus on what data are available rather than what is useful to measure the linkage between system objectives and child and family outcomes (Devaney, 2004). One study has noted that the Getting to Outcomes accountability framework employed within the context of performance-based contracting demonstrated positive results related to understanding outcome accountability, contract quality and collaboration (Hannah, Ray, Wandersman, & Chien, 2010). Additionally, collaborative capacity has been linked to performance improvement when shared goals and investment are present in the partnership (Gazley, 2010). The field needs to examine whether strategies such as performance-based contracting speak to bottom line–minded agency administrators and board members, policymakers and stakeholders, while leveraging the stewardship goals which may be motivating to human service professionals. One multistate study suggested that administrators in both public and private agencies did not agree regarding which would be most effective in promoting outcome achievement—i.e., incentives or penalties (Garstka et al., 2012). The interrelationship among goals, organizational investment and performance deserves scholarly and practitioner attention.

Certainly, rigorous experimentation is in order with different performance-based contracting models to promote outcome achievement in child welfare. Because contracts exist to tie the two sectors together in a very real fashion, there is a clear need for future demonstration projects that can examine the performance contracting using sufficiently rigorous designs permitting the drawing of credible inferences about the comparative effectiveness of alternative market-pricing and equality-matching incentive structures.

Continuous quality improvement (CQI) strategies on a cross-sector level involving shared access to agency data and authentic dialogue around what the data mean has the potential to elevate the child welfare system as a whole. Such processes should delve deeply into building the evidence base around the relationship between frontline practices, agency characteristics and outcome achievement (Moulin, 2009). Some states are experimenting with the use of data dashboards to compare and manage performance across providers (Cash, Ingram, Biben, McKeever, & Thompson, 2012; Kapp, Ah Hahn, & Rand, 2011). Research is needed to distinguish between individual versus organizational determinants of outcomes, with such studies potentially benefiting from automated randomized controlled comparative research designs or quasi-experimental, risk adjustment strategies (Raghavan, 2010). While empirical research in this area is evolving, systems that collect, analyze, share and use practice and outcome data across private providers and public agencies transparently will have the tools to begin to answer those questions to inform contracting decisions as well as managerial and frontline practice.

Given possible challenges associated with performance achievement across a service network, the development of cross-provider performance monitoring, a learning organizational approach implemented on a system level, and a focus on system impact may be used (Lynch-Cerullo & Cooney, 2011). Comparative performance measurement can help child welfare policymakers and agency leaders manage within and across organizations and sectors to develop a shared vision and then to operationalize it through performance indicators (Tilbury, 2007). There is a lack of research into the administration of comparative performance approaches (Wulcyzn, Chen, & Orlebeke, 2010), which are influenced by competition and fiscal implications. However, there is evidence to suggest that collaborative, cross-sector approaches to developing performance and contracting schemas, within the parameters allowed in procurement regulations, are being piloted (Johansen, Kim, & Zhu, 2016; Benjamin, Voida, & Bopp, 2018). It is important to think about performance achievement, and contracting for it, as a process that evolves over time, which does not end when the contract is executed (Garstka et al., 2012).

Joint commitment to rigorous research design to test the questions policymakers and agency leaders deem most important to move the system forward, based on overall system improvement as opposed to private agency competition or a "thinning the herd" mentality is an important continuous quality improvement (CQI) approach. In some ways, systemic CQI necessitates an enlightened provider community that is willing to suspend the reactive tendency to hold cards close to the chest in order to maintain market share and compete. This may only be possible in an environment in which there is not tremendous resource scarcity, and the system is not in the mode of weeding out providers. Only when such comparative data analysis can be focused on elevating the system as a whole, and there is a sense that outcome achievement at a systemic level is only as good as its weakest provider, can such efforts thrive.

The importance of infrastructure and evaluative collaborative mechanisms to support partnership development over time has been noted in multisite research around performance-based contracting and quality assurance systems (Garstka et al., 2012). A meta-analysis of collaborative governance cases revealed a number of variables associated with successful collaboration including (1) the use of incentives for participation; (2) strategies for addressing power and resource imbalances, and institutional decision-making; and (3) infrastructural supports for regular and reciprocal communication and collaboration (Ansell & Gash, 2008). In a political and highly scrutinized arena such as child welfare, gains achieved through previously discussed strategies (which can be extremely time-consuming to implement) can be easily lost without established infrastructural supports.

CONCLUSION

On its worst day, the relationship between the public and private sectors in child welfare is no more than a contractual relationship that fails to deliver the goods. Testing and refinement of promising market-based contracting approaches should without question be a priority for research; and initiatives should be explored to compare fiduciary agency relationships and contractual agency relationships along criteria including effectiveness, efficiency and overall accountability. It is important that public and private agency managers share with each other what they are learning, and with what consequences for diverse stakeholders.

On its best day, however, the contract may be the mere overarching playbook by which public and private agency partners work together regularly to fulfill their complementary roles to contribute to the collective achievement of systemic outcomes. This benefits from business practices keeping agencies focused on system priorities and using data for performance improvements; but the use of economically based incentives and disincentives is not necessarily central to the purpose and success of the partnership. Public-private partnerships vary tremendously, from the hierarchical agency (funder-service provider) relationship, to a communal sharing (joint venture) arrangement, and ultimately to a fiduciary agency (network broker) model oriented towards a shared interest in the well-being of principals and agents—a true partnership—as opposed to a narrowly focused contractual relationship that invites defections from broader public interests (Schaeffer & Loveridge, 2002). Such a schema has the potential to harvest the organizational strengths of each sector in order to tackle the complex and high-stakes challenges experienced by the child welfare population.

We move from a brokered or lead organization governance approach to one of shared network governance in which trust is high, agencies are committed to collectively established goals and outcomes are viewed as attainable only through collaboration and information sharing (Provan & Kenis, 2008). Through such a fiduciary agency approach, joint decision-making can exist driven by the shared goal of improved child well-being. If there is agreement that child welfare is challenged to ascertain how to promote optimal performance in its purchase of service contracts, then the answer cannot be found in the components of the contract alone. By supporting the partnership between agencies across sectors with different strengths and weaknesses, we see the most promising and sustainable path forward for achieving desired child and family outcomes.

KEY POINTS

- Current efforts in child welfare contracting reflect historical partnerships, new performance pressures and continued accountability concerns.
- Research is limited regarding different models of service contracting among the private child welfare sector.
- Several practical, programmatic and policy-focused strategies are proposed to organize service contracting to enhance child welfare outcomes:

1. Alignment of contracts within a shared vision of family continuity and child well-being;

2. Linking incentive-based contracts with performance measurement systems to move the system forward;
3. Continuous quality improvement (CQI) strategies on a cross-sector level involving shared access to agency data and authentic dialogue around what the data mean;
4. Joint public and private commitment to rigorous research design to test the questions policymakers and agency leaders deem most important to move the system forward; and,
5. Development of infrastructure and evaluative collaborative mechanisms to support partnership development.

*Acknowledgment: The authors would like to acknowledge the input of Dr. Mark Testa on early versions of this chapter.

REFERENCES

Abbott, G. (1968). *The child and the state, volume II: The dependent and the delinquent child; The child of unmarried parents*. New York: Greenwood Press.

Administration for Children and Families. (n.d.). *Results of the 2007 and 2008 child and family services reviews*. Retrieved from www.acf.hhs.gov/programs/cb/cwmonitoring/results/agencies_courts.pdf

Adoption and Safe Families Act of 1997, Pub. L. No. 105–89, § 111 Stat. 2115 (1997).

Agranoff, R., & McGuire, M. (2001). American federalism and the search for models of management. *Public Administration Review*, *61*(6), 671–681.

Alexander, J., Brudney, J. L., & Yang, K. (2010). Introduction to the symposium: Accountability and performance measurement: The evolving role of nonprofits in the hollow state. *Nonprofit and Voluntary Sector Quarterly*, *39*(4), 565–570.

Amirkhanyan, A. (2009). Collaborative performance measurement: Examining and explaining the prevalence of collaboration in state and local government contracts. *Journal of Public Administration, Research and Theory*, *19*, 523–554.

Ansell, C., & Gash, A. (2008). Collaborative governance in theory and practice. *Journal of Public Administration, Research and Theory*, *18*, 543–571.

Austin, M. J. (2003). The changing relationship between nonprofit organizations and public social service agencies in the era of welfare reform. *Nonprofit and Voluntary Sector Quarterly*, *32*(1), 97–114.

Austin, M. J. (2008). Strategies for transforming human service organizations into learning organizations: Evidence-based practice and the transfer of learning. *Journal of Evidence-Based Social Work*, *5*, 569–596.

Behn, R., & Kant, P. (1999). Strategies for avoiding the pitfalls of performance contracting. *Public Productivity and Management Review*, *22*, 470–489.

Benjamin, L. M., Voida, A., & Bopp, C. (2018). Policy fields, data systems, and the performance of nonprofit human service organizations. *Human Service Organizations: Management, Leadership & Governance*, *42*(2), 185–204.

Bertilli, A., & Smith, C. (2010). Relational contracting and network management. *Journal of Public Administration, Research and Theory*, *20*(S1), 21–40.

Bess, R., Andrews, C., Jantz, A., Russell, V., & Geen, R. (2002). *The cost of protecting vulnerable children III: What factors affect states' fiscal decisions?* Occasional Paper Number 61. Washington, DC: The Urban Institute.

Brousseau, E., Dedeurwaerdere, T., & Siebenhuner, B. (Eds.). (2012). *Reflexive governance for global public goods*. Cambridge, MA: The MIT Press.

Brown, T., Potoski, M., & Van Slyke, D. (2010). Contracting for complex products. *Journal of Public Administration Research and Theory*, *20*(Supp 1), 41–58.

Bunger, A. C., Cao, Y., Girth, A. M., Hoffman, J., & Robertson, H. A. (2017). Constraints and benefits of child welfare contracts with behavioral health providers: Conditions that shape service access. *Administration and Policy in Mental Health and Mental Health Services Research*, *43*(5), 728–739.

Carnochan, S., Samples, M., Myers, M., & Austin, M. J. (2014). Performance measurement challenges in nonprofit human service organizations. *Nonprofit and Voluntary Sector Quarterly*, *43*, 1014–1032.

Cash, S. J., Ingram, S. D., Biben, D. S., McKeever, S. J., & Thompson, J. (2012). Moving forward without looking back: Performance management systems as real-time evidence-based practice tools. *Children and Youth Services Review*, *34*(4), 655–659.

Chaffin, M., Hecht, D., Bard, D., Silovsky, J. F., & Beasley, W. H. (2012). A statewide trial of the SafeCare home-based services model with parents in child protective services. *Pediatrics*, *129*, 509–515.

Child Welfare League of America. (1958). *Statement of principles and policies on private and public child welfare administration*. Minneapolis: Child Welfare League of America Records, Social Welfare History Archives, University of Minnesota, box 43, folder 9.

Collins-Camargo, C., Chuang, E., McBeath, B., & Bunger, A. C. (2014). Private child welfare agency managers' perceptions of the effectiveness of different performance management strategies. *Children and Youth Services Review*, *38*, 133–141.

Collins-Camargo, C., Ensign, K., & Flaherty, C. (2008). The national quality improvement center on the privatization of child welfare services: A program description. *Research on Social Work Practice*, *18*(1), 72–81. http://doi.org/10.1177/1049731507303495

Collins-Camargo, C., McBeath, B., & Ensign, K. (2011). Privatization and performance-based contracting in child welfare: Recent trends and implications for social service administrators. *Administration in Social Work*, *35*(5), 494–516. http://doi.org/10.1080/03643107.2011.614531

Conlan, T. (1988). *New federalism: Intergovernmental reform from Nixon to Reagan*. Washington, DC: Brookings Institution Press.

Courtney, M. E. (2000). Managed care and child welfare services: What are the issues? *Children and Youth Services Review*, *22*(2), 87–91.

Davis, J. H., Schoorman, F. D., & Donaldson, L. (1997). Toward a stewardship theory of management. *Academy of Management Review*, *22*(1), 20–47.

Devaney, J. (2004). Relating outcomes to objectives in child protection. *Child and Family Social Work*, *9*, 27–38.

Dubnick, M. J., & Fredrickson, H. G. (2010). Accountable agents: Federal performance measurement and third party government. *Journal of Public Administration, Research and Theory*, *20*(1), i143–i159.

Elder, J. K., DeStefano, D., Blazevski, J., & Schuler, C. (2012). Key recommendations for developing a foundation and framework for successful implementation of performance-based contracting: A case study of a child welfare lead agency in Florida. *Journal of Public Child Welfare*, *6*(1), 42–66.

Embry, R. A., Buddenhagen, P., & Bolles, S. (2000). Managed care and child welfare: Challenges to implementation. *Children and Youth Services Review*, *22*(2), 93–116.

Faith, J., Panzarella, C., Spencer, R. C., Williams, C., Brewer, J., & Covone, M. (2010). Use of performance-based contracting to improve effective use of resources for publicly funded residential services. *The Journal of Behavioral Health Services & Research*, *37*(3), 400–408.

Flaherty, C., Collins-Camargo, C., & Lee, E. (2008). Privatization of child welfare services: Lessons learned from experienced states regarding site readiness assessment and planning. *Children and Youth Services Review*, *30*(7), 809–820.

Garstka, T., Collins-Camargo, C., Hall, J., Neal, M., & Ensign, K. (2012). Implementing performance-based contracts and quality assurance systems in child welfare services: Results from a national cross-site evaluation. *Journal of Public Child Welfare*, *6*(1), 12–41.

Gazley, B. (2010). Linking collaborative capacity to performance measurement in government-nonprofit partnerships. *Nonprofit and Voluntary Sector Quarterly*, *39*(4), 653–673.

Hanleybrown, F., Kania, J., & Kramer, M. (2012). Channeling change: Making collective impact work. *Stanford Social Innovation Review*. Retrieved from www.ssireview.org/blog/entry/channeling_change_making_collective_impact_work

Hannah, G., Ray, M., Wandersman, A., & Chien, V. H. (2010). Developing performance-based contracts between agencies and services providers: Results from a getting to outcomes support system with social service agencies. *Children and Youth Services Review*, *32*(10), 1430–1436.

Hasenfeld, Y. (2010). The attributes of human service organizations. In Y. Hasenfeld (Ed.), *Human services as complex organizations* (2nd ed., pp. 9–32). Thousand Oaks, CA: Sage Publications.

Hood, C. (2000). Paradoxes of public-sector managerialism, old public management, and public service bargains. *International Public Management Journal*, *3*, 1–22.

Jansson, B. S. (2001). *The reluctant welfare state: American social welfare policies—past, present and future* (4th ed.). Belmont, CA: Brooks, Cole.

Johansen, M., Kim, T., & Zhu, L. (2016). Managing for results differently: Examining managers' purposeful performance information use in public, nonprofit, and private organizations. *The American Review of Public Administration*, *48*(2), 133–147.

Jolles, M. P., Collins-Camargo, C., McBeath, B., Bunger, A. C., & Chuang, E. (2017). Managerial strategies for frontline worker understanding of performance measures in nonprofit child welfare agencies. *Nonprofit and Voluntary Sector Quarterly*, *46*(6), 1166–1188.

Kahn, A. J., & Kamerman, S. B. (1999). *Contracting for child and family services: A mission sensitive guide*. Baltimore, MD: The Annie E. Casey Foundation.

Kapp, S. A., Ah Hahn, S., & Rand, A. (2011). Building a performance information system for statewide residential treatment services. *Residential Treatment for Children and Youth*, *28*(1), 39–54.

Katz, M. B. (2001). *The price of citizenship: Redefining the American welfare state*. New York: Owl Books.

Kearney, K. A., Bloom-Ellis, B., & Thompson, R. (2012). Breaking down the Silos: Lessons learned from the expansion of performance-based contracting to residential treatment services in Illinois. *Journal of Public Child Welfare*, *6*(1), 83–107.

Kettl, D. F. (2002). *The transformation of governance: Public administration for twenty-first century America*. Baltimore, MD: The Johns Hopkins University Press.

Kettner, P. M., & Martin, L. L. (1990). Purchase of service contracting: Two models. *Administration in Social Work*, *14*(1), 15–30.

Kramer, R., & Grossman, B. (1987). Contracting for social services: Process management and resource dependencies. *Social Service Review*, *61*(1), 32–55.

Lamothe, S., & Lamothe, M. (2008). *Examining the link between competition and accountability in social service delivery: Does competition increase adherence to contract terms?* Western Political Science Association Annual Meeting.

Lindsey, D., & Shlonsky, A. (Eds.). (2008). *Child welfare research: Advances for practice and policy*. New York: Oxford University Press.

Lynch-Cerullo, K., & Cooney, K. (2011). Moving from outputs to outcomes: A review of the evolution of pm in the human service nonprofit sector. *Administration in Social Work*, *35*(4), 364–388.

Martin, L. L. (2003). *Performance-based contracting (PBC) for human services: A review of the literature*. Orlando, FL: Center for Community Partnerships.

Martin, L. L. (2005). Performance-based contracting for human services: Does it work? *Administration in Social Work*, *29*(1), 63–77.

Marwell, N. P., & Calabrese, T. (2016), A deficit model of collaborative governance: Government-nonprofit fiscal relations in the provision of child welfare services. *Journal of Public Administration Research and Theory, 25*, 1031–1058.

McBeath, B. (Spring, 2016). *Performance based contracting in child welfare: Lessons learned to date.* Child Welfare 360: A Comprehensive Look at a Prevalent Child Welfare Issue, 14–15.

McBeath, B., Collins-Camargo, C., Chuang, E., Wells, R., Bunger, A. C., & Jolles, M. P. (2014). New directions for research on the organizational and institutional context of child welfare agencies: Introduction to the symposium on "the organizational and managerial context of private child welfare agencies". *Children and Youth Services Review, 38*, 83–92.

McBeath, B., & Meezan, W. (2010). Governance in motion: Service provision and child welfare outcomes in a performance-based, managed care contracting environment. *Journal of Public Administration Research and Theory, 20*(Suppl 1), i101–i123.

McCullough, C., & Schmitt, B. (1999). *1998 managed care & privatization tracking project: State and county survey results*. Washington, DC: CWLA Press.

McCullough, C., & Schmitt, B. (2000). Managed care and privatization: Results of a national survey. *Children and Youth Services Review, 22*(2), 117–130.

McCullough, C., & Schmitt, B. (2003). *2000–2001 management, finance, and contracting survey final report*. Washington, DC: CWLA Press.

Meezan, W., & McBeath, B. (2008). Market-based disparities in foster care outcomes. *Children and Youth Services Review, 30*(4), 388–406.

Meezan, W., & McBeath, B. (2011). Moving toward performance-based, managed care contracting in child welfare: Perspectives on staffing, financial management, and information technology. *Administration in Social Work, 35*(2), 180–206.

Mirafab F. (2004). Public-private partnerships: The Trojan horse of neoliberal development? *Journal of Planning Education and Research, 24*(1), 89–101.

Mitchell, L., Walters, R., Thomas, M. L., Denniston, J., McIntosh, H., & Brodowski, M. (2012). Children's bureau's vision for the future of child welfare. *Journal of Public Child Welfare, 6*(4), 550–567.

Monkkonen, E. H. (1988). *America becomes urban: The development of U.S. cities and towns, 1780–1980*. Berkeley, CA: University of California Press.

Moulin, M. (2009). Public sector scorecard. *Nursing Management, 16*(5), 26–31.

Noonan, K., Sabel, C., & Simon, W. (2009). Legal accountability in the service-based welfare state: Lessons from child welfare reform. *Law & Social Inquiry, 34*(3), 523–568.

Pecora, P. J., Whittaker, J. K., Maluccio, A. N., & Barth, R. P. (2000). *The child welfare challenge: Policy, practice, and research* (2nd ed.). New York: Aldine de Gruyter.

Personal Responsibility and Work Opportunity Reconciliation Act of 1996, Pub. L. No. 104–193, § 11 Stat. 2168 (1996).

Provan, K., & Kenis, P. (2008). Modes of network governance: Structure, management, and effectiveness. *Journal of Public Administration Research and Theory, 18*, 229–252.

Purdy, J. M. (2012). A framework for assessing power in collaborative governance process. *Public Administration Review, 72*(3), 409–417.

Raghavan, R. (2010). Using risk adjustment approaches in child welfare performance measurement: Applications and insights from health and mental health settings. *Children and Youth Services Review, 32*(1), 103–112.

Rhodes, R. (1996). The new governance: Governing without government. *Political Studies, 44*, 652–667.

Romzek, B. S., & Johnston, J. M. (2005). State social services contracting: Exploring the determinants of contract accountability. *Public Administration Review, 65*(4), 436–449.

Romzek, B. S., LeRoux, K., & Blackmar, J. (2012). A preliminary theory of informal accountability among network organizational actors. *Public Administration Review, 72*, 442–453.

Rosenthal, M. G. (2000). Public or private children's services? Privatization in retrospect. *Social Service Review, 74*(2), 281–305.

Salamon, L. M. (1995). *Partners in public service: Government-nonprofit relations in the modern welfare state*. Baltimore, MD: Johns Hopkins University Press.

Schaeffer, P., & Loveridge, S. (2002). Toward and understanding of public-private cooperation. *Public Performance and Management Review, 26*(2), 169–189.

Smith, S. R. (1989). The changing politics of child welfare services: New roles for the government and the non-profit sectors. *Child Welfare, 68*(3), 289–299.

Smith, S. R. (2012). Social services. In L. M. Salamon (Ed.), *The state of nonprofit America* (2nd ed., pp. 192–128). Washington, DC: The Brookings Institute.

Smith, S. R., & Lipsky, M. (1993). *Nonprofits for hire: The welfare state in an age of contracting*. Cambridge, MA: Harvard University Press.

Taylor, K., & Shaver, M. (2010). Performance based contracting: Aligning incentives with outcomes to produce results. In M. Testa & J. Poertner (Eds.), *Fostering accountability: Using evidence to guide and improve child welfare policy*. Oxford: Oxford University Press.

Testa, M. F., & Poertner, J. (2010). *Fostering accountability: Using evidence to guide and improve child welfare policy*. Oxford: Oxford University Press.

Tilbury, C. (2007). Shaping child welfare policy via performance measurement. *Child Welfare, 86*(60), 115–135.

U. S. Department of Health and Human Services, National Clearinghouse on Child Abuse and Neglect Information. (2002). *National child abuse and neglect data system summary of key findings from the calendar year 2000*. Retrieved from www.calib.com/nccanch/pubs/factsheets/canstats.cfm

Van Slyke, D. M. (2003). The mythology of privatization in contracting for social services. *Public Administration Review, 63*(3), 296–315.

Van Slyke, D. M. (2007). Agents or stewards: Using theory to understand the government-nonprofit social service contracting relationship. *Journal of Public Administration Research and Theory, 17*(2), 157–187.

Webster, D., Usher, C. L., Needell, B., & Wildfire, J. (2008). Self-evaluation: Using data to guide policy and practice in public child welfare agencies. In D. Lindsey & A. Shlonsky (Eds.), *Child welfare research: Advances for practice and policy* (pp. 261–270). New York: Oxford University Press.

Weigensberg, E. C. (2009). *Child welfare agency performance: How are child, agency, and county factors related to achieving timely permanency outcomes for children in foster care?* (Doctoral dissertation), The University of North Carolina, Chapel Hill.

Wells, R., Jolles, M. P., Chuang, E., McBeath, B., & Collins-Camargo, C. (2014). Trends in local public child welfare agencies 1999–2009. *Children and Youth Services Review, 38*, 93–100. http://doi.org/10.1016/j.childyouth.2014.01.015

Wulcyzn, F., Chen, L., & Orlebeke, B. (2010). Measuring contract agency performance with administrative data. *Child Welfare, 79*(5), 457–474.

5

Contracting for Mental Health Services

Melissa Hirschi and Sara S. Bachman

INTRODUCTION

According to the U.S. Surgeon General (2010), and more recently by the National Institute of Mental Health (2018), an estimated 20% of the adult population in the United States is affected by mental disorders that range in severity from mild to serious. Some mental disorders such as anxiety can be managed by the patient individually or with medication and/or professional counseling. Other mental disorders such as schizophrenia or bipolar disorder are more debilitating (U.S. Surgeon General, 2010). Individuals living with mental illness can obtain treatment through various agencies and organizations.

Over time, the United States has used various practices to care for and manage individuals with mental health issues (Conrad & Schneider, 1980). Prior to the 1960s, individuals with mental illness were cared for and treated in large psychiatric institutions. After the deinstitutionalization policies of 1963 (Mental Retardation and Facilities Community Mental Health Centers (CMHC) Act, 2012) treatment and care for this vulnerable population shifted from large institutions to community mental health centers (e.g., Brown, 1985; Mechanic & Rochefort, 1990; Morrissey, 1989). As treatment migrated from large state-run institutions to community-based care, payment for these services also shifted, including increased use of contracting (e.g., Demone & Gibelman, 1989).

In this chapter, we will discuss the broad landscape of the use of contracting as a method of transferring payment for mental health services from one entity to another. We will begin by presenting a history of mental health contracting in our country. We will then discuss current trends in financing and reimbursement that might be included in contracting mechanisms, such as capitation, pay for performance and value-based purchasing. Contracting can be used to integrate mental health services with other sectors in order to promote more comprehensive care and better meet the treatment needs of individuals with mental health problems. We will discuss integration of mental health services with other areas such as substance use, primary care, child welfare, criminal justice and schools. We will end this chapter by presenting lessons learned and key points on contracting for mental health services.

HISTORY OF MENTAL HEALTH CONTRACTING

Throughout our country's history, the use of contracting for services by the government, including mental health services, has shifted based on the evolving roles of government and private organizations, the functions of each, as well as the influence of public opinion and broader legislation (Demone & Gibelman, 1989). In Colonial America, caring for the poor and needy was first seen as the responsibility of the church but as a last resort, the government would provide services. Often these services were provided through an early form of contracting in which the needs of orphans, individuals who were poor, or older adults, were auctioned to private individuals who were then paid to care for these individuals (Demone & Gibelman, 1989). Contracting for medical services was a forerunner to contracting for mental health services and began with physicians providing care in the nineteenth century for various industries such as the railroad (Ameringer, 2008). Over time, abuses to these systems brought change such as government direct subsidies for services. As the growth of the need for social welfare services continued, so too did the growth of subsidies for those services (Demone & Gibelman, 1989).

Other factors also influenced the use of subsidies and contracting for services. Proponents of contracting argued that it was less costly to contract for services than it was to build facilities, maintain them and staff them in order to provide those services. It was also thought that contracting for services rather than providing those services directly through the government, would keep the services free of political influence. Additionally, many believed that higher standards of care and service would be provided through contracting because they would not be limited by government control (Demone & Gibelman, 1989).

During the 1930s with the influence of the Great Depression, public sentiment as to the range and role of government responsibility in providing services further evolved. The size and scope of the need for services during this time was expansive and the Social Security Act increased the government's role in providing services. Subsidies decreased as the role of the government in providing services increased (Demone & Gibelman, 1989). In the following decades, the increasing client population expanded government role in both funding and providing services (Demone & Gibelman, 1989).

Changes in provision of services, in particular for mental health services, moved from large state run psychiatric facilities to community-based mental health providers after the passing of the Community Mental Health Centers Act of 1963 (Dorwart, Schlesinger, & Pulice, 1986; Frank & Gaynor, 1993; Libby, 1997). During the 1960s, the government began using an open match for social services and purchase of services was more formally introduced for these types of services (Demone & Gibelman, 1989). Further changes came in 1967 with increased contracting for services as the growing dislike of public social services and the ever-increasing belief that government provided services were inefficient (DeHoog, 1984; Demone & Gibelman, 1989). Fewer restrictions in the language of contracting also increased the scope of contracted services during this time (Demone & Gibelman, 1989).

The loosening of definitions and restrictions for services continued in the mid 1970s and states were able to go so far as to define the services and decide where, how much and to whom services would be provided (Demone & Gibelman, 1989). This greatly increased the ability of states to determine the ways in which federal funding would be used and influenced the use of contracting by the states for services (Demone & Gibelman, 1989). The expanded ability of states to determine the use of federal funding came at a time when mental health parity was at the forefront of public and legislative purview. The recognition of the inequity in provision for mental health and substance use disorders when held against the provision of services for medical conditions, led legislation mandating more equitable coverage of services by insurance providers (Ettner et al., 2016).

With an ever-increasing focus on efficiency and cost-containment, finding ways to minimize expenditures and increase services becomes a central focus. Beginning in 1981 with Title XX, block grants were used as a way to pay for mental health services. Block grants reduced the level of federal funding, helped eliminate some regulations over services and freed states from needing to provide a match for federal funding (Frank & Gaynor, 1993; Demone & Gibelman, 1989; Libby, 1997). Additionally, in order for states to further reduce their level of expenditures for social services with providers, they moved to terminate purchase of services contracts or asked agencies to match funds in order to maintain the contract for services (Demone & Gibelman, 1989). Whereas the legislation surrounding mental health parity has shifted repeatedly since the first parity legislation (Sipe et al., 2015), a focus on parity for these services has continued to be a common rationale to fund mental health services (e.g., Ettner et al., 2016; Frank & Gaynor, 1993; Demone & Gibelman, 1989; Libby, 1997).

TRENDS IN FINANCING AND REIMBURSEMENT IN MENTAL HEALTH CONTRACTING

Since the trend toward contracting for mental health services in the 1980s, other financing and reimbursement strategies have evolved and become more prevalent in multiple health and social support sectors. These strategies may serve as the framework for a contract between a payer and a provider or provider network organization. These arrangements may focus on mental health services specifically, or include mental health services in a broader array of health services and supports. In this section, we discuss several of these strategies, describing their key attributes and how they might be used in contracting for mental health services, including capitation or bundled payments, pay for performance and value-based purchasing strategies.

Capitation

For many years, Medicare has promoted capitation or bundled payments to control program spending. Capitation is often implemented through contract specifications. The Medicare Payment Advisory Commission endorsed bundled payments, noting the intent of this method: to decrease spending by reducing the number of unnecessary physician services during a hospitalization; to encourage more judicious use of health care resources during the hospital stay; and to reduce post-discharge costs, including unnecessary post-acute care services and avoidable readmissions (MedPAC, 2008). Medicaid programs have also long advanced agendas that include use of capitated purchasing of health care services for eligible populations. However, the impact of these payment systems on vulnerable populations, such as those with serious mental illness, has not been well documented, and the incentives to withhold care under capitation are powerful, with potentially devastating consequences. High-risk or high need patients are particularly vulnerable to underservice if provider payment systems are not linked to meaningful quality and outcome measures that are included in the contract. Inadequate payment rates that do not cover the costs of serving high-risk or high-need patients may cause providers to skimp on necessary services or avoid serving vulnerable patients entirely, thus exacerbating existing inequities according to income, severity of illness, race, ethnicity or other characteristics.

One solution to this issue is the inclusion of risk adjustment mechanisms in contracts in order to "level the playing field" among capitated plans. Through risk adjustment, health plans under contract to different payers receive a greater capitation amount for individual patients who have greater health care needs. Bundled payment rates are often risk-adjusted in an effort to account for differences in patient-level characteristics or severity of illness. However, the accuracy of risk-adjustment methodologies remains imperfect, especially for potentially high-cost populations such as people with serious mental health problems. The development of accurate risk adjustment strategies has not kept pace with the trend toward moving to bundled payments (Salinsky, 2013). As a result, some very-high-risk (and, thus, high-cost) populations may be excluded from bundled payment arrangements or be at risk for inadequate care. Risk adjustments or patient exclusions are relevant for all the provider payment reforms that may be used together with contracting. Attention to those issues is critical when payment innovation methods replace rather than supplement known fee-for-service reimbursement mechanisms.

The Patient Protection and Affordable Care Act (ACA) included provisions for the development of a new type of bundled payment strategy—the Accountable Care Organization (ACO). The ACO model can be used in contracting arrangements in order to promote care integration and provide financial incentives (shared savings) for improved outcomes including quality (Bachman, 2011). However, there is little evidence about the impact of ACOs, especially with respect to quality of care (Damberg et al., 2014). Moreover, ACOs are nearly uniformly being used for the general adult population and there is little information about how this strategy might be applied particularly to people with specific, potentially more severe disorders such as serious mental illness (Salinsky, 2013).

Payers can use contracts as the vehicle for purchasing bundled services from a health plan or ACO. The contract will ideally include provisions that clearly identify the population to be covered, the services and benefits that will be provided, mechanisms for monitoring the contract, financing specifications including the risk adjustment methods to be used, quality assurance monitoring strategies, benefit exception policies and other specifications that will clarify the relationship between the payer and the capitated entity. Contracting with a health plan offers the benefit of simplifying the purchasing strategy for the payer, perhaps requiring just one contract rather than several for different types of services. For people with mental health problems, it is essential for a specialist in mental health services and supports to be engaged in planning, implementing and monitoring the contract.

Pay for Performance

Pay for Performance (P4P) strategies can be used in contracts in order to offer financial incentives for provider performance measured against a standard set of metrics, including quality outcomes. A key concern with P4P strategies is the lack of specific quality outcome measures, and performance is often assessed against process measures (Korda & Eldridge, 2011). Further, there is not consensus in the design or effectiveness of the programs, although programs that are more likely to be effective have a specific focus on individual providers and greater communication about the program (Salinsky, 2013). There are few studies that have focused on the impact of P4P for mental health service and there is not consistency with respect to the outcome measures that are used (Korda & Eldridge, 2011). Evidence about the impact of P4P is mixed and efforts to determine impact have been hindered by confounding from other innovations that were being implemented simultaneously (Damberg et al., 2014).

Value-Based Purchasing

Value-based purchasing (VBP) includes a set of health care payment and delivery strategies that can be implemented through contracting in order to emphasize cost effectiveness and achieving the best possible outcomes given available resources. Value-based purchasing, especially for Medicare, has been promoted by the ACA beginning early after the law was passed in 2010. However, VBP programs were initiated by employers before the ACA took effect, such as the program begun by Pitney Bowes in 2002 (Mahoney et al., 2013). VBP is thus an example of employer sponsored contracting initiatives, begun in the last several decades, aimed at achieving value in health benefit provision for employees (Bachman, Pomeranz, & Tell, 1988). More recently, employers implementing VBP strategies ask health plans to achieve both cost and quality outcomes (Rosenthal et al., 2007). Although VBP contracting strategies have been used by employers for many years, there is little published data about the results of these efforts, primarily because the initiatives are being implemented in the private sector. Some results suggest that VBP is more likely to be implemented by larger employers or employer collaboratives (Rosenthal et al., 2007) who likely have more purchasing power to incentivize health plans to drive cost and quality outcomes. There is also a cost to implementing VBP programs, such as the need to identify and implement measures of quality as well as the need to educate employees to make them "smart buyers" of health care. Large employers are more likely to have the resources to develop and support this needed infrastructure (Rosenthal et al., 2007).

Under VBP, employers are responsible for making purchasing and contracting decisions based on the results of data analysis associated with estimating cost and quality outcomes. Benefits managers in private employer human resource departments may decide not to pay for services that are determined to be high cost or low quality, without the counterbalancing positive outcome, and these decisions may be controversial within the company (Mahoney et al., 2013). Without good data to justify benefit design decisions, the uncertainty about the impact of VBP may diminish decision-makers' enthusiasm for taking on the controversy. Some data suggest that the impact of VBP and value-based insurance design (VBID) may vary across benefit design options for different conditions. As a result, employers may not be best served by a "one size fits all" VBP approach, further complicating the employer strategic benefit design choices (Mahoney et al., 2013). For VBP to be effective, employers must have access to and use cost and quality data. Robst, Rost and Marshall (2013) examined survey findings to determine whether employers knew the results of the quality measures available to them. Larger employers were more likely to know the quality measures of their health plans, although a majority of all employers did not know this information (Robst et al., 2013).

Employers must also be prepared for the unintended consequences of using VBP strategies for contracts in various health plan designs. For example, under VBP, as well as other health plan designs, costs may be shifted to the employee and result in increases in out of pocket expenditures. This outcome may have devastating consequences for those at the low to moderate end of the pay range, or if the employee has a family member with high health care needs, including people with serious mental health problems (Ghandour et al., 2015).

A number of strategies have been implemented under the general framework of value-based purchasing. In this section, we provide brief descriptions of various models used to achieve value in health care purchasing.

Value-Based Purchasing—Insurance Design

A specific type of VBP that can be used with contracting mechanisms is value-based insurance design (VBID). Chernew and Fendrick (2009) have identified two general approaches to VBID programs: one targets services that are especially cost effective such as specific medications, and the second targets groups of patients that are likely to respond to selected treatments such as people with type II diabetes (Chandran et al., 2015). For these two overall strategies, VBID programs use financial or program incentives to encourage patient behaviors, thus reducing overall health care costs, even if the VBID program requires some additional expenditures. For example, Choudry et al. (2014) found that VBID programs that used selected pharmacy benefit management strategies such as mail order pharmacy demonstrated greater patient medication adherence and lower cost sharing. There is some evidence that VBID can improve medication adherence by lowering or eliminating patients' payments for some medications, although the longer-term business case for VBID has still not been made (Maciejewski et al., 2014).

Value-based insurance designs frequently lower consumers' cost sharing to motivate healthy behavior, such as adhering to medication regimens. Few health care purchasers have followed the more controversial approach of using increased cost sharing to reduce demand for high-cost, low-value medical care (Ginsberg, 2010). A lingering question, however, is whether risk, responsibility and rewards are being equitably shared among patients, providers and payers under plans that include VBID (Berry, 2015). The greater treatment costs associated with more serious conditions such as serious mental health disorders may not be responsive to cost-sharing incentives.

Value-Based Purchasing—High-Deductible Health Plans (HDHPs)

High-deductible health plans (HDHPs) are health care coverage options that offer lower premiums but higher deductibles than typical plans (AAP, 2014). HDHPs often appeal to subscribers that have few identified health care needs, because the associated short-term out-of-pocket costs are an incentive to enroll. However, for individuals and families with higher health care needs, these plans are associated with increased out of pocket costs and potentially, financial hardship associated with health care spending. Family financial hardship resulting from increased out of pocket costs associated with the greater health care needs of people with mental illness may impact their families disproportionately (Bachman, Comeau, Dworetzky, Hamershock, & Hirschi, 2015). Thus, although HDHPs may be included in the set of options considered for contracting through VBP designs, this strategy has potentially devastating consequences, especially in the absence of adequate quality and outcome measures that can be used in the contract to assure value (AAP, 2014).

The Evidence About Value-Based Purchasing

A recent report produced by the Government Accountability Office (GAO, 2015) found little impact of Medicare's hospital VBP program (HVBP). For the most part, the quality measures that were evaluated did not change, the exception being the readmissions indicators that are subject to financial penalties, rather than financial rewards. Interestingly, hospital leaders who were interviewed for the report suggested that any changes that were seen were a result of the hospital's ongoing quality improvement efforts that were in place prior to the VBP program (GAO, 2015). Another study confirmed these results, and noted that the timing of the financial incentives in Medicare's HVBP was not associated with improved quality of care. It is unclear whether improvement for the clinical process measures prior to the start of HVBP was driven by the expectation of the program or was the result of other factors (Ryan, Burgess, Pesko, Borden, & Dimick, 2015). These results suggest that—although contracts based on VBP principles are moving forward—there is little evidence base on which to build these advancements. We still know little about how best to design and implement VBP programs to achieve stated goals (Korda & Eldridge, 2011; Damberg et al., 2014). And, the information we do have does not apply to many members of vulnerable populations.

Value-Based Purchasing and Health Care Inequities

The financial incentives that are an essential element of VBP encourage biased selection of less complex cases, and without adequate risk adjustment protections, certainly do not encourage providers to address the social determinants of health that drive some health inequities. VBP includes the provision that more costs are shifted to the consumer, especially in the context of HDHPs. However, for people with low incomes or high health care costs, such as those with serious mental illness, costs are a barrier to care. Without reliable and valid outcome measures, there is an associated risk that VBP programs will not mitigate and may exacerbate existing health inequities.

INTEGRATION OF MENTAL HEALTH SERVICES INTO OTHER SERVICE AREAS

This chapter has focused on emerging strategies to pay for and manage the costs of mental health services through contracting. In this section we will address more specifically areas in which contracts might be used to integrate mental health services with other services when clients receive cross sectoral services. The literature is rich with calls for the integration of services (e.g., Adelsheim, 2014; Child & McIntyre, 2014; Dobmeyer, 2018; Dutmers, 2017; Frailing, 2010; He & Phillips, 2017; Michael & Jameson, 2017; Osher, 2013). Integration can fall along a spectrum, including coordinated care, care that is co-located and fully integrated care (e.g., Waugh, Voyles, Shore, Lippolis, & Lyon, 2017). The level of integration may vary depending on the specific systems and providers. This section will use the terms "integrated" and/or "integration" to cover the full spectrum of the ways that a contract might be used to promote integration of mental health and other services.

Substance Use

Substance use and mental health are an important pairing. According to the Substance Abuse and Mental Health Services Administration (SAMHSA), whereas approximately 8.2 million adults in the United States have a co-occurring mental illness and substance use disorder (SUD) (SAMHSA, 2015); the majority of these individuals (51.9%) receive no treatment. Of the remaining individuals, 38.2% receive mental health services only and less than 10% receive specialty substance use treatment only (2.9%) or mental health services and specialty substance use treatment combined (6.9%) (SAMHSA, 2015). As we continue to study and evaluate effective treatments for both mental health and SUD, the link between both and the importance of treating them in concert, is increasing (e.g., Johnson et al., 2015; Osher, 2013; Rossheim, Livingston, Lerch, Taxman, & Walter, 2018).

Several effective SUD treatments make use of mental health techniques, including motivational interviewing SUD (Sayegh, Huey, Zara, & Jhaveri, 2017), seeking safety (Hien et al., 2012; Morgan-Lopez et al., 2014), cognitive behavior therapy (CBT) and trauma informed CBT (TF-CBT) (Badour et al., 2017; Beck, 2011), integrated dual diagnosis treatment (IDDT) (Drake, O'Neal, & Wallach, 2008; Harrison, Spybrook, Curtis, & Cousins, 2017; Osher, 2013) and integrated assertive community treatment (I-ACT) (Cooper et al., 2010). In addition, medically assisted therapy (MAT) incorporates therapy (Carroll et al., 2011; Kampman & Jarvis, 2015), including treatment for alcohol (Agency for Healthcare Research and Quality (AHRQ), 2016), opioids (Ali, Tahir, Jabeen, & Malik, 2017; HSER et al., 2015; Moore et al., 2016; Potter et al., 2015; Weiss & Rao, 2017; Williams, 2018), cannabis (Squeglia et al., 2016, 2018), Methamphetamine (Elkashef et al., 2008; Spiller et al., 2008) and cocaine (Castells, Cunill, Merez-Mana, Vidal, & Capella, 2016).

The National Institute on Drug Abuse (NIDA, 2018) has current treatment principles that can be thought of as best practice when working with individuals who have SUD: (1) Treatment needs to be readily available. By integrating mental health services and SUD services, agencies and organizations will be able to provide a more holistic approach to treatment for clients as well as more efficiently utilize scarce resources and personnel to meet the treatment needs for individuals with mental health, SUD, or those who are dually diagnosed. (2) Remaining in treatment for an adequate period of time is critical. Using contracts to integrate mental health and SUD treatment has the potential to more effectively address this principle by having the same treatment provider(s) working closely with individuals on both their mental health and SUD issues, thereby allowing treatment providers to have a more complete picture of the individual's overall progress in both areas. Treatment providers will then be able to more confidently make recommendations on length of time in treatment, ensuring it is adequate to meet the needs and treatment goals of the individual. (3) Counseling, whether group, individual or both, and other behavioral therapies (e.g., DBT, MI, trauma informed treatment) are the most commonly used forms of drug treatment. These treatment modalities use trained mental health practitioners and therefore, a more targeted integration of mental health and SUD treatment is a natural blending of personnel, training and skills. (4) Medications are an important element of treatment for many patients, especially when combined with counseling and other behavioral therapies. (5) An individual's treatment and services plan must be assessed continually and modified as necessary to ensure that it meets his or her changing needs (NIDA, 2009). Integrating mental health and SUD services makes use of the natural opportunity mental health practitioners often have to spend more time with clients than do medical providers. As such, they are more likely to be able to assess and modify treatment plans as necessary to ensure the individual's treatment goals are being addressed.

Guidelines and recommendations for best practices in treating co-morbid mental health and SUD can be helpful when working to integrate these services. However, missing from the literature is specific information on how best to provide these services; make use of contracts to pay for these services, and work across providers to effectively and efficiently deliver these services. More information on strategies to negotiate service delivery and contracts to pay for integrated mental health and SUD services would help. Additionally, more research focused specifically on outcomes and metrics used for evaluation would bolster our ability to more confidently integrate mental health and SUD services.

Primary Care

Contracts can be used to integrate mental health services with SUD treatments to effectively address the range of needs for individuals with dual diagnosis. Further integrating mental health services with primary care is another way to provide services for individuals who may need MAT for a SUD as discussed previously, however, the benefits of integrating mental health and primary care can go well beyond MAT. Connections have been seen between poor mental health condition and poor physical health (Siantz, Henwood, Xu, Sarin, & Gilmer, 2017; Zivin et al., 2017). The integration of mental health services and screenings in primary care settings may provide greater opportunity to meet individuals where they are and more easily identify their needs. This can happen through having a relationship and greater level of comfort between the individual and provider (Adelsheim, 2014; Dobmeyer, 2018; Feldman, 1994), early detection (Adelsheim, 2014; Dobmeyer, 2018; Feldman, 1994; Talmi et al., 2016), a decrease in the gap between identification of need and service delivery (Adelsheim, 2014) and the ability to provide services over the course of the disease (Dobmeyer, 2018).

Several barriers to integrating mental health care in primary care settings include a lack of specific mental health training for primary care providers (Adelsheim, 2014; Delbridge, Zubatsky, & Fowler, 2017; Khatri, Perry, & deGruy, 2017; Saillant, Hudelson, Dao, & Perron, 2016; Siantz et al., 2017), providers not asking questions or probing in areas of mental health (Saillant et al., 2016), lack of appropriate screening tools (Dobmeyer, 2018; Shedler, 2017) and a lack of collaboration and communication across providers (Adelsheim, 2014; Khatri et al., 2017; Waugh et al., 2017). Understanding the benefits and barriers to integration of mental health services in primary care settings is useful. However, with a dearth of applicable research on how to make use of contracts to streamline payment of screenings and services, this knowledge is often relegated to ideal best practice that lacks practical application. More research should be focused on how contracts are implemented within these settings to pay for services as well as contracts or memoranda of understanding across providers to communicate with each other when delivering these services.

Child Welfare

Another area to examine when integrating mental health services through contracting, is the child welfare system. Research has shown improved outcomes for children and youth in the child welfare system when mental health treatment is part of the child and family service plan (Child & McIntyre, 2014; Okpych & Courtney, 2018; Oppenheim, Lee, Lichtenstein, Bledsoe, & Fisher, 2012; Wells & Chuang, 2012). When integrating mental health services in child welfare, it is important to find ways to ensure timely and accurate assessment (Cappelli et al., 2016; He, & Phillips, 2017; He, Lim, Lecklitner, Olson, & Traube, 2015; Okpych & Courtney, 2018), collaboration across providers and members of the child and family team (Cappelli et al., 2016; Drabble, 2007; He & Phillips, 2017; He, 2015; He et al., 2015; Oppenheim et al., 2012), adequate training for staff and providers (He & Phillips, 2017; He, Traube, & Young, 2014) and continuity of care for youth transitioning to adulthood (Braciszewski et al., 2018; Cappelli et al., 2016).

Because child welfare is necessarily a cross-sectoral discipline for children in need of services, it is crucial to effectively and efficiently integrate mental health services for this vulnerable population. More information on the use of contracts to provide these services is needed. Similar to SUD and primary care, more robust research focused on outcomes and evaluation of implementation methods for contracting would provide greater insight into how best to integrate these services across systems.

Criminal Justice

There are multiple layers to the criminal justice system or points of intervention and all have opportunities for integrating mental health services. Osher (2013) highlighted four specific areas: police, courts, jails and prisons, and discharge planning. Each have unique avenues for integrating mental health services. Police can and do play a role in integrating mental health services within the criminal justice system whether through providing specialized responses based on specific training, integrating mental health providers more closely in the work they do such as with a co-responder or consultant, or through larger community-based mental health responses such as mental health first aid (Deane, Steadman, Borum, Veysey, & Morrissey, 1999).

Mental health services are also being integrated in the court system, including mental health specialty courts, which emerged in the late 1990s (Cooper, 2017; Cosden, Ellens, Schnell, & Yamini-Diouf, 2005; D'Emic, 2015; Frailing, 2010; Han & Redlich, 2018; Honegger, 2015; Hughes & Peak, 2012; Johnston & Flynn, 2017), substance abuse courts (Dutmers, 2017; Fisher, 2014; Zettler, 2018) and juvenile courts (Howell, Kelly, Palmer, & Mangum, 2004). Mental health services can also be integrated within jails and prisons whether through diagnosis (Al-Rousan, Rubenstein, Sieleni, Deol, & Wallace, 2017) or treatment (Hinton & Reister, 2015; Van Dorn et al., 2017). Upon release, mental health services are integrated into discharge planning and re-entry (Bonfine, Ritter, & Munetz, 2016; Johnson et al., 2015; Zettler, 2018) as well as through probation and parole (Belenko, Johnson, Taxman, & Rieckmann, 2016).

Across the criminal justice system when integrating mental health services, evaluation, assessment and identification of need are important (Bonfine et al., 2016; Grudzinskas, Clayfield, Roy-Bujnowski, Fisher, & Richardson, 2005; Hinton & Reister, 2015; Rossheim et al., 2018). So, too, is the understanding of the importance of dual diagnosis treatment (Grudzinskas et al, 2005; Johnson et al., 2015; Osher, 2013; Rossheim et al., 2018; Van Dorn et al., 2017; Zettler, 2018), training for staff and providers (Osher, 2013) and communication across all points of contact (Grudzinskas et al., 2005; Hinton & Reister, 2015; Johnson et al., 2015; Kriegel, Henwood, & Gilmer, 2016).

Although an individual's mental health can contribute to their criminal involvement, it generally is the criminal justice system driving treatment (Wilson & Draine, 2006). Therefore, the knowledge needed to better understand this integration and how these services are paid for, provided and monitored is extremely important. The use of contracts to pay for delivery of these services is one avenue but requires greater assessment, monitoring of outcomes and communication across disciplines to ensure individuals mental health needs are being treated. Additionally, important is the advocacy for sufficient treatment for individuals within a system focused primarily on criminality and recidivism and secondarily on the individual's mental health. Contracts written to link mental health services to the individual's criminal sanctions may be an effective way to leverage the unique focus of each system and draw on the power held within the criminal justice system to promote the utilization of and access to mental health services, which can help promote reentry for those leaving the criminal justice system.

Schools

Integrating mental health services in schools can help increase access by minimizing delays in service delivery or location barriers that may exist because youth access mental health services at the schools where they are already present (Adelsheim, 2014; Lai, Guo, Maghsoodi, Puffer, & Kataoka, 2016; Michael & Jameson, 2017). Providing services where the child is already located, the schools, can be very important for youth to be able to receive those services, especially in rural areas where access to mental health services and providers is more limited (Adelsheim, 2014; Michael & Jameson, 2017). Similar to other areas just discussed, assessment, identification and early intervention of mental health needs is important for successful integration of services within schools (Adelsheim, 2014). So, too, is coordination and timely follow-up (Adelsheim, 2014; Atkins, Hoagwood, Kutash, & Seidman, 2010; Berzin et al., 2011; George et al., 2014; Lai et al., 2016) and working across systems, understanding limitations of different service sectors and confidentiality (Dinkmeyer, Carlson, & Dinkmeyer, 1994; George et al., 2014).

Mental health services can be integrated within schools in different ways including the use of mental health consultants or direct service providers for the individual child (Berzin et al., 2011; Dinkmeyer et al., 1994; Erchul, 1993; Marks, 1995). The differing ways in which mental health services can be integrated in schools provides various methods for contracting to provide and pay for these services. More research is needed to understand these processes and the mechanisms required to work within school systems to more completely integrate mental health services. Additionally, more research is needed to assess these services and the outcomes on mental health of the child as well as assessing and attending to educational outcomes and addressing both in concert.

Because individuals cross paths with and can be touched by many of these systems (mental health, substance use, primary care, child welfare, criminal justice and schools), integration of services within and among these systems can be important for streamlining services and meeting individual needs. As an example, if we considered a child and his or her family who are involved with the juvenile court, it is not unreasonable to think that the court would have an interest in the outcomes for this child and family and these may be impacted by mental health of the child and/or their family. Substance use issues may also be present and can play a role as well. Additionally, the child welfare system would naturally be involved and the academic outcomes for the child would be important to the overall success and work with this child and family. Assessment, identification, treatment and measuring outcomes are all important hen working to integrate mental health services into other systems of care. Integration in and among systems can be a great way to have a more holistic approach when working with individuals and their mental health needs, and contracting can be an effective and efficient way to pay for and deliver these services across multiple systems.

LESSONS LEARNED ABOUT MENTAL HEALTH CONTRACTING

Contracting for mental health services is not a new idea. Since the earliest days of United States history, government has played a role in providing services to people with mental health problems. In the mid-twentieth century, as individuals with mental illness were moved from large institutions to community-based service systems, these services were increasingly provided by private entities. Funding for mental health services was thus transferred from government organizations to private, typically not for profit, entities. And, contracts were the mechanism that was used to accomplish this transfer of funds, accompanied by the responsibility for providing services to this vulnerable population.

Later, in the 1980s and 1990s, new research contributed to our understanding of mental health contracting (Bachman, 1996a, 1996b). These inquiries suggested that contracting served as a mechanism for accomplishing government strategic aims, rather than as a symbol of a particular perspective on the role of government. Privatization, as a governing value was supported through contracting. However, those that implemented contracts for mental health services were generally more focused on getting services to those who needed them, and contracting helped to accomplish this aim. Contracting enabled government officials to work with more flexibility than the system of checks and balances that characterizes government operations.

Since the 2000s however, research related to contracting has often been linked to financing and reimbursement mechanisms, such as capitation, value-based purchasing or pay for performance. Although contracts are the mechanisms by which these purchasing strategies are implemented, the contracts themselves are not often the focus of inquiry. There has also been little advancement in terms of metrics that enable government or the private sector to determine the value of the mechanisms that are the subject of the contracts. These results suggest that—even though contracts based on principles such as value-based purchasing are moving forward—there is little evidence base on which to build on these advancements. We still know little about how best to design and implement value-based purchasing programs to achieve stated goals (Korda & Eldridge, 2011; Damberg et al., 2014). Further, we do not have a strong evidence base to inform how we structure contracts to ensure we achieve desired outcomes with respect to financing and organization of services.

Contracting can be used to promote the integration of services that members of vulnerable populations often need. As described previously, people with mental health problems may require services for substance use disorder, primary care or other health and social support services. A contract could help facilitate this integration through specifications around how service delivery and payment mechanisms will be bundled, coordinated and monitored. However, little is known about how contracting can accomplish these goals, especially with respect to building the evidence base about metrics of success.

KEY POINTS

Drawing on information we have presented in this chapter, there are four key points to highlight.

- Contracting as a means of transferring payment for various services from one entity to another has been used for a long time.

- The practice of contracting for mental health services in particular, grew as a result of the privatization of mental health services following deinstitutionalization in the 1960s.
- Contracting could further evolve to include other services and systems.
- We know very little about the outcomes for clients and systems related to contracting for mental health services.

In order to ensure the most comprehensive and effective care for individuals, more study needs to be done to have a better picture of the impact of contracting for mental health services.

REFERENCES

Adelsheim, S. (2014). From school health to integrated health: Expanding our children's public mental health system. *Academic Psychiatry, 38*(4), 405–408.

Agency for Healthcare Research and Quality (AHRQ). (2016). *Pharmacotherapy for adults with alcohol use disorder in outpatient settings*. Retrieved from https://effectivehealthcare.ahrq.gov/sites/default/files/pdf/alcohol-misuse-drug-therapy_policymaker.pdf

Ali, S., Tahir, B., Jabeen, S., & Malik, M. (2017). Methadone treatment of opiate addiction: A systematic review of comparative studies. *Innovations in Clinical Neuroscience, 14*(7–8), 8–19.

Al-Rousan, T., Rubenstein, L., Sieleni, B., Deol, H., & Wallace, B. (2017). Inside the nation's largest mental institution: A prevalence study in a state prison system. *BMC Public Health, 17*(342), 1–9.

American Academy of Pediatrics, Committee on Child Health Financing. (2014). High deductible health plans. *Pediatrics, 133*, e1461–e1470.

Ameringer, C. F. (2008). *The health care revolution: From medical monopoly to market competition.* Los Angeles, CA: University of California Press.

Atkins, M., Hoagwood, K., Kutash, K., & Seidman, E. (2010). Toward the integration of education and mental health in schools. *Administration and Policy in Mental Health and Mental Health Services, 37*(1–2), 40–47.

Bachman, S. S. (1996a). Monitoring mental health service contracts: Six states' experiences. *Psychiatric Services (Formerly Hospital and Community Psychiatry), 47*(8), 837–841.

Bachman, S. S. (1996b). Why do states privatize mental health services? Six state experiences. *Journal of Health Politics, Policy and Law, 21*(4), 807–824.

Bachman, S. S. (2011). Accountable care organizations: Opportunities for social workers. *Health and Social Work, 36*(4), 245–247.

Bachman, S. S., Comeau, M., Dworetzky, B., Hamershock, R., & Hirschi, M. (2015). The Louisiana family opportunity act medicaid buy-in program. *Maternal and Child Health Journal, 19*(12), 2568–2577.

Bachman, S. S., Pomeranz, D., & Tell, E. J. (1988). Making employers smart buyers of health care. *Clinical Laboratory Management Review, 2*(5), 273–279.

Badour, C. L., Flanagan, J. C., Gros, D. F., Killeen, T., Pericot-Valverde, I., Korte, K. J., . . . Back, S. E. (2017). Habituation of distress and craving during treatment as predictors of change in PTSD symptoms and substance use severity. *Journal of Consulting and Clinical Psychology, 85*(3), 274–281.

Beck, J. S. (2011). *Cognitive behavior therapy: Basics and beyond* (2nd ed.). New York: The Guilford Press.

Belenko, S., Johnson, I., Taxman, F., & Rieckmann, T. (2016). Probation staff articles toward substance abuse treatment and evidence-based practices. *International Journal of Offender Therapy and Comparative Criminology, 62*(2), 313–333.

Berry, K. (2015). *"Volume to value" still needs an ethics consult.* Petri-Flom Center at Harvard Law School's Bill of Health blog. Retrieved from http://blogs.harvard.edu/billofhealth/petrie-flom-center/

Berzin, S. C., O'Brien, K. M., Frey, A., Kelly, M., Alvarez, M., & Shaffer, G. (2011). Meeting the social and behavioral health needs of students: Rethinking the relationship between teachers and school social workers. *Journal of School Health, 81*(8), 493–501.

Bonfine, N., Ritter, C., & Munetz, M. (2016). Exploring the relationship between criminogenic risk assessment and mental health court program completion. *International Journal of Law and Psychiatry, 45*, 9–16.

Braciszewski, J. M., Wernette, G. K. T., Moore, R. S., Tran, T. B., Bock, B., Stout, R. L., . . . Vose-O'Neal, A. (2018). Developing a tailored substance use intervention for youth exiting foster care. *Child Abuse & Neglect, 77*, 211–221.

Brown, P. (1985). *The transfer of care: Psychiatric deinstitutionalization and its aftermath.* Boston, MA: Routledge & Kegan Paul.

Cappelli, M., Davidson, S., Racek, J., Leon, S., Vloet, M., Tataryn, K., . . . Lowe, J. (2016). Transitioning youth into adult mental health and addiction services: An outcomes evaluation of the youth transition project. *The Journal of Behavioral Health Services & Research, 43*(4), 597–610.

Carroll, K. M., Ball, S. A., Jackson, R., Martino, S., Petry, N. M., Stitzer, M. L., . . . Weiss, R. D. (2011). Ten take home lessons from the first 10 years of the CTN and 10 recommendations for the future. *The American Journal of Drug and Alcohol Abuse, 37*(5), 275–282.

Castells, X., Cunill, R., Merez-Mana, C., Vidal, X., & Capella, D. (2016). Psychostimiulant drugs for cocaine dependence. *Cochrane Database of Systematic Reviews 2016*, 9. Art. No: CD007380. doi:10.1002/1465158.CD007380.pub4. Retrieved from http://cochranelibrary-wiley.com/doi/10.1002/14651858.CD007380.pub4/full

Chandran, A., Bonafede, M., Nigam, S., Saltiel-Berzin, R., Hirsch, L., & Lahue, B. (2015). Adherence to insult pen therapy is associated with reduction in healthcare costs among patients with type 2 diabetes mellitus. *American Health and Drug Benefits, 8*(3), 148–158.

Chernew, M. E., & Fendrick, A. M. (2009). Value based insurance design: Restoring health to the health care cost debate. In *Visions for the future of the US health care system.* Schaumberg, IL: Society of Actuaries.

Child, H., & McIntyre, D. (2014). Examining the relationships between family drug court program compliance and child welfare outcomes. *Child Welfare, 94*(5), 67–87.

Choudry, N. K., Fischer, M. A., Smith, B. F., Brill, G., Girdish, C., Matlin, O. S., . . Shrank, W. H. (2014). Five features of value based insurance design plans were associated with higher rates of medication adherence. *Health Affairs, 33*, 1–9.

Conrad, P., & Schneider, J. W. (1980). *From badness to sickness.* St. Louis: The C.V. Mosby Company.

Cooper, J. (2017). Trapped: The limits pf care in California's mental health courts. *Social Justice, 44*(1), 121–141.

Cooper, R. L., Seiters, J., Davidson, D. L., MacMaster, S. A., Rasch, R. R., Aadams, S., & Darby, K. (2010). Outcomes of integrated assertive community treatment for homeless consumers with co-occurring disorders. *Journal of Dual Diagnosis, 6*(2), 152–170.

Cosden, M., Ellens, J., Schnell, J., & Yamini-Diouf, Y. (2005). Efficacy of a mental health treatment court with assertive community treatment. *Behavioral Sciences and the Law, 23*(2), 199–214.

D'Emic, M. (2015). Mental health courses: Bridging two worlds. *Touro Law Review, 31*(3), 369–376.

Damberg, C. L., Sorbero, M. E., Lovejoy, S. L., Martsolf, G., Raaen, L., & Mandel, D. (2014). *Measuring success in health care value based purchasing programs.* Santa Monica, CA: The RAND Corporation.

Deane, M. W., Steadman, H. J., Borum, R., Veysey, B. M., & Morrissey, J. P. (1999). Emerging partnerships between mental health and law enforcement. *Psychiatric Services, 50*(1), 99–101.

DeHoog, R. H. (1984). *Contracting out for human services.* Albany, NY: State University of New York Press.

Delbridge, E., Zubatsky, M., & Fowler, J. (2017). Integrating mental health professionals in residencies to reduce health disparities. *The International Journal of Psychiatry in Medicine, 52*(3), 286–297.

Demone, H. W., & Gibelman, M. (1989). *Services for sale: Purchasing health and human services.* New Brunswick, CT: Rutgers University Press.

Dinkmeyer, D., Carlson, J., & Dinkmeyer, D. (1994). *Consultation: School mental health professionals as consultants.* Levittown, PA: Accelerated Development, Inc.

Dobmeyer, A. C. (2018). *Psychological treatment of medical patients in integrated primary care.* Washington, DC: American Psychological Association.

Dorwart, R. A., Schlesinger, M., & Pulice, R. T. (1986). The promise and pitfalls of purchase-of-service contracts. *Hospital and Community Psychiatry, 37*(9), 875–878.

Drabble, L. (2007). Pathways to collaboration: Exploring values and collaborative practice between child welfare and substance abuse treatment fields. *Child Welfare and Substance Abuse Treatment, 12*(1), 31–42.

Drake, R. E., O'Neal, E. L., & Wallach, M. A. (2008). A systematic review of psychosocial research on psychosocial interventions for people with co-occurring severe mental health and substance use disorder. *Journal of Substance Abuse Treatment, 34*(1), 123–138.

Dutmers, J. (2017). Campus drug courts: How universities may be best equipped to tackle crime and substance abuse in young adults. *Law & Psychology Review, 41*, 191–207.

Elkashef, A., Vocci, F., Hanson, G., White, J., Wickes, W., & Tiihonen, J. (2008). Pharmacotherapy of methamphetamine addiction: an update. *Substance Abuse, 29*(3), 31–49.

Erchul, W. P. (Ed.). (1993). *Consultation in community, school, and organizational practice: Gerald Caplan's contributions to professional psychology.* Washington, DC: Taylor & Francis.

Ettner, S. L., Harwood, J. M., Thalmayer, A., Ong, M. K., Xu, H., Bresolin, M. J., Wells, K. B., . . . Azocar, F. (2016). The mental health parity and addiction equity act evaluation study: Impact on specialty behavioral health utilization and expenditures among "carve-out" enrollees. *Journal of Health Economics, 50*, 131–143.

Feldman, S. (1994). Dialogue: Integrated or carved out: The future of behavioral health programs. A marriage unconsummated. *Behavioral Healthcare Tomorrow, 3*(6), 40–48.

Fisher, C. (2014). Treating the disease or punishing the criminal? Effectively using drug court sanctions to treat substance use disorder and decrease criminal conduct. *Minnesota Law Review, 99*(2), 747–781.

Frailing, K. (2010). How mental courts function: Outcomes and observations. *International Journal of Law and Psychiatry, 33*(4), 207–213.

Frank, R. G., & Gaynor, M. (1993). State government choice of organizational structure for local mental health systems: An exploratory analysis. *Advances in Health Economics and Health Services Research, 14*, 181–196.

George, M., Trumpeter, N., Wilson, D., McDaniel, H., Schiele, B., Prinz, R., & Weist, M. (2014). Feasibility and preliminary outcomes from a pilot study of an integrated health-mental health promotion program in school mental health services. *Family & Community Health, 37*(1), 19–30.

Ghandour, R. M., Comeau, M., Tobias, C., Dworetzky, B., Hamershock, R., Honberg, L., & Bachman, S. S. (2015). Assuring adequate health insurance for children with special health care needs: Progress from 2001 to 2009–2010. *Academic Pediatrics, 15*, 451–460.

Ginsberg, M. (2010). Value based insurance design: Consumers views on paying more for high-cost, low value care. *Health Affairs, 29*, 2022–2026.

Grudzinskas, A. J., Clayfield, J. C., Roy-Bujnowski, K., Fisher, W. H., & Richardson, M. H. (2005). Integrating the criminal justice system into mental health service delivery. *Behavioral Science Law, 23*(2), 277–293.

Han, W., & Redlich, A. (2018). Racial/ethnic disparities in community behavioral health service usage. *Criminal Justice and Behavior, 45*(2), 173–194.

Harrison, J., Spybrook, J., Curtis, A., & Cousins, L. (2017). Integrated dual disorder treatment: Fidelity and implementation over time. *Social Work Research, 41*(2), 111–119.

He, A. (2015). Examining intensity and types of interagency collaboration between child welfare and drug and alcohol service providers. *Child Abuse & Neglect, 46*, 190–197.

He, A., Lim, C., Lecklitner, G., Olson, A., & Traube, D. (2015). Interagency collaboration and identifying mental health needs in child welfare: Findings from Los Angeles County. *Children and Youth Services Review, 53*, 39–43.

He, A., & Phillips, J. (2017). Interagency collaboration: Strengthening substance abuse resources in child welfare. *Child Abuse & Neglect, 64*, 101–108.

He, A., Traube, D., & Young, N. (2014). Perceptions of parental substance use disorders in cross-system collaboration among child welfare, alcohol and other drugs, and dependency court organizations. *Child Abuse & Neglect, 38*(5), 939–951.

Hien, D. A., Morgan-Lopez, A. A., Campbell, A. N. C., Saavedra, L. M., Wu, E., Cohen, L., . . . Nunes, E. V. (2012). Attendance and substance use outcomes for the seeking safety program: Sometimes less is more. *Journal of Consulting and Clinical Psychology, 80*(1), 29–42.

Hinton, M., & Reister, S. (2015). The interface of mental health and the realities of the correctional system. *DePaul Law Review, 64*(817), 817–822.

Honegger, L. N. (2015). Does the evidence support the case for mental health courts? A review of the literature. *Law and Human Behavior, 39*(5), 478–488.

Howell, J. C., Kelly, M. R., Palmer, J., & Mangum, R. (2004). Integrating child welfare, juvenile justice, and other agencies in a continuum of services. *Child Welfare, 83*(2), 143–156.

Hughes, S., & Peak, T. (2012). Evaluating mental health courts as an ideal mental health intervention. *Best Practices in Mental Health, 8*(2), 21–37.

Johnson, J., Schonbrun, Y. C., Peabody, M., Shefner, R., Fernandes, K., Rosen, R., & Zlotnick, C. (2015). Provider experiences with prison care and aftercare for women with co-occurring mental health and substance use disorders: Treatment, resource, and systems integration challenges. *The Journal of Behavioral Health Services & Research, 42*(4), 417–436.

Johnston, E. L., & Flynn, C. (2017). Mental health courts and sentencing disparities. *Villanova Law Review, 62*(4), 685–746.

Kampman, K., & Jarvis, M. (2015). American society of addiction medicine (ASAM) national practice guideline for the use of medications in the treatment of addiction involving opioid use. *Journal of Addiction Medicine, 9*(5), 358–367.

Khatri, P., Perry, G., & deGruy, F. V. (2017). Integrated health care at Cherokee health systems. In R. E. Feinstein, J. V. Connelly, & M. S. Feinstein (Eds.), *Integrating behavioral health and primary care* (pp. 17–30). New York: Oxford University Press.

Korda, H., & Eldridge, G. N. (2011). How can we bend the cost curve? Payment incentives and integrated care delivery: Levers for health system reform and cost containment. *Inquiry 48*, 277–287.

Kriegel, L., Henwood, B., & Gilmer, T. (2016). Implementation and outcomes of forensic housing first programs. *Community Mental Health Journal, 52*(1), 46–55.

Lai, K., Guo, S., Maghsoodi, R., Puffer, M., & Kataoka, S. (2016). Bringing wellness to schools: Opportunities for and challenges to mental health integration in school-based health centers. *Psychiatric Services, 67*(12), 1328–1333.

Libby, A. M. (1997). Contracting between public and private providers: A survey of mental health services in California. *Administration and Policy in Mental Health and Mental Health Services Research, 24*(4), 323–338.

Maciejewski, M. L., Ansink, D., Lindquist, J. H., Parker, J. C., & Farley, J. F. (2014). Value based insurance design program in North Carolina increased medication adherence but was not cost neutral. *Health Affairs, 33*, 300–308.

Mahoney, J. J., Lucas, K., Gibson, T. B., Ehrlich, E. D., Gatwood, J., Moore, B. J., & Heithoff, K. A. (2013, June). Value based insurance design: Perspectives, extending the evidence, and implications for the future. *The American Journal of Managed Care*.

Marks, E. S. (1995). *Entry strategies for school consultation*. New York: The Guilford Press.

Mechanic, D., & Rochefort, D. A. (1990). Deinstitutionalization: An appraisal of reform. *Annual Review of Sociology, 16*, 301–327.

Medicare Payment Advisory Commission (MEDPAC). (2008). *Report to the congress: Reforming the delivery system*. Retrieved from www.medpac.gov/documents/reports/Jun08_EntireReport.pdf

Mental Retardation Facilities and Community Mental Health Centers Construction Act of 1963, 24 U.S.C. §§ 2670–2697b (2012).

Michael, K. D., & Jameson, J. P. (Eds.). (2017). *Handbook of rural school mental health*. Cham, Switzerland: Springer International Publishing.

Morgan-Lopez, A. A., Saavedra, L. M., Hien, D. A., Cambell, A. N., Wu., E., Ruglass, L., . . . Bainter, S. C. (2014). Indirect effects of 12-session seeking safety on substance use outcomes: Overall and attendance class-specific effects. *The American Journal on Addictions, 23*(3), 218–225.

Morrissey, J. P. (1989). The changing role of the public mental hospital. In D. A. Rochefort (Ed.), *Handbook on mental health policy in the United States* (pp. 311–338). New York: Greenwood Press.

National Institute of Drug Abuse (NIDA). (2009). *Principles of effective treatment: A research based guide*. Retrieved from www.drugabuse.gov/publications/principles-drug-addiction-treatment/principles-effective-treatment

National Institute on Drug Abuse (NIDA). (2018, January 17). *Treatment approaches for drug addiction*. Retrieved from www.drugabuse.gov/publications/drugfacts/treatment-approaches-drug-addiction

Okpych, N. J., & Courtney, M. E. (2018). Characteristics of foster care history as risk factors for psychiatric disorders among youth in care. *American Journal of Orthopsychiatry, 88*(3), 269–281.

Oppenheim, E., Lee, R., Lichtenstein, C., Bledsoe, K., & Fisher, S. (2012). Reforming mental health services for children in foster care: The role of child welfare class action lawsuits and systems of care. *Reforming Mental Health Services for Children in Foster Care, 93*(4), 287–294.

Osher, F. (2013, August). *Integrating mental health and substance abuse services for justice-involved persons with co-occurring disorders*. SAMHSA's Gains Center. Retrieved from http://gainscenter.samhsa.gov

Robst, J., Rost, K., & Marshall, D. (2013). Do employers know the quality of health care benefits they provide? The use of HEDIS depression scores for health plans. *Psychiatric Services, 64*, 1134–1139.

Rosenthal, M. B., Landon, B. E., Normand, S. T., Frank, R. G., Ahmad, T. S., & Epstein, A. M. (2007). Employers use of value based purchasing strategies. *JAMA, 298*, 2281–2288.

Rossheim, R., Livingston, M., Lerch, J., Taxman, F., & Walter, S. (2018). Serious mental illness and negative substance use consequences among adults on probation. *Health & Justice, 6*(1), 1–9.

Ryan, A. M., Burgess, J. F., Pesko, M. F., Borden, W. B., & Dimick, J. B., (2015). The early effects of Medicare's mandatory hospital pay for performance program. *Health Services Research, 50*, 81–97.

Saillant, S., Hudelson, P., Dao, M. D., & Perron, N. J. (2016). The primary care physician/psychiatrist joint consultation: A paradigm shift in caring for patients with mental health problems? *Patient Education and Counseling, 99*(2), 279–283.

Salinsky, E. (2013). *Effect of provider payment reforms on maternal and child health services*. Washington, DC: National Governors Association.

Sayegh, C. S., Huey, S. J., Zara, E. J., & Jhaveri, K. (2017). Follow-up treatment effects of contingency management and motivational interviewing on substance use: A meta-analysis. *Psychology of Addictive Behaviors, 31*(4), 403–414.

Shedler, J. (2017). Automated mental health assessment for integrated care: The quick psychodiagnostics panel meets real-world clinical needs. In R. E. Feinstein, J. V. Connelly, & M. S. Feinstein (Eds.), *Integrating behavioral health and primary care* (pp. 134–145). New York: Oxford University Press.

Siantz, E., Henwood, B., Xu, Z., Sarin, A., & Gilmer, T. (2017). Health care decisions among mental health services consumers in San Diego County: Implications for integrated care. *Health & Social Work*, *42*(1), 48–56.

Sipe, T. A., Finnie, R. K., Knopf, J. A., Qu, S., Reynolds, J. A., Thota, A. B., Hahn, R. A., . . . Community Preventive Services Task Force. (2015). Effects of mental health benefits legislation: A community guide systematic review. *American Journal of Preventive Medicine*, *48*(6), 755–766.

Spiller, K., Xi, ZX, Peng, XQ, Newman, A.H., Ashby, C.R., Heidbreder, C., Gaai, J., & Gardner, E.L. (2008). The selective dopamine D3 receptor antagonists SB-277011A and NGB 2904 and the putative partial D3 receptor agonist BP-897 attenuate methamphetamine-enhanced brain stimulation reward in rats. *Psychopharmacology, 196*(4), 533–542.

Squeglia, L.M., Baker, N.L., McClure, E.A., Tomko, R.L., Adisetiyo, V., & Gray, K.M. (2016). Alcohol use during a trial of N-acetylycysteine for adolescent marijuana cessation. *Addictive Behaviors, 63*, 172–177.

Squeglia, L.M., Tomko, R.L., Baker, N.L., McClure, E.A., Book, G.A., & Gray, K.M. (2018). The effect of N-acetylcysteine on alcohol use during a cannabis cessation trial. *Drug and alcohol Dependence, 185*, 17–22.

Substance Abuse and Mental Health Services Administration (SAMHSA). (2015). *Results from the 2014 National Survey on Drug Use and Health: Summary of National Findings, NSDUH, HHS Publication No. SMA 15-4927.* Rockville, MD: Substance Abuse and Mental Health Services Administration, 2015.

Talmi, A., Muther, E., Margolis, K., Buchholz, M., Asherin, R., & Bunik, M. (2016). The scope of behavioral health integration in a pediatric primary care setting. *Journal of Pediatric Psychology, 41*(10), 1120–1132.

United States Government Accountability Office. (2015). *Hospital value based purchasing*. Washington, DC: GAO Report to Congressional Committees.

U.S. National Institutes of Mental Health. (2018). *Mental illness*. Retrieved from www.nimh.nih.gov/health/statistics/mental-illness.shtml

U.S. Surgeon General. (2010). *Mental health: A report of the surgeon general*. Retrieved from www.surgeongeneral.gov/library/mentalhealth/chapter2/sec2_1.html

Van Dorn, R., Desmarais, S., Rade, C., Burris, E., Cuddeback, G., Johnson, K., . . . Mueser, K. (2017). Jail-to-community treatment Continuum for adults with co-occurring substance use and mental disorders: Study protocol for a pilot randomized controlled trial. *Trials, 18*(365), 1–12.

Waugh, M., Voyles, D., Shore, J. H., Lippolis, L. C., & Lyon, C. (2017). Telehealth in an integrated care environment. In R. E. Feinstein, J. V. Connelly, & M. S. Feinstein (Eds.), *Integrating behavioral health and primary care* (pp. 121–133). New York: Oxford University Press.

Wells, R., & Chuang, E. (2012). Does formal integration between child welfare and behavioral health agencies result in improved placement stability for adolescents engaged with both systems? *Child Welfare, 91*(1), 79–100.

Williams, R. (2018). Responding to the opioid epidemic and expanding access to quality treatment. *Psychiatric Times, 35*(5), 31–34.

Wilson, A. B., & Draine, J. (2006). Collaborations between criminal justice and mental health systems for prisoner reentry. *Psychiatric Services, 24*(6), 875–878.

Zettler, H. (2018). Exploring the relationship between dual diagnosis and recidivism in drug court participants. *Crime & Delinquency, 64*(3), 363–397.

Zivin, K., Miller, B., Finke, B., Bitton, A., Payne, P., Stowe, E., . . . Sessums, L. (2017). Behavioral health and the comprehensive primary care initiative: Findings from the 2014 CPC behavioral health survey. *BMC Services Research, 17*(612), 1–9.

6

Contracting for Employment and Training Programs

Burt S. Barnow and Shayne Spaulding

INTRODUCTION

The publicly funded U.S. employment and training system is complex, with funding primarily at the federal level, and service delivery mainly at the state and local levels through a number of funding streams and administrative structures aimed at meeting a variety of goals for workers, businesses and industry, and communities. The trends in contracting out for employment and training services are linked to this diffuse administrative structure and diverse goals. Throughout the history of public workforce programs, there has been the desire to both create a more efficient system through competition, and to control the delivery of services and manage performance in meeting the system's diverse goals.

In this chapter, we focus on the main federal employment and training programs funded through the U.S. Department of Labor, currently the Workforce Innovation and Opportunity Act (WIOA) and the Wagner-Peyser Act, but we will note other programs in the system; in addition to the main employment and training programs covered by this chapter, other federal programs include Job Corps, National Farmworkers Jobs Program, Trade Adjustment Assistance, Disabled Veterans Outreach Program, Local Veterans Employment Representatives, YouthBuild and the Homeless Veterans Reentry Program. Major programs funded outside the Department of Labor include Pell grants, the Supplemental Nutrition Assistance Program Employment and Training, adult education, career and technical education, vocational rehabilitation and Temporary Assistance for Needy Families.[1]

The chapter proceeds as follows. In the next section, rationales for and against contracting out are presented. This is followed by a brief discussion of service delivery for the Employment Service. The following section presents the experiences with contracting out for federal employment and training programs from the 1960s through the 1990s—the Manpower Development and Training Act, the Comprehensive Employment and Training Act, and the Job Training Partnership Act. The next section discusses the current major national program and its immediate predecessor, WIOA and the

Workforce Investment Act (WIA), respectively, as well as the American Recovery and Reinvestment Act (ARRA, which provided additional funding during the Great Recession) because of its role in influencing the development of contracting in workforce programs. The final section provides lessons learned and key points to inform future directions in contracting out in federal workforce programs.

REASONS FOR AND AGAINST CONTRACTING OUT EMPLOYMENT AND TRAINING SERVICES

Contracting out issues apply to two distinct aspects of the employment and training system. Most commonly, the discussion applies to the delivery of services themselves—should services be delivered by government workers, or should they be contracted out to a service provider? Most of the discussion in this chapter applies to service delivery, but interesting and important issues have arisen regarding management of those services, and that issue is covered in the discussion of WIA and WIOA.

Several arguments have been offered as to why employment and training services should be offered by government workers or contracted out.[2] One argument for using government workers is the concept of "inherently governmental." The Congressional Research Service (2014) notes that the statutory definition in the Federal Activities Inventory Reform Act of 1998 is "a function so intimately related to the public interest as to require performance by federal government employees."[3] Note that the concept of inherently governmental relates to which workers provide the service rather than whether the service is funded with public funds. The concept of "merit goods," proposed by Musgrave (1959) argues that some goods and services are so important that they should be paid for with government funds, but inherently governmental deals with who provides the services rather than who pays for the services; thus, the issue of who provides the service is independent of whether the government should pay for the services.

Balducchi and Pasternak (2004, p. 44) summarize the thinking that led to the requirement for merit staffing for the Employment Service (ES):

> Shortly after the Wagner-Peyser Act was enacted, the USES adopted a requirement that states must administer a merit personnel system in which appointments and promotions are based upon competence. This requirement ensures that hiring is not affected by patronage, that the execution of program services is impartial and nonpartisan, and that the delivery of services is not affected by favoritism (Balducchi & Pasternak, 2001, p. 159). . . . to insure the highest quality of state ES operations, USDOL concluded that state staff must be of superb quality and politically impartial. It seemed to USDOL that a merit personnel system—in which individuals are rated objectively on their experience, education, understanding of the job, and personality—was the most reliable way to ensure the highest quality of ES operations.

If one accepts the assumptions here, then employment and training programs (or at least the Employment Service) are inherently governmental, and the people providing services should be government employees, and the programs should therefore not be contracted out.

Of course, the argument for merit staffing—instead of contracted services—in government employment and training programs is not necessarily a valid one. The public choice literature is built on the premise that government programs are not necessarily efficient and may not act in the public's behalf. For example, Niskanen (1968, 1971) argues that government agencies may be interested in maximizing their budget rather than efficiently providing services. Perhaps less radically, Osborne and Gaebler (1992) argued that government agencies can become stale and inefficient. One proposed remedy to underperforming public agencies proposed by Osborne and Gaebler (1992) was the institution of competition between agencies to determine which agency will deliver particular services. Niskanen (1971) also advocated the use of competition among government agencies as one way to improve performance, although he preferred contracting out with competition as a superior approach.

In addition to competitive procurement as a means of ensuring quality services by contracted service providers, performance management has been used to incentivize high performance in contracted services. Performance management is the broad category of management tools that attempts to make public programs more accountable for their performance and results. Barnow (1992) defines performance management as "a system whereby programs are systematically judged against specified objectives." Performance management involves establishing goals and objectives, finding ways to measure success in meeting goals and objectives, and using information about performance to shape the continuous improvement of contracted service provider performance and government programs. Increasingly, performance management has involved a focus on outcomes and outputs rather than inputs and design specifications (Heinrich, 2003; Kettner & Martin, 1993). Performance-based contracts go a step further and tie service provider payments to the achievement of certain results or benchmarks (Kettner & Martin, 1993; GMAS, 1989; Behn & Kant, 1999).

As we present the history of contracting out in employment and training programs in the following sections, the various reasons for government delivery or contracting out are noted, as well as the issues that have occurred with each approach, and steps taken to meet the goals of government workforce programs through a diffuse delivery system of services that are largely contracted out.

THE WAGNER-PEYSER ACT EMPLOYMENT SERVICE

The first major U.S. employment and training program was the Employment Service, which was established under the Wagner-Peyser Act of 1933. The Employment Service provides labor exchange services to individuals seeking jobs and employers with vacancies. In summarizing the history of the Wagner-Peyser Act, Balducchi and Pasternak (2004) note that from the beginning DOL required states to deliver services through state merit staff employees, and services were not contracted out. Wagner-Peyser stands apart from the other employment and training programs we discuss in this section in the way that services have historically been and continue to be provided almost exclusively by government employed merit staff instead of being provided by contracted external agencies.

During the 1990s, several states considered alternative arrangements for providing Wagner-Peyser services, and ultimately three states were permitted to deviate from the usual structure of having services delivered by merit staff employees of a state agency.[4] The new approaches were implemented during the Clinton administration when Osborne and Gaebler's (1992) reinventing government ideas were popular and the Clinton administration sought to improve services through its National Performance Review.

Massachusetts was the first state to implement major changes to the delivery of Wagner-Peyser services. As part of an implementation grant in 1994 from the Department of Labor, Massachusetts was permitted to allow local competition for delivery of Wagner-Peyser and other Department of Labor programs; contracts were made to eligible local service providers, including private nonprofit and for-profit organizations. In 1998, the Department of Labor restricted the competition to four local areas.[5] Massachusetts is the only case where the Department of Labor has granted permission for Wagner-Peyser services to be contracted out to a for-profit organization. At this time, we believe that no local area in Massachusetts provides Wagner-Peyser services through a for-profit organization, and only one local area contracts with a nonprofit organization.[6]

Colorado received permission to provide Wagner-Peyser services through county governments in 1997. In 1999, The U.S. Department of Labor instructed Colorado to assure that county staff providing the Wagner-Peyser services were covered by merit-staffing systems similar to what was used in other states. Colorado still provides Wagner-Peyser services through county merit staff employees. Thus, whereas Wagner-Peyser services are provided at the county rather than the state level, services are still provided directly by government employees and not contracted out.

Michigan is the final example of a state that does not use state merit staff workers to provide Wagner-Peyser services. Michigan reorganized delivery of Wagner-Peyser services in 1997 and engaged in what Balducchi and Pasternak (2004, p. 46) characterize as a "pitched brawl" over how the services would be delivered. Ultimately, the state and U.S. Department of Labor agreed that Wagner-Peyser services in the state would be delivered by local agencies (city and county governments) using a merit staffing system.

The three Wagner-Peyser demonstration sites involved both devolution from the state level to the local level and contracting out from the state government to local levels of government and/or private organizations. Massachusetts and Michigan appear to have been motivated by the idea of adding competition to increase efficiency, whereas Colorado's effort was more of an effort to devolve services to the local level. Over time, the focus on introducing competition in service delivery appears to have decreased in importance, and, to our knowledge, none of the states currently make use of for-profit firms for service delivery. The three demonstration states were included in an evaluation of the Employment Service by Jacobson, Petta, Shimshak and Yudd (2004), but it is difficult to make comparisons in effectiveness and in a cost-benefit framework because of the non-experimental nature of the evaluations and the fact that the demonstration states tended to serve a more disadvantaged population than traditional Wagner-Peyser states.

In the Final Rule for implementing Title I and Title III of WIOA, DOL indicated that it intended to continue authorizing the demonstrations in Colorado, Massachusetts, and Michigan, and that it did not intend to expand this authority to other states: "The benefits of merit staffing in promoting greater consistency, efficiency, accountability, and transparency have been well established, and the Department intends to continue Wagner-Peyser Act merit staffing requirements under WIOA" (*Federal Register*, August 19, 2016, p. 56267.) More recently, however, after the change in administrations, the Department of Labor has indicated that it is exploring an expansion of the opportunity to offer Wagner-Peyser services other than through state merit staff employees:

> The Department of Labor (Department) will solicit public comment on a proposed rule to provide additional flexibility to states in providing labor exchange services under the Wagner-Peyser Act, including services to veterans. The Wagner-Peyser Act section 3(a) provides the Secretary legal authority to set staffing standards and requirements to ensure effective service delivery of services provided under the Wagner-Peyser Act. The Secretary and Department propose to use that authority to remove excessive staffing standards and requirements, and provide States with maximum flexibility to use staffing approaches other than State merit staffing that allow for high quality and cost-efficient service delivery. This interpretation is consistent with the Michigan v. Herman court ruling (81 F. Supp. 2nd 840 (W.D. Mich., 1998)) establishing that continuing or eliminating the merit staffing policy was at the discretion of the Department.[7]

CONTRACTING IN WORKFORCE PROGRAMS: 1960S TO 1990S

The Manpower Development and Training Act[8]

The Manpower Development and Training Act of 1962 (MDTA) was the first federal program to provide training on a larger scale, necessitating development of a system for providing that training.[9] The history of MTDA is important context for understanding the evolution of contracting out in federal employment and training programs because decisions to contract out for human services are driven not only by the desire for competition but also by the potential lack of capacity, particularly in times of economic downturn or mass layoffs, to meet the demand for training through government provided services. MDTA was one of the first steps in the local provision of job training services, paving the way for contracted services at the local level under subsequent federal legislation.

The original intent of MDTA was to retrain workers who lost their jobs due to "automation," the term used at that time (and experiencing a resurgence now) for technical change. From the beginning, the program also served disadvantaged workers, and services to the economically disadvantaged soon predominated, as job losses due to automation failed to materialize. A total of approximately 1.9 million workers enrolled in MDTA between 1963 and 1972, with about two-thirds of the participants enrolled in classroom training and one-third enrolled in on-the-job training (OJT, which is informal training by employers who receive subsidies of up to 50% of wages for up to six months).[10]

Administration of MDTA was complex. The original legislation called for states to eventually pay for half the program, but these requirements were postponed and diluted, and eventually states were only required to make a 10% match that could be an "in-kind" contribution. Administration of the OJT component of the program was eventually shifted from the U.S. Department of Labor to the Job Opportunities in the Business Sector (JOBS) program, which was operated by the National Alliance of Business, a nonprofit business trade association. The institutional classroom training was largely administered by the U.S. Department of Labor, with relatively minor roles played by state and local governments.

Mangum (1968) observes that vocational education facilities were inadequate to meet their regular enrollments, so alternative arrangements were required for the MDTA training. Initially, MDTA training was conducted in vocational education public facilities during off hours, but the program soon became too large for this arrangement. Local programs developed their own training facilities, which were called "skill centers," and some of these facilities are still in use. Unlike vocational education facilities, the skill centers were not constrained to operate on an academic year, and unlike facilities that were developed to house Area Redevelopment Act (ARA) projects, the skill centers included training programs for a number of occupations.[11] By 1967, MDTA programs had established 108 training facilities exclusively for MDTA training. Although literature on contracting arrangements during this period is sparse, based on site visits to local sites in the 1970s and discussions with individuals who operated such institutions, we believe that the skill centers were typically established as captive nonprofit organizations and that state and local governments typically negotiated contracts with the skill centers on a sole source basis.

THE COMPREHENSIVE EMPLOYMENT AND TRAINING ACT[12]

In 1973, MDTA was replaced by the Comprehensive Employment and Training Act (CETA). The new program included a change in the mix of activities offered and in the responsibilities of different levels of government, with local city and county agencies being given greater power, leading to variation in the types of service providers offering training and in the extent to which such training was contracted out.

President Nixon was a strong advocate for the "New Federalism," which sought to give state and local governments more control over who was served and how they were served. The CETA program represented a major departure from MDTA in several ways. First, decisions about who would be served and how they would be served were primarily made at the local level rather than at the federal or state level; in fact, CETA was the high point for local authority compared to the MDTA program that preceded it and the Job Training Partnership Act (JTPA), Workforce Investment Act (WIA), and Workforce Innovation and Opportunity Act (WIOA) programs that succeeded it.

Under CETA Title I, funds were distributed by formula to cities, counties, or consortia of local governments. Any jurisdiction with a population of 100,000 or more was entitled to be recognized as a "prime sponsor." Areas that were ineligible for designation on their own and failed to join a consortium were included in a "balance of state" prime sponsor that was administered by the state. Prime sponsors were required to submit an annual plan to the U.S. Department of Labor for approval, and they were also required to establish a planning council with representatives of various constituencies, including the private sector. Prime sponsors had significant latitude in determining their mix of activities and participants under Title I, as well as who provided these services; activities available included classroom and on-the-job training, public service employment, and work experience.

Levitan and Mangum (1981) conducted 12 case studies of training provided under CETA, and they also described the overall system. The authors note that delivery varied significantly among the 12 sites studied. In three locations, the major providers were the skill centers established under MDTA with services being typically provided by employees of the captive nonprofit organizations that operate the skill centers. The other locations reflected either partial or exclusive reliance on contracted training providers. In San Francisco, community based organizations (CBOs) were favored, with minor use of a skills center and individual referrals to proprietary schools and community colleges. In North Carolina and Penobscot (Maine), community colleges and technical institutes were key, with some use of private colleges. In Dallas, two CBOS and two school districts did most of the training. Baltimore and Worcester used a mix of public and private schools with some done by employers. Rural Ottawa County (Michigan) paid living expenses and sent trainees to other places with more training opportunities available. Montgomery County (Maryland) used public and private schools. Indianapolis used individual referrals to public and private schools. Levitan and Mangum (181, p. 18) conclude:

> To generalize from the case studies, public postsecondary schools seem to provide most of the training, with skill centers in second place, followed by CBO-run schools and then private proprietary schools. In contrast to the national picture where individual referral purportedly predominates, enrollments in class-size groups were more common than individual referrals in all of the study locations, but this was true primarily because of the unusual CBO delivery system in San Francisco, Seattle, and Dallas.

Thus, the CETA program, which provided local areas with great authority to provide training as they saw fit, saw movement from the dominant use of local captive skill centers with their own staff providing training to entire classes for specific occupations toward a mix of postsecondary schools contracted to provide class-size training and individual referrals.

THE JOB TRAINING PARTNERSHIP ACT[13]

CETA was due to expire in 1982, and the replacement program, the Job Training Partnership Act (JTPA) was a bipartisan effort sponsored by Senators Edward Kennedy and Dan Quayle. The new law reflected President Reagan's view of federalism, which included a larger role for state government and smaller roles for the federal government and local government. Thus, under JTPA, state governments played a larger role in decisions about contracting out for services. Some key features of JTPA included: programs for economically disadvantaged youth and adults continued to be locally administered; states assumed a much greater role in monitoring the performance of local programs; private sector employers were given the opportunity to play a major role in guiding and/or operating the local programs; and the system was to be "performance driven," with local programs rewarded or sanctioned based on their performance. As we describe later, both the role of private sector employers and the performance measurement system remain important but unsettled issues that connect to the structure of contracted employment and training services.

JTPA continued the trend of moving from direct provision of training at skill centers run by the local program to contracting the training out, largely to public postsecondary institutions. Levitan and Gallo (1988, p. 81) note that "Only one of six SDAs provided all training directly in 1985, and about two-thirds subcontracted at least half their training funds." Levitan and Gallo state that about 30% of the local programs used proprietary schools to provide training, which is higher than was the case under MDTA and CETA.[14] Community based organizations, such as Opportunities Industrialization Centers of America (OIC), SER-Jobs for Progress and the Urban League, which were commonly relied upon under MDTA and CETA, played a smaller role under JTPA. Although the literature is sparse on how contracts were awarded under JTPA, based on observations and discussions with programs, we believe that contracts were awarded primarily on a sole source basis. Johnston (1987, p. 45) notes that while under previous legislation CBOs were "presumptive deliverers of service," under JTPA it was only required that "proper consideration shall be given to community-based organizations as service providers" while primary consideration was to be given to effectiveness and demonstrated performance.

As noted previously, there was an increased use of performance-based contracting under JTPA as part of the focus on effectiveness and quality under the law. In the early stages of JTPA, the U.S. Department of Labor (DOL) encouraged the use of performance-based contracts, but backed away from this position when it discovered a number of abuses and violations. Such improprieties included large profits for service providers, a tendency to focus on short-term strategies rather than training, and inadequate state monitoring. These problems led DOL to place restrictions on the use of performance-based contracting in the late 1980s (DOL, 1987, 1989). Performance-based contracting has also been criticized for providing incentives for service providers to select only the most qualified applicants, commonly known as "cream-skimming" or "creaming," and for placing unreasonable risk on nonprofit service providers (Koning & Heinrich, 2013; Heinrich & Lynn, 2000; Behn & Kant, 1999; Dickinson et al., 1988).

CONTRACTING IN WORKFORCE PROGRAMS: 1990S TO THE PRESENT

The Workforce Investment Act

The Workforce Investment Act (WIA) was enacted August 7, 1998, to replace JTPA. States had the option of being "early implementers," but most states began implementing the new law July 1, 2000.[15] The WIA program maintained the formulas used to distribute funds to states and sub-state areas. The utilization of a one-stop system began several years prior to enactment of WIA on a voluntary basis in local areas, but the 1998 statute required many workforce development programs to co-locate and coordinate services in One-Stop Career Centers, which the U.S. Department of Labor has recently rebranded as American Job Centers (AJCs). The One-Stop centers were intended to provide the "core" and "intensive" services mandated by WIA (described later); to provide access to workforce development programs and services offered by One-Stop partners; and to provide access to the labor market information, job search, placement, recruitment and labor exchange services offered by the Employment Service (Bradley, 2013). The introduction of new partnerships and collaboration, not necessarily involving contractual relationships or payment for services, created new challenges in managing a system where services were primarily contracted out.

Another challenge under WIA was the notion of individual empowerment, an important feature of the law, implemented largely through voucher-like instruments called Individual Training Accounts (ITAs).[16] Although vouchers were used by some local areas under JTPA, ITAs were the default approach for training under WIA. Local areas had a great deal of flexibility in administering the ITAs, and some local areas tended to give customers wide latitude in using their ITA, whereas others restricted customers in terms of cost, past performance of the service provider, and qualifications and aptitude of the customer for the course; see D'Amico and Salzman (2004), Barnow (2009) and King and Barnow (2011).

Although vouchers are not contracts per se, they are a mechanism for service provision by nongovernmental entities, and the requirements placed by local areas created contracting-like requirements to ensure accountability. When ITAs were used, the participant would select an eligible provider, and the local program would either establish or modify a contract with the service provider.

The goal of increased accountability was addressed in two ways—changes were made to the performance measurement system used under JTPA, and states and local areas were asked to establish an eligible training provider (ETP) list of service providers with strong performance. Only those on the list could accept ITAs from WIA participants. With customers having a greater role in selecting their field of training and service providers through the use of ITAs, there was a risk that customers might select service providers based on service provider claims rather than the performance of the programs and the customer's suitability for the program selected. Governors were thus asked to establish an ETP list that only included service providers who had a good track record for that program. Evidence indicates that although some states were able to develop satisfactory ETP lists, there were severe challenges in meeting this requirement of WIA, and 35 states received waivers that permitted them to implement only a portion of the ETP requirements or to delay implementation (Van Horn & Fichter, 2011).

The American Recovery and Reinvestment Act

An important event in the evolution of contracting for workforce programs was the Great Recession, which lasted from 2007 to 2009, and the corresponding American Recovery and Reinvestment Act, signed into law in February 2009, which included a stimulus package aimed at immediately boosting job growth and employment. The law focused on infusing funds via "shovel ready" projects, meaning those that could be implemented quickly. It also included expanded funding for WIA programs and the Wagner-Peyser Act. As part of the effort to get money out quickly and for targeted purposes, changes were made to rules about how training could be funded. In the statute, WIA placed an emphasis on customer choice through ITA vouchers. Under ARRA, there were changes in the rules, which allowed for states to contract directly with institutions of higher education to allow for expanded training capacity. It also became possible for states and localities to contract directly with education and training providers for class-size training. These changes in policy made it possible for a large expansion in the number of people served, as well as increased use of class-sized training and improvements in the training available (Trutko & Barnow, 2013).

With millions of people out of work, the unemployment insurance and reemployment service systems were faced with large increases in demand. A challenge related to government-provided services under these programs was the fact that as interpreted, the law mandated that merit staff covered by civil service rules provide services. It could take months to hire new merit staff workers, making it difficult to expand capacity during this national economic crisis. Several states also instituted hiring freezes because of their fiscal distress, which also hampered efforts to meet the high demand for services, even with ARRA funding available to pay for the workers (Kaiser, 2013). In this case, the rules regarding workforce services provided directly by government were an impediment to the flexibility required to respond to the crisis of the Great Recession. ARRA funding ended in 2012, and service levels began again to decline. However, some elements remained beyond the term of the funding, laying the groundwork for the Workforce Innovation and Opportunity Act.

The Workforce Innovation and Opportunity Act

The Workforce Innovation and Opportunity Act (WIOA) was enacted in 2014, maintaining the approach of formula funding to states and substate areas, oversight by employer-majority boards at the state and local levels, involvement of a set of mandatory partners in oversight and service provision, and service delivery through the American Job Center network. The law aims to strengthen the strategic role of state and local boards in meeting the needs of employers and create a more aligned system for meeting the needs of job seekers throughout their working lives, especially individuals with barriers to employment. The law also includes the implementation of six common measures of performance across the six core programs under WIOA,[17] requiring increased coordination across the administrators of these programs and across levels of government. The changes in WIOA most relevant to understanding contracted services are the requirements for competitive procurement, expansion of mandatory partners and roles, increased flexibility for local areas to contact out for training as opposed to only using vouchers (ITAs), and new language allowing limited funding to be used for pay for performance-based contracts. We discuss each of these changes in this section and their relevance to contracted employment services.

First, new requirements related to the competitive procurement of contracts for One-Stop Operators aim to create a more efficient system, but also greater transparency about the selection of One-Stop Operators in local areas. Under WIA, LWDBs were able to function as One-Stop Operators without a procurement process. WIOA allows Local Workforce Development Boards (LWDBs) to serve as One-Stop Operators, but only as the result of a competitive process certified by the Governor. Contracts must be bid out at least once every four years (TEGL 16–16, pp. 20–21). Once selected, the law requires the establishment of Memorandum of Understanding between the LWDB and the One-Stop Operator specifying the terms of service. The rationale for this requirement is articulated in federal guidance as follows: "Competition is intended to promote efficiency and effectiveness of one-stop operators by providing a mechanism for Local WDBs to regularly examine performance and cost against original expectations."[18] Federal guidance also urges, but does require, the use of a competitive procurement process in the selection of contracted providers of other services, including career services[19] and training services.[20] Youth program providers, on the other hand, must compete for awards based on specific requirements and quality standards, established by the governor and detailed in a state's plan (P.L. 113–128, §123).

To build a more aligned system, WIOA includes new requirements for the involvement of partners in the oversight of the program by workforce development boards (WDBs) at the state and local levels, and in the co-location of services at American Job Centers. Career services are to be provided through the One-Stop delivery system either directly by One-Stop Operators or under contract with the LWDB (§107(d)(10)(D)). Federal guidance further clarifies that career services must be available in local areas and that certain career services must be provided by comprehensive American Job Centers, and that services can be provide directly on site by One-Stop Operators or partners, or virtually through use of technology (TEGL 16–16, p. 7). This is relevant to the consideration of contracted workforce services because some essential services are provided not only through contracts nor directly by government, but also through partnerships with other service providers, not necessarily involving contracts for those services.

Like WIA, WIOA emphasizes customer choice and maintains the use of ITAs for training by providers on the ETP list; however, the law expands the options for contracted training, allowing contracted class-size training in the following circumstances:

- For employer-based training, such as on-the-job training, customized training and incumbent worker training; this reflected the goal of building a system that is responsive to employer needs. Contracted training allows for training cohorts of workers and also may be a more simplified and familiar mechanism than vouchers like ITAs.
- When there are insufficient providers in a local area or region; this is often the case in rural areas.
- When the board decides there is a program of demonstrated effectiveness to meet the needs of customers with barriers to employment; contracted training may serve as a more attractive vehicle for realizing WIOA's goals of prioritizing job seeker customers with barriers to employment and facilitating access to effective programs.
- When the Board determines the need to train multiple individuals in an in-demand industry; this aligns with WIOA's goal of building a system that is responsive to business demands for a skilled workforce (P.L. §134 (3)(G)(ii)).

The changes in the rules under ARRA laid the groundwork for these new rules under WIOA and reflect multiple goals of the program, including design of a system responsive to industry needs and the focus on individuals with barriers to employment.

A final area of change under WIOA of importance in understanding the role of contracted services is the specific allowance in the statute for the use of "pay-for-performance" contracts. These contracts are a type of procurement mechanism and performance management tool where performance targets are set and the government only outlays funding if the contactor realizes performance targets. Typically pay-for-performance contracts involve private funders that contribute resources to ostensibly bear the risk of the program not meeting established targets.[21] WIOA allows for states to spend up to 10% of funding on pay-for-performance contracts, as long as certain conditions are met, such as requirements for a feasibility study prior to implementation of the contract and independent validation the contactor has reached performance targets (P.L. 113–128, §116(b)(2)(A)). Pay for performance contracts are different from typical performance-based contracts where service providers are paid to meet certain milestones because the government pays zero if contracted service providers do not reach their goals. Pay for performance contracts involve the private sector as a direct financial stakeholder in the outcomes of programs—as opposed to a stakeholder through the contribution of taxes and the election of government officials (Urban Institute, 2018). It is unclear the extent to which states, regions and local areas are using pay for performance contracts, but this will be important to follow as more time passes and new research and evidence emerges on the implementation of WIOA.

LESSONS LEARNED

The public workforce system is complex and the evolution of contracted services reflects that complexity. There are multiple goals of the system, including increased earnings and employment for participants and helping employers gain workers they need. The system is also driven by the sometimes competing principles of customer choice and efficiency of programs. These all affect use and desirability of contracting out. Beyond these driving goals and principles, there are legal and institutional constraints on use of contracting out in the public workforce system in that Wagner-Peyser services for the unemployed cannot be contracted out, but One-Stop Operators and under current law running AJCs must be contracted out.

We do not know as much as we should about what rules are best to have in place when contracting out for workforce program services, yet evolution in policy has led to strong rules being put in place over time, such as rules around service provision by merit-based government employees, performance-based contracts, competitive procurement or customer choice through ITA vouchers. More research and evaluation studies are clearly needed to test the underlying hypotheses about how different variations in contracting out affect outcomes and efficiency in the employment and training area.

KEY POINTS

- It can be argued that employment and training services are inherently governmental, where provision by government workers is in the public interest. This is one of the arguments advanced for requiring Wagner-Peyser labor exchange services to be delivered by government (in this case, state government) merit staff workers.
- Balducchi and Pasternak (2004, p. 44) note that some have argued that, at least for the Employment Service, government provision of employment and training services is "the most reliable way to ensure the highest quality of ES operations," but we are unaware of any evidence that this is the case.
- Although services provided directly by government, such as those provided under the Wagner-Peyser Act, might offer some advantages in terms of oversight and administration, they may lack the flexibility needed to respond to significant changes in service needs or demands, such as those that occurred during the Great Recession. They also may not offer the diversity of options required in a system that has multiple customers and goals, and emphasizes state and local control in response to varied needs.

- If consumer choice is an important consideration, then some contracting out is a necessity. Consumer choice was not a major part of the U.S. employment and training system from the 1960s through the 1990s, but it became an important feature under WIA beginning in 1998.
- The arguments made by Osborne and Gaebler (1992) and Niskanen (1968, 1971) about the virtues of competition for government service provision suggest that contracting out might improve efficiency, but they do not prove that contracting out and competition will increase the productivity and efficiency of employment and training services (or any other services).
- Whereas competition has been touted as the mechanism that might improve the efficiency in contracted versus government run programs, there is a lack of evidence that enhanced productivity and efficiency will occur in employment and training programs
- Contracted services offer diverse service delivery options, but they require mechanisms to ensure that programs are effective and high performing. Competitive procurement and various performance management strategies, including performance-based and pay-for-performance contracts have been used in the public system to manage the performance of service providers, but there is scant evidence that these approaches improve the performance of the programs, and there is some evidence that the mechanisms may waste resources or lead to inappropriate behavior. Examples noted in this chapter include that performance measures lead to cream-skimming in selecting participants, performance-based contracting was believed to have been abused and led to extraordinary profits for service providers, and efforts to restrict providers to those with good track records have resulted in widespread efforts to circumvent the system.
- How contracted service providers are selected and services accessed must consider the various goals, customers and principles of service provision, but these can sometimes come in conflict. For example, the principle of job seeker customer choice may be in conflict with the goals and strategies being implemented to meet the needs of business and industry, and there is evidence that participants may make poor choices.[22] Likely a mix of contracting mechanisms—such as allowing for customer choice through ITAs as well as contracts for class-size training—makes it possible to realize varied goals and serve multiple customers.
- The diverse service delivery might be good in a system designed to meet the needs of a diverse group of stakeholders and promote quality through competition, but it can also make the system difficult to navigate for employers and job seekers, and difficult to monitor performance.

NOTES

1. See Barnow and Smith (2016) for a list and description of these major federal employment and training programs, the history of the federal programs, and the budgets of the programs.

2. For a more general discussion of how and when government should be involved in the provision of government services, see Blank (2000).

3. The Congressional Research Service (214, p. 4 notes that the Office of Management and Budget has a slightly different definition and that "In addition to the FAIR Act, other statutes have 'definitions' sections that include *inherently governmental function* or *functions closely associated with inherently governmental functions*."

4. The material in this section is based on Balducchi and Pasternak (2004).

5. The four local areas where competition was permitted were Boston, Brockton, Cambridge, and Springfield.

6. Information on the current status of Wagner-Peyser service providers in Massachusetts was provided by David Balducchi in personal communications. We have asked the U.S. Department of Labor if more recent information is available.

7. Retrieved from www.reginfo.gov/public/do/eAgendaViewRule?pubId=201804&RIN=1205-AB87 on July 21, 2018.

8. Material in this section is based on Barnow and Smith (2016).

9. The Area Redevelopment Act of 1961 also funded vocational training, but the scale was much smaller, and the program was superseded by MDTA the following year.

10. See Mangum (1968).

11. The Area Redevelopment Act (ARA) was a small and brief predecessor to MDTA.

12. Material in this section is based on Barnow and Smith (2016).

13. Material in this section is based on Barnow and Smith (2016).

14. Interestingly, the concerns with proprietary schools during the JTPA period were high cost, which continues to be a concern relative to community colleges, and great selectivity, which appears to be much less a concern today.

15. Some states implemented some of the reforms included in WIA during the JTPA era. See Grubb et al. (1999).

16. Although WIA required that ITAs be available to training customers in most circumstances, exceptions included when on-the-job training and customized training are provided, when the local board determines that there are too few providers available to meet the intent of vouchers, and when the local board determines that there is a local program of demonstrated effectiveness for meeting the needs of special low-income participant populations that face multiple barriers to employment (Patel & Savner, 2001, p. 1).

17. The six core programs of WIOA are Title I Adult; Title I Youth; Title I Dislocated Worker; Title II Adult Education and Family Literacy; Title III Wagner-Peyser Employment Services; and Title IV Vocational Rehabilitation. The six core indicators of performance are Employment Rate in 2nd Quarter after Exit; Employment Rate in 4th Quarter after Exit; Median Earnings in 2nd Quarter after Exit; Credential Attainment; Measureable Skill Gains; and Effectiveness in Serving Employers. The common measures apply to all six programs, with slight differences in indicators for Title I Youth programs

18. TEGL 15–16, p. 2.

19. Career services are those that must be available to adults and dislocated workers through the one-stop delivery system and include the full range of services from eligibility determination and skills assessment, career planning, supportive services and follow-up services, but do not include training. See P.L. 113–128, Section 134 (c) (2) for a full list of career services as defined under the law. Career services are further clarified in TEGL 16–16 and 19–16, which divide career services into basic, individualized and follow-up services with definitions and requirements for each with respect to the availability of services in local areas and to specific populations.

20. TEGL 15–16, p. 2

21. Urban Institute. Retrieved August 1, 2018, from https://pfs.urban.org/pfs-101/content/what-pay-success-pfs

22. See Barnow (2000) and Barnow (2009) for reviews of the evidence on how well vouchers for employment and training programs affect outcomes for participants

REFERENCES

Balducchi, D. E., & Pasternak, A. J. (2001). *One-stop statecraft: Restructuring workforce development programs in the United States*. Labour Market Policies and the Public Employment Service, Prague Conference, July 2000. Paris: Organization for Economic Cooperation and Development.

Balducchi, D. E., & Pasternak, A. J. (2004). Federal state relations in labor exchange policy. In D. E. Balducchi, R. W. Eberts, & C. J. O'Leary (Eds.), *Labor exchange policy in the United States* (pp. 33–71). Kalamazoo, MI: The W.E. Upjohn Institute for Employment Research.

Barnow, B. S. (1992). The effects of performance standards on state and local programs. In C. Manski & I. Garfinkel (Eds.), *Evaluating welfare and training programs*. Cambridge, MA: Harvard University Press.

Barnow, B. S. (2000). Vouchers for federal targeted training programs. In E. Steurele, V. D. Ooms, G. Peterson, & R. Reischauer (Eds.), *Vouchers and related delivery mechanisms: Consumer choice in the provision of public services*. Washington, DC: Brookings Institution Press.

Barnow, B. S. (2009). Vouchers in U.S. vocational training programs: An overview of what we have learned. *Journal for Labour Market Research, 42*(1), 71–84.

Barnow, B. S., & Smith, J. (2016). Employment and training programs. In R. E. Moffitt (Ed.), *Economics of means-tested transfer programs in the United States* (Vol. II, pp. 127–234). Chicago, IL: University of Chicago Press.

Behn, R., & Kant, P. (1999). Strategies for avoiding the pitfalls of performance contracting. *Public Productivity in Management Review, 22*(4), 470–489.

Blank, R. M. (2000). When can public policy makers rely on private markets? The effective provision of social services. *110*, C34–C49.

Bradley, D. (2013). *The workforce investment act and the one-stop delivery system*. CRS Report for Congress. Washington, DC: Congressional Research Service.

Congressional Research Service. (2014). *Definitions of "inherently governmental function" in federal procurement law and guidance*. Washington, DC: Congressional Research Service.

D'Amico, R., & Salzman, J. (2004). Implementation issues in delivering training services to adults under WIA. In C. J. O'Leary, R. A. Straits, & S. A. Wandner (Eds.), *Job training policy in the United States* (pp. 101–134). Kalamazoo, MI: The W.E. Upjohn Institute for Employment Research.

Dickinson, K., West, R., Kogan, D., Drury, D., Franks, M., Schlichtmann, L., & Vencill, M. (1988, September). *JTPA performance standards: Effects on clients, services, and costs*. Report No. 88–17. Washington, DC: National Commission for Employment Policy Research.

Grants Management Advisory Service. (1989, June 5–7). DOL clarifies policy on the use of performance-based contracts under JTPA. In *Current developments*. Washington, DC: GMAS.

Grubb, W. N., Badway, N., Bell, D., Chi, B., King, C., Herr, J., . . . Taylor, J. C. (1999). *Toward order from chaos: State efforts to reform workforce development systems*. Berkeley, CA: National Center on Vocational Education, University of California.

Heinrich, C. J. (2002). Outcomes—based performance management in the public sector: Implications for government accountability and effectiveness. *Public Administration Review, 62*, 712–725.

Heinrich, C. J. (2003). Measuring public sector performance and effectiveness. In B. Guy Peters & J. Pierre (Eds.), *The Sage handbook of public administration* (pp. 24–38). Los Angeles, CA: Sage Publications.

Heinrich, C. J., & Lynn Jr., L. E. (2000). Governance and performance: The influence of program structure and performance on the job training partnership act (JTPA) program outcomes. In *Governance and performance: New perspectives*. Washington, DC: Georgetown University Press.

Jacobson, L., Petta, I., Shimshak, A., & Yudd, R. (2004). *Evaluation of labor exchange services in a one-stop delivery system environment*. Final Report submitted to the U.S. Department of Labor, Employment and Training Administration. Rockville, MD: Westat.

Johnston, J. W. (1987). *The job training partnership act*. Washington, DC: National Commission for Employment Policy.

Kaiser, J. (2013). Wagner-Peyser employment services. In B. S. Barnow & R. A. Hobie (Eds.), *The American recovery and reinvestment act: The role of workforce programs*. Kalamazoo, MI: The W.E. Upjohn Institute for Employment Research.
Kettner, P. M., & Martin, L. L. (1993). Performance, accountability, and purchase of service contracting. *Administration in Social Work, 17*(1), 61–79.
King, C. T., & Barnow, B. S. (2011). The use of market mechanisms. In D. J. Besharov & P. H. Cottingham (Eds.), *The workforce investment act: Implementation experiences and evaluation findings*. Kalamazoo, MI: The W.E. Upjohn Institute for Employment Research.
Koning, P., & Heinrich, C. J. (2013). Cream-skimming, parking and other intended and unintended effects of high-powered, performance-based contracts. *Journal of Policy Analysis and Management, 32*, 461–483.
Levitan, S. A., & Gallo, F. (1988). *A second chance: Training for jobs*. Kalamazoo, MI: The W.E. Upjohn Institute for Employment Research.
Levitan, S. A., & Mangum, G. L. (Eds.). (1981). *The T in CETA: Local and national perspectives*. Kalamazoo, MI: The W.E. Upjohn Institute for Employment Research.
Mangum, G. L. (1968). *MDTA: Foundation of federal manpower policy*. Baltimore, MD: The Johns Hopkins Press.
Musgrave, R. (1959). *The theory of public finance: A study in public economy*. New York: McGraw-Hill.
Niskanen, W. A. (1968). The peculiar economics of bureaucracy. *American Economic Review*.
Niskanen, W. A. (1971). *Bureaucracy and representative government*. New York and Chicago, IL: Aldine Publishing Company.
Osborne, D., & Gaebler, T. (1992). *Reinventing government: How the entrepreneurial spirit is transforming the public spirit*. Reading, MA: Addison-Wesley Publishing Company, Inc.
Patel, N., & Savner, S. (2001). *Implementation of individual training account policies under the workforce investment act: Early information from local areas*. Washington, DC: Center for Law and Social Policy.
Trutko, J., & Barnow, B. S. (2013). Workforce investment act adult and dislocated worker programs. In B. S. Barnow & R. A. Hobbie (Eds.), *The American recovery and reinvestment act: The role of workforce programs*. Kalamazoo, MI: The W.E. Upjohn Institute for Employment Research.
Urban Institute. (2018). *What is pay for success?* Retrieved November 19, 2018, from https://pfs.urban.org/library-new/content/what-pay-success-pfs
U.S. Department of Labor, Employment and Training Administration. (1987). *Mounting concerns regarding "problem contracts" written under 20 CFR 629.38 (e)(2)*. Training and Employment Guidance Letter No. 3–87.
U.S. Department of Labor, Employment and Training Administration. (1989, March 13). *Job training partnership act: Requirements for acceptable fixed-unit price contracts*. 54 FR 10459.
Van Horn, C., & Fichter, A. (2011). Eligible training provider lists and consumer report cards. In D. Besharov & P. Cottingham (Eds.), *The workforce investment act: Implementation experiences and evaluation findings* (pp. 153–172). Kalamazoo, MI: W.E. Upjohn Institute for Employment Research.

7

Contracting for Human Services in New York City

James Krauskopf

INTRODUCTION

Historically, the "voluntary" sector preceded public financing for social services in New York City in the form of settlement houses and other religious and secular nonprofit organizations, some dating back to the nineteenth century. Prior to the 1960s, city government formed relationships with organizations providing child welfare, job training and a few other services for people with particular needs. Subsequent to the enactment of the federal anti-poverty and Great Society programs of Presidents Kennedy and Johnson, a large and diverse nonprofit human services system has developed over more than 50 years utilizing federal, state and local government financing, as well as private funds.

The system provides delivery of government-funded employment, community development, housing, homeless shelter, legal services, healthcare, mental health, substance abuse treatment, senior citizen centers, home meals, child welfare, childcare, youth development, after school, educational support, immigration services, adult literacy, criminal justice and many other social services. Nonprofit advocacy and program development, followed by government financing, has produced services responsive to emerging issues, such as HIV-AIDS outreach and treatment, supportive housing for homeless mentally ill, universal pre-kindergarten and other initiatives that required ingenuity and flexibility to address critical social needs.

Government contracts with nonprofit organizations became the primary vehicle for utilizing public funds to support human services during the twentieth century, and the role of contracting has continued to expand in the twenty-first. Today's pattern of services in New York City derives from programmatic responses to social and economic conditions over this long period of time, with many originating in the 1960s and some even before (Smith & Lipsky, 1993; Fabricant & Fisher, 2002; Smith, 2016, 2017).

CONTRACTING FOR HUMAN SERVICES IS EXTENSIVE

In fiscal year 2017, New York City approved more than 7,200 human services contracts totaling nearly $6.5 billion; and in 2018 more than 7,400 with a total value exceeding

$6.8 billion—consistently constituting 30% to 35% of all city contracts. Accountability for both program performance by nonprofit providers and the contracting process are essentially internal processes of city government managed by the substantive city departments and procedurally through the Mayor's Office of Contract Services (MOCS) (Mayor's Office of Contract Services, 2017, 2018).

Eight different departments (as follows) contract for most of the city's human services. Annual reports by the mayor's Office of Contract Services aggregate the numbers of contracts and the total amounts approved by each department. These reports describe the different methods and procedures utilized by city government for overall procurement, rather than analyzing program performance data.

The eight city departments that contract with human service providers are:

Human Resources Administration/Department of Social Services—career services (workforce, job skills), WeCare (wellness, rehabilitation), domestic violence shelters, legal assistance, HIV/AIDS services;
Department of Homeless Services (recently made part of Dept. of Social Services)—shelters for single adults, families with children, and adult families; Homebase prevention; homeless outreach;
Administration for Children's Services—foster care, preventive services, EarlyLearn centers, child care vouchers, juvenile justice detention and Close to Home Services;
Department of Youth and Community Development—after school (K-12 and high school), Beacons, Cornerstone centers, adult and young adult literacy programs, immigrant services, Neighborhood Development Areas, Summer Youth Employment and other youth workforce programs, Runaway Homeless Youth, Family Support;
Department for the Aging—senior centers, Naturally Occurring Retirement Communities, home-delivered meals, Housekeeping, ThriveNYC Geriatric Mental Health and Friendly Visiting programs, Senior Employment Services;
Department of Health and Mental Hygiene—community health centers, Primary Care Development Corporation, Public Health Solutions, mental health services, substance abuse resources;
Department of Probation—alternative to placement programs, Justice Community, Justice Plus, Youth Wrap, Young Adult Success Corps;
Mayor's Office of Criminal Justice.

(Mayor's Office of Contract Services, 2014, 2015, 2017, 2018)

Today, city government delivers very few human services directly, with the exception of eligibility determinations for large so-called entitlement programs—Cash Assistance (welfare), Supplemental Nutrition Assistance (Food Stamps), Medicaid (with overall management by New York State), Child Support Enforcement and rental assistance (Section 8 housing vouchers and other subsidies). Considered government safety net assistance for people in and near poverty, these programs constitute large items in local, state and federal expenditure budgets and continue to be directly administered by government. Although final eligibility decisions have remained government responsibilities, non-governmental organizations do play roles, such as "facilitated" enrollers and navigators who assist people to prepare their applications for health insurance and other safety net benefits.

City government also directly performs particularly sensitive human services functions. Child Protective Service caseworkers investigate child abuse and neglect allegations, making initial determinations of where and how to protect children at risk of physical or psychological harm. City caseworkers provide some adult protective services; government outreach workers bring aid to homeless people on the streets and in public transportation venues; and public health doctors staff health and mental health clinics—among a limited number of other directly provided public human services. Private nonprofit organizations are active providers of many of these service areas, as well, in joint or parallel operations with their government counterparts.

In brief, New York exemplifies in abundance all of the three categories found in Dennis Young's typology of government-nonprofit relations—supplemental, complementary and adversarial (Young & Casey, 2017). As examples, nonprofit organizations supplement government early education and community healthcare programs; complement provision of homeless shelters and senior centers; and advocate for new public services in response to HIV/AIDS and service-enriched affordable housing. As the partial list of contracted services from the eight city departments attests, the scope of services is extensive.

CONTRACT DELAYS AND OTHER ADMINISTRATIVE PROBLEMS PERSIST, DESPITE REFORMS

However, long-standing administrative problems—especially delays in contract registration and payments—continue to affect the operations of nonprofit providers and the clients who need services. Late registration of contracts after their designated starting dates lead to cash shortfall that have plagued the contracting system for decades. Providers feel obligated to initiate their services at the planned time, which is often before the contract is registered. Because the city cannot make reimbursement and fee payments until the comptroller registers the contract, many providers experience cash flow problems that cause them to utilize their reserve funds (if they have them), draw down on lines of credit, adopt emergency fundraising campaigns and undertake other borrowing or coping strategies—none of which correct the underlying problem of delayed contracts.

The city responded by creating a low-interest loan facility at the Fund for the City of New York for providers waiting for contract registration. Whereas some city departments now provide advance payments against approved contracts, not all do.

Official reports from city and state officials previously tracked by department the continuing delays in human services contracts, and the information was regularly reported in the annual *Agency Procurement Indicators* reports by the Mayor's Office of Contract

Services. (Mayor's Office of Contract Services, 2014, 2015; DiNapoli, 2011; Office of the State Comptroller, 2015). Subsequently, the mayor's office no longer reports on delayed contracts, and the separately elected New York City comptroller recently issued a report showing departmental lateness.

The city continues to address the problem, but this shift in reporting has reduced the previously visible commitment of the mayor's office to reform the process by tracking department-by-department late contracts. (Mayor's Office of Contract Services, 2017; NYC Comptroller, 2018)

The frequent delays in final approvals of government contracts occur for a variety of reasons involving government contracting departments, mayor's office and central management and program functions, city comptroller, and nonprofit service providers themselves. The city Law Department and the Office of Management and Budget also provide oversight of the contracting process. As a result, nonprofits too often find they must and do begin to provide employment, homeless, child care and other vital service programs before reimbursement mechanisms are in place. An essential question is why these conditions persist. It is answered in part by a recent report from SeaChange Capital, which examines the complexity and number of steps by multiple agencies in the public contracting process (SeaChange, 2018).

Complaints about cash flow problems from services providers continue, and nonprofit leaders view with concern the ongoing effects of related contracting practices. They perceive that government sets rates for some services that are too low and provides inadequate reimbursement amounts. Despite federal policies to establish a basic level of administrative overhead, the city has not yet made sufficient funding allowances for overhead that covers actual and federally recommended levels. Many nonprofits in New York operate without financing for their reasonable administrative overhead costs—a topic regularly addressed in different formats for many years by city government and nonprofit leaders, but still not fully resolved (Human Services Council, 2016, 2018; United Neighborhood Houses, 2015–2018).

Extensive reporting required by different city departments causes additional back office compliance work for nonprofits. Performance contracts can put providers at risk for receiving the expected funding for these services. Executive directors and other senior staff have described anecdotally, but consistently, examples from their own and other organizations.

From a national perspective, Steven Rathgeb Smith identified many of these problems in a review of nonprofit contracting with government. They are not unique to New York City (Smith, 2016). The Urban Institute conducted with the National Council on Nonprofits a series of surveys that document issues in government-nonprofit contracting on a state-by-state basis. Collaborative efforts began subsequently to address problems in other states that are similar to those in New York (Urban Institute, 2013; National Council of Nonprofits, 2013).

A key question in New York City is why the well-established and generally positive government relationships with nonprofit organizations in delivering human services have not led to correcting more of the fundamental operational problems. Leaders in both sectors express appreciation for the importance of an effective process, and, as indicated, both have invested considerable time and effort to make essential improvements.

Over nearly two decades, two city administrations have addressed these problems.

A joint committee of city officials and nonprofit leaders advised the administration of former Mayor Michael Bloomberg on the design and implementation of initiatives to improve contracting with nonprofits, including a Health and Human Services Accelerator to manage the human services proposal process online and a payment system for contractors. A "vault" for basic nonprofit documents forms the basis for pre-qualifying prospective human services providers without requiring them to make redundant submissions. A common city human services contract facilitates new programs by focusing negotiations on the scopes of work, rather than more technical legal issues.

These and other initiatives to strengthen nonprofit organizations and their relationships to city government resulted from attention and commitment of top staff under a new position of deputy mayor for Health and Human Services. Bloomberg's appointee, Linda Gibbs, had been commissioner of the Department of Homeless Services and had other relevant senior management and budget experience in city government.

The current administration of Mayor Bill de Blasio, which began in 2014, has continued implementation and further developed these initiatives. With responsibilities assigned to several deputy mayors, management and policy are perhaps less concentrated in a single official in the mayor's office than in the previous city administration. The significant reforms under Mayors de Blasio and Bloomberg, as well as actions by the mayors who preceded them, have not eliminated persistent problems in the management of New York City's contracting system.

A particular shock to the system occurred when FEGS (formerly Federation Employment and Guidance Service), which had been the city's largest human services nonprofit with a budget of $250 million, declared bankruptcy in 2015. There appear to be multiple causes, including internal decisions and practices at the agency, as well as government financing and contracting issues.

Initially, the rapid demise of FEGS presented major challenges for maintaining client services and employment. Government officials working intensively with leaders of an experienced nonprofit organization were able to transfer $75 million New York State Office of Mental Health contracts from FEGS to the Jewish Board of Family and Children's Services, which thereby became the city's largest human services organization.

FEGS workforce programs under the New York City Human Resources Administration transferred to another large employment agency, Fedcap Rehabilitation Services. Other government agencies and UJA-Federation of New York enabled willing nonprofits with capacity for growth to assume additional contracts for substantial, but lesser amounts. Transferring contracts was the mechanism for government and UJA to preserve essential services for vulnerable clients and to continue employment for many former FEGS workers, demonstrating the overall capacity and flexibility of the human services system in New York.

There was been much speculation, and some analysis, about the causes of the collapse of such a large and seemingly capable organization, and public reports have varied.

Media coverage, opinion pieces and documents submitted to the bankruptcy court point to multiple reasons. There were weak central financial systems and reporting, contracts that were losing money, subsidiary ventures that drained reserves rather than adding to them as intended, under-utilized leases, multiple capital debt financings from public agencies, large layers of middle and senior management compensated at high levels, and more (Woodlock, 2015; Prakash, 2015).

For some observers, inadequate payment rates for government-funded services, including both the cost of the services and a reasonable overhead for agency administration, were a primary cause (Nocenti, 2015). Indeed, the affidavit submitted to the bankruptcy court by Kristin Woodlock, who assumed the CEO role at FEGS after the 2014 deficit announcement, notes that consultants determined that 74% of its 350 programs were in deficit and that "financial performance on its workforce governmental contracts was among the worst in all its business lines" (Woodlock, 2015, pp. 32–33).

However, as indicated previously and in the affidavit overall, there were many contributing factors to the demise of FEGS. Contracting issues are part, but by no means all, of the story. FEGS may be a unique case because of its size, range and extensive problems, but other agency closings and acquisitions designed to appear as mergers indicate there are more organizations that are weak financially and vulnerable in the future. The high risk of operations for even the largest human services agency with its wide scope of services caught the attention of other nonprofit human service provider organizations.

The Human Services Council (HSC), which represents the nonprofit service providers and their membership organizations in discussions with government, convened a commission to examine both government financing practices for nonprofit programs and the need for greater attention by nonprofit service providers to identifying and minimizing their own risks to their organizations (Human Services Council, 2016). So-called unfunded mandates and costs of operating and reporting to different government departments resonate throughout the human services field. HSC subsequently developed for nonprofit providers a voluntary survey of the contracting practices of city and state government departments to rank them and identify problems for advocacy purposes. Together with other nonprofit leaders, HSC is also encouraging organizations to determine the aggregated risks due to inadequate rates for contracted services, payment delays and other potentially harmful factors in particular contract solicitations (Human Services Council, 2018; GovGrader 2018).

New systems, although praised in concept, take many years to implement fully. Some city department representatives continued requesting duplicate documents from the staff of nonprofits, even after creation of the central database made them available, in Accelerator. The Accelerator payment module is still phasing in for contracts in some city departments, and the online PASSPort system for vendor information will not be fully operating until 2019 (Human Services Council, 2016, 2018; Mayor's Office of Contract Services, 2018; NYC Comptroller, 2018; SeaChange, 2018; United Neighborhood Houses, 2015–2018).

These and related contract management issues are on the agenda of a joint city government-nonprofit leader Nonprofit Resiliency Committee established in April 2016 by the administration of Mayor de Blasio under the deputy mayor for Strategic Policy Initiatives and the deputy mayor for Health and Human Services. Staffed by the mayor's Office of Contract Services, this committee has reported progress in multi-year funding by the city for nonprofit overhead and services rates and in administrative improvements for electronic procurement and digitized human service agency audits (Nonprofit Resiliency Committee, 2017, 2018). The City Council has held hearings on contract issues, and several members have introduced legislation aimed to reduce delays. (City Council, 2018).

Beyond administrative issues, nonprofit organization leaders have long noted their desire to participate more fully in designing new and revised programs and in setting program performance targets. In this view, ensuring sound program determinations depends on prior consultation by city officials with experienced providers of services. Policy decisions made without sufficient lead-time for such consultation negatively affects the feasibility and impact of programs (Human Services Council, 2016).

Recent commitments to collaborative program design by the city with nonprofit service providers is a promising step. The Nonprofit Resiliency Committee is developing a manual to enable more productive and permissible pre-discussions between city departments and nonprofits before issuance of requests for proposals and concept papers (Nonprofit Resiliency Committee, 2018).

ENSURING A VIABLE CONTRACTING SYSTEM FOR THE FUTURE REQUIRES SUSTAINED MUTUAL ACTION BY GOVERNMENT AND NONPROFITS

New York City government continues to expand its publicly financed human services to needy residents. The scope of services is already broad and deep, and program development is responding actively to newly identified problems and opportunities. The de Blasio administration has utilized a favorable city economic and fiscal climate to expand pre-school education, after school programs, legal representation in housing eviction cases, homeless shelter, outreach, and mental health support largely through contracts with nonprofit organizations.

Adequate fiscal capacity for such growth does not always coincide with a mayoral philosophy of expanding government. Their current juxtaposition at city hall is certainly not guaranteed for the future. New York is not immune from effects of the nation's business cycle, and most mayors have had more austere governing policies than the current occupant of city hall. Future downturns in the national economy, New York City constraints caused by inadequate affordable housing supply and conditions, mass transit failures, results of local elections, and other factors could quickly change mayoral priorities.

It is not enough to expand services during such a rare period of favorable conditions. Officials should devote sufficient sustained attention to correct administrative problems that prevent the nonprofit-government contracting system from working effectively. Resources to correct the longstanding contract delays, cash flow issues, overhead cost, and other management issues discussed here and in referenced reports should receive attention and allocations, ahead of prioritizing fresh program and services commitments.

New York City's large and complex system of government contracts with nonprofit service providers is difficult to manage and requires continuous high level attention. Partial fixes, such as emergency loans and advances against contract payments, are compromises that add to system complexity. The new systems for contract solicitations and payments need full implementation to improve the operations of both government departments and nonprofit organizations. If city departments continue to make independent decisions about their contracting practices, nonprofit providers will still have to endure multiple administrative and reporting requirements that complicate their operations and require unreimbursed staff.

Nonprofit organizations became providers of publicly supported services because they could reconcile their independent missions with the realities of being a government contractor. Differences in perspective exist. A nonprofit's mission may be more specific and particularistic on a geographic, demographic or cultural basis than the more universal intentions of government. Elected officials are responsible for providing services equitably and consistently throughout their service areas (Smith, 2017; Smith & Lipsky, 1993).

Being a public service provider can change the character of a nonprofit organization. With roots in certain communities and particular approaches to service provision, nonprofits make compromises in joining a universal public mission. Do they maintain a more limited program that expresses their roots and origins? Or, do they broaden their funding and scope while accepting both requirements and contracts from government?

As noted, many New York nonprofit organizations seek opportunities to participate in program design, as well as provision, of publicly funded services. Recognizing that there will be constraints imposed by government, nonprofits seek to be active participants in program development and standard-setting as essential aspects of working with government. In administrative theory, ideally nonprofits and government would mutually share objectives and obligations in joint stewardship, rather than in a more typically hierarchical principal-and-agents relationship (Van Slyke, 2007).

Consultation and advisement do occur in New York to a certain extent and may happen more in the future if the Nonprofit Resiliency Committee—or similar vehicle—can sustain and deepen joint policy, planning and practice by the government and nonprofit sectors. Effective services depend on a complex system of delivery for many different human services—some of which each sector provides separately and some by both operating together (Krauskopf & Chen, 2010).

Although the sectors may be mutually dependent, government is ultimately accountable, and power is not equal. Government officials need a mechanism to share decision-making as partners with private nonprofit leaders without surrendering control. The ongoing task is to continue engagement and commitment of senior people in both sectors.

The city sets policy, provides some services directly and contracts for others.

Given its multiple roles, government should consider what kinds of consultations are needed with nonprofit service providers before policy and planning decisions are made. How should such consultations be managed with the nonprofits and government departments in particular circumstances involving new and revised programs? Acknowledgment of the value of jointly conceived objectives could encompass determinations to start new programs, conduct needs assessments for ongoing services, change or terminate programs, or take other pre-solicitation actions. The city's development of a manual that will facilitate communications with nonprofits prior to RFP development, as well as the use of concept papers to gather of feedback about new initiatives, is a constructive step to draw upon nonprofit provider experience in program design.

At the back-end—*i.e.*, measuring and reporting—the metrics and means are currently set by government, often without sufficient joint determination with providers. More effort should be made to establish joint discussion and decision-making. Consolidating multiple measures and separate program reports would benefit nonprofit providers and improve operations overall.

Another factor in the contracting process stems from New York City's political structure with its three top officials each separately elected on a citywide basis. The mayor, comptroller and public advocate can all claim that they are independently accountable to citizens of the city. Media attention feeds on conflict and controversy more often than on smooth process. In recent years, for example, the comptroller held or returned contracts to provide homeless shelters because of his finding of poor conditions in the facilities. In other instances, responses by city officials to questions from the comptroller about pending contracts led to registration delays when the comptroller deemed the responses inadequate. Resolving such issues between mayor and comptroller and their staffs in a manner that avoids contract delays should be a mutual objective.

CITY DEPARTMENTS MEASURE AND REPORT PERFORMANCE WITHOUT DISTINGUISHING BETWEEN DIRECT OPERATIONS AND CONTRACTOR SERVICES

The Mayor's Management Report (MMR), which the mayor announces via press release, is the primary government document that tracks the performance of public services. The preliminary document in February reports on the first four months of the July 1 to June 30 fiscal year, and the final form in September covers the full fiscal year. Throughout its 40-year history, the MMR has been a regular source for information and data on city government performance in New York city. The report now appears online and provides key indicators in a chapter for each department.

Generally, the unit of a city department responsible for human service programs sets the performance and reporting measures for both its directly operated and contracted services. The measures reported do not distinguish government operations from nonprofit provider services. Each program area, such as childcare or homeless shelter, includes a series of specific indicators that may include services from either or both government or nonprofits. The chapter for human services departments describes priorities, goals, variances and relevant data indicators for the most recent five fiscal years (Mayor's Management Report, 2018).

The Citywide Performance Reporting (CPR) system integrates with the MMR online through the Office of Operations website. Citywide Themes group all departments with related functions together, although their indicators are each reported separately. Indicators are color-coded to identify whether a program element is improving or stable (green), declining 10% or more (tan) or declining more than 10% (red).

To provide a more complete picture, public reporting on government performance should identify nonprofit-managed services that are publicly financed, as well as those directly run by the government. It would be useful to know what the contributions of contractors are to city departments' performance in each program area, because nonprofits provide most social services in New York City under contracts with government departments. Making it possible to discern the contributions by nonprofits can enhance the transparency of the reports issued by government.

Although city government directly determines eligibility for such entitlements as cash and food assistance, investigates child abuse and neglect, and participates with New York state in managing medical assistance—among other government-provided human services—the interactions of both government and nonprofit-provided services impact social conditions in the city. Clarifying the roles of each can help to explain how broad goals are being achieved, or not, as well as to facilitate assessment and responsibility for individual human services programs.

The city tracks provider performance by program to inform decision-making about renewal of specific providers and for new contracts. The nonprofits report extensively in accord with city requirements, and consultations to involve them in setting performance objectives and reporting requirements should occur on a more consistent basis. When discussions occur, they are often a post-implementation adjustment to performance indicators in response to provider complaints about feasibility.

Reporting to city departments is program-by-program. Effective performance measurement requires consensus on which indicators to use and how to simplify reporting so that nonprofit providers with multiple government contracts can feasibly carry out accountable reporting while maintaining appropriate focus of their staffs on the essential tasks of providing the services. Streamlining reporting so that government gets the data necessary to determine performance and nonprofits can track the data that matters for assessing their own work is an analytic and operational challenge that remains to be resolved.

The information in both city MMR and CPR reports is primarily *output* data that does not easily translate into broader *outcomes*. Outputs quantify what programs do—people trained for jobs, day care slots available, cash assistance provided and the like. *Outcomes*, on the other hand, are the results achieved by such programs—gainful employment, improved education and reduced poverty for the program participants. Do public program outcomes relate to social conditions in the city?

Human services indicators pertain to large commitments of government funds from all levels. Caseloads and policies for these programs have often been the center of major public controversies in New York and nationally. Reporting on the many indicators can be complex and difficult to integrate into an overall picture. Discussions in the MMR can be detailed and nuanced. Reports that accurately convey the data, trends and issues does not lead easily to broad generalizations or quick sound bites.

There have been many critics of the MMR, including some who commented regularly on social conditions such as homelessness, poor school performance, high unemployment and other indicators of distress following the recession a decade ago (Pasanen, 2010).

Concerns for current social condition should include questions that cut across departments and indicators:

> Administration for Children's Services (ACS) indicators show a long-term consistent reduction in the number of children in out-of-home foster care, now below 9,000 from a high near 50,000 in the 1980s. As a positive indicator of child and family well-being, some of this improvement may result from the provision of preventive services to meet families by ACS own case management work together with its contracted nonprofit social services agencies.
>
> Looking at the growth of homeless families with children over another long-term timeframe, however, raises questions about greater family stress with effects on children's behavior and school performance. The Department of Homeless Services' (DHS) is making efforts to mitigate these effects with school attendance and other initiatives. How can the MMR develop indicators to measure what is happening to families with children in these two systems and what the relationships are between these seemingly disparate trends in their well-being?

Fiscal watchdogs have frequently argued for a combined budget and performance focus by requiring that the MMR provide unit costs to match indicators for the reported services. Although each agency does report budget and spending information, explicitly connecting performance of programs with their units of expenditure is not assured:

> Where possible, the relationship between an agency's goals and its expenditures and planned resources, by budgetary unit of appropriation (UA), is shown in the "Applicable MMR Goals" column. Each relationship is not necessarily exhaustive or exclusive. Any one goal may be connected to multiple UAs, and any UA may be connected to multiple goals.
>
> (Mayor's Management Report, 2018, p. 353)

> Spending and Budget Information—Shows the relationship, where possible, between an agency's goals and its expenditures and planned resources, by budgetary unit of appropriation.
>
> (Mayor's Management Report, 2018, p. 435)

Another reform to advance public engagement in the official city reporting process would establish citizen surveys of public services as a measure of satisfaction and quality in the MMR (Khurshid, 2016, 2017).

PERFORMANCE REPORTING SHOULD INFORM ABOUT SOCIAL GOALS

Beyond these fiscal reforms, city reporting could emphasize major social conditions that affect residents in the city. The city could work with nonprofits to modify its reports to add definitions of social outcomes that cross program and department lines. Indicators from both directly operated city government programs and those managed by nonprofit contract service providers could help to determine direction, progress and trends in social conditions in the city, such as:

- Earnings, income, and poverty
- School performance and education
- Social services and family well-being
- Shelter and stable housing
- Healthcare and public health

Using the relevant program areas, report analysts could aggregate program indicators to measure performance. Social conditions are not directly attributable solely to particular public programs because broad national and international socioeconomic factors play important roles. Nevertheless, enabling public program reporting to contribute evidence toward illuminating effects on these larger social conditions would be constructive.

Because the city's various performance reports tend to be program-specific, going beyond the current measures to test feasibility of broader indicators should be an objective for these reports. Providing the information to public officials, nonprofit executives and their boards, and to the general public would inform about whether the city's major social goals are being.

Goals set by venerable social advocacy organizations in New York City provide useful examples. Citizens' Committee for Children advocates that "every child is healthy, housed, educated and safe" (CCC). The Community Service Society wants to "create opportunity and prosperity for all New Yorkers" emphasizing low-income and people of color receiving access to healthcare, affordable housing, economic security, imprisonment and reentry, and opportunities for youth (CSS). These organizations have further elaborated these broad social goals, which could potentially relate to the program-by-program public indicators from current city reports.

DOES ORGANIZATION MATTER?

In addition to reviewing the issues in the contracting process and in public reporting of outcomes, it is important to consider how the organization of government affects human services contracting. How has the structure of city departments administering human services developed and evolved to its present configuration, and what are the implications for contracting and services?

For the most part, the organization and reorganization of human services in New York City government has proceeded over time in an *ad hoc* manner in response to particular program priorities, events, and crises publicized in the media. An exception was the creation of the Human Resources Administration (HRA) in 1966, following a six-month planning period conducted for Mayor John Lindsay by the Institute of Public Administration. The resulting plan created a comprehensive structure for welfare, public medical insurance, food stamps, foster care, day care, employment, youth development, senior citizen centers, addiction treatment, and other social services. HRA was a broad umbrella "super-agency" for human services, one of several such administrations created in housing, environmental protection, and other substantive areas of government.

After more than 50 years, the Human Resources Administration/Department of Social Services remains in name, but many of the services functions have become separate city departments. (Aspen, 2001). Many services transferred out of HRA, and some later returned as a result of separate decisions by subsequent mayors. The eight city departments described earlier in this chapter represent the current structure of New York City human services.

One especially important change was the establishment under Mayor Rudolph Giuliani in 1995 of a separate department for child welfare and early childhood education functions, following a tragic and well-publicized death of a child known to city child abuse investigators and education authorities. A study led by Nicholas Scoppetta—a former deputy mayor, prosecutor and foster child—recommended removing investigations of child abuse and neglect, foster care and family services programs from HRA in order to establish them in an independent Administration for Children's Services (ACS). ACS continues to manage these child welfare programs currently.

As indications of ongoing structural evolution, however, child support enforcement, which was previously included in ACS, soon transferred back to HRA. Juvenile justice, which Mayor Koch had moved into an independent agency, has again become associated with child welfare as a division within ACS. And forthcoming in 2019, early childhood education programs (child care centers, Head Start and family day care) will transfer from ACS into the city's Department of Education.

One other example of the many structural changes that occurred, illustrates the ever-evolving reorganization of human services in New York City government. In 1992, Mayor David Dinkins created a new Department of Homeless Services, following the recommendations of a commission headed by Andrew Cuomo (now governor of New York State and then head of a nonprofit homeless shelter and housing organization). The mayor transferred then burgeoning city shelters and services from the Human Resources Administration into this new department to make it more responsive to the needs of the homeless and their nonprofit providers. In its recent plan to combat growing homelessness, the de Blasio administration moved the Department of Homeless Services back under HRA where it could get the attention of the current commissioner.

Many of these and other organizational changes were responses by different mayors to particular problems that became immediate public issues involving unmet social needs, tragedies, or scandals. Little overall human services planning has guided the many structural changes since the Lindsay administration executive order that implemented the original design for HRA.

There is little evidence to suggest, however, that either the original planned HRA structure, which proved difficult to manage, or subsequent reorganizations, has produced a "best way" to organize human services. As human services have continued to evolve and grow throughout this long period, reorganization of departments and functions does not seem to be the key to better contracting. Addressing problems directly with adequate resources, appropriate staffing, and focused program development is likely to be more productive than undertaking reorganizations that cause anxiety for staff of government departments and nonprofit service providers while disrupting their assistance to constituents.

The more *ad hoc*, but pragmatic, approach to adapting social services functions to shifting needs and priorities in New York City government may have served New York better than the carefully designed super-agency that faced frequent and challenging operating problems. (Aspen, 2001; Krauskopf, 2015)

The looser federation of agencies has functioned well when there has been a coordinating function in the mayor's office to set priorities and undertake inter-agency projects, as demonstrated by the deputy mayor for Health and Human Services in the Bloomberg administration—a model that Mayor de Blasio is also utilizing but perhaps with less concentrated authority. For such a structure to work well, the senior mayoral officials must exercise administrative authority over human services departments and be accessible and responsive to advocacy by nonprofit organizations that contract with city government.

Threats to the city from climate change and terrorism call for effective mechanisms to bring city departments and nonprofit human services organizations together for disaster preparedness, response, and recovery. Twenty-first-century events, including the 9/11 attack on the World Trade Center in 2001 and Hurricane Sandy in 2012, demonstrated that coordinating capacity between government and nonprofit contractors and other community organizations had to be built anew for each of these very different disasters.

Currently, the Human Services Council and city departments are building relationships and supporting coordinating structures that operate between vulnerable communities and government during periods after these disasters in anticipation of establishing greater joint readiness in advance of any future events. Once again, mechanisms are developing through evolving joint efforts by government departments—especially Health and Mental Hygiene and New York City Emergency Management—working with the nonprofit Human Services Council and local organizations that are representative of their communities. They are identifying changes in contract forms and practices that can enable neighborhood-based human services organizations to respond flexibly to disaster events that may require response work that is different from the social services prescribed in their existing contracts.

To conclude, should there be a more established overall framework for human services providers and government to interact on a regular basis about broad policy?

Structural and programmatic solutions do develop as new needs appear. Although this evolutionary process has demonstrated strength built on its flexibility and responsiveness to changing conditions and the dynamics of new social problems, this creative process could occur more consistently if there were a regular process for the government and nonprofit service sectors to establish mutual objectives.

KEY POINTS

- Contracting is the essential means of delivery of human services in NYC. The contracting problems described in this paper have implications for immediate and long-term provision and management of services to people in need, especially in low-income areas of the city.
- Despite implementation of important administrative reforms, the contracting system does not deliver consistent, on-time contract approvals. Serious delays cause cash flow problems for nonprofit providers and undermine service delivery capacity.
- Persistent administrative problems should command more attention from top city officials in order to develop consistent solutions across the government that minimize idiosyncratic approaches to contracting issues by each city department separately. See recent City initiatives at: https://www1.nyc.gov/site/nonprofits/about/about.page
- The mayor's Office of Contract Services should track each city department and report status in order to focus the necessary high-level attention on solving administrative problems, such as delayed contracts, as visible mayor's office management objectives. The mayor and comptroller should resist allowing these problems to become political issues between them.
- Contracting problems occur against the background of a well-established system of collaborative government-nonprofit services delivery that goes back many decades. The two sectors should sustain and strengthen joint committees and similar vehicles that address problems at a high level in both city government and nonprofit organizations.
- Human services constitutes a complex shared system in which both government departments and nonprofit organizations operate. Yet it does not function as a system of equals, because government must hold its contractors accountable for their performance, while they also work jointly to provide services. Within that framework, there should be mutual policy-making, planning, program development and goal-setting measures.
- Improvements in the city's reporting system can better engage city residents, as well as public officials and the nonprofit services community, in understanding trends and progress in achieving important objectives to improve social conditions in New York.

REFERENCES

City of New York, Mayor's Management Report. (2018, September). *Fiscal 2018.*

City of New York, Mayor's Office of Contract Services, Agency Procurement Indicators, and Appendix B "Agency Procurement by Industry". 2014, 2015, 2017, 2018.

City of New York, NYC Nonprofits, "Nonprofit Resiliency Committee," 2017, 2018, 2019. Retrieved from https://www1.nyc.gov/site/nonprofits/funded-providers/nonprofit-resiliency-committee.page. Retrieved from https://www1.nyc.gov/site/nonprofits/funded-providers/indirect-implementation.page?utm_medium=email&utm_source=govdelivery

Fabricant, M. B., & Fisher, R. (2002). *Settlement houses under siege: The struggle to sustain community organizations in New York City*. New York: Columbia University Press. 2019.

Glenn Pasanen, *Gotham Gazette*, Citizens Union Foundation, 2010.

GovGrader, Human Services Council. (2018). *GovGrader series 2018*. Retrieved from www.surveygizmo.com/s3/4472707/GovGrader-Survey-2018

Human Services Council. (2016). *New York nonprofits in the aftermath of FEGS: A call to action*. Human Services Council.

Human Services Council. (2018). Interviews with Executive Director on July 27, 2018, with Associate Director/General Counsel on August 8, 2018, and observations by author at meetings sponsored by HSC.

Krauskopf, J. A. (2001, November). *Recommendations on human services policy for the next New York City mayor and city council*. Aspen Institute, Roundtable on uH. Comprehensive Community Initiatives for Children and Families.

Krauskopf, J. A. (Jack). (2015). Nonprofit-government relationships in New York City. In J. Brothers (Ed.), *Rebalancing public partnership: Innovative practice between government and nonprofits from around the world*. VT and United Kingdom: John Brothers, Gower, Burlington.

Krauskopf, J. A., & Chen, B. (2010). "Administering services and managing contracts: The dual role of government human services officials". In Professional practice, Steven Rathgeb Smith, Guest Editor. *Journal of Policy Analysis and Management*, *29*(3).

National Council of Nonprofits, Partnering for Impact: Government-Nonprofit Contracting Task Force Produces Results for Taxpayers. (2013, April).

New York City Comptroller Scott M. Stringer. (2018, May). *Running late: An analysis of NYC agency contracts*.

New York City Council, Committees on Contracting and General Welfare, Hearing on June 21, 2018, NYCC-PV-250-14_180621-131516.mp4. Retrieved from https://councilnyc.viebit.com/player.php?hash=3zxGtttX6sw0

Nocenti, D. (2015, March 9). Starving those who help the poor: How state and city systematically underfund social-service nonprofit groups. *New York Daily News*.

Nonprofit Resiliency Committee, City of New York. (2018, May 24). *Update from nonprofit resiliency committee*.

Prakash, N. (2015, March 18). *Bankruptcy filings detail FEGS descent*. Capital New York.

Samar Khurshid, *Gotham Gazette*, Citizens Union Foundation, 2016, 2017.

SeaChange Capital Partners. (2018, August). *New York City contract delays: The facts, research note*.

Smith, S. R. (2016). Managing the challenges of government contracts. In D. O. Renz (Ed.), *The Jossey-Bass handbook of nonprofit leadership and management* (4th ed.) Jossey-Bass.

Smith, S. R. (2017). Cross-sector nonprofit-government financing. In E. T. Boris & C. E. Steuerle (Eds.), *Nonprofits and government: Collaboration and conflict* (3rd ed.). Rowman & Littlefield.

Smith, S. R., & Lipsky, M. (1993). *Nonprofits for hire: The welfare state in the age of contracting*. Cambridge, MA: Harvard University Press.

United Neighborhood Houses, Author Observations During Board, Committee, and Other Discussions. (2015–2018).

Urban Institute, National Survey of Nonprofit-Government Contracts and Grants. (2013).

Van Slyke, D. M. (2007, April). Agents or stewards: Using theory to understand the government-nonprofit social service contracting relationship. *Journal of Public Administration Research and Theory*.

Woodlock, K. (2015, March 18). *Affidavit pursuant to local bankruptcy rule 1007–4 and in support of first day motions*. United States Bankruptcy Court Eastern District of New York, *in re* Federation Employment and Guidance Service Inc. d/b/a FEGS.

Young, D. R., & Casey, J. (2017). Complementary, supplementary, or adversarial? Nonprofit-government relations. In E. T. Boris & C. E. Steuerle (Eds.), *Nonprofits and government: Collaboration and conflict* (3rd ed.). Rowman & Littlefield.

Part 3

Contracting for Human Services in Other Countries

8

Contracting for Children and Youth Mental Health Services in Ontario, Canada, Using a Modified Lead Agency Approach

Rosemary Vito

INTRODUCTION

In Ontario, Canada, the Ministry of Children and Youth Services (MCYS), has shifted to "lead agencies" and an accountability framework in the children and youth mental health (CYMH) sector. Specifically, MCYS (2013) has designated 31 lead agencies (one per region) across the province who are responsible for overseeing new service requirements and service coordination with other CYMH agencies in their regions, with increased expectations for accountability and performance outcomes. In 2014/15, CYMH agencies who were interested in becoming a lead agency in their region submitted a lengthy application process to MCYS for review. To date, 31 lead agencies have been established across the province of Ontario. Originally, these lead agencies had multiple designated responsibilities: establishing a regional service delivery plan; creating clear service pathways for clients and service partners; delivering or sub-contracting services with local CYMH agencies and holding them accountable; making services effective and accountable to clients; and establishing and maintaining inter-agency and inter-sectoral partnerships (MCYS, 2013). Lead agencies are also accountable for reporting regional data to the ministry on key performance indicators regarding clients served, service efficiency, responsiveness, access and effectiveness (MCYS, 2013).

However, in 2016, MCYS decided to retain the funding and contracting function for all CYMH agencies in the province, removing the expectation of lead agencies to hold funding for agencies within their service region (Consortium, 2018). At the same time, lead agencies continued to be primarily responsible for developing an annual "Core Services Delivery Plan" and a broader "Community Mental Health Plan," which the ministry would use to inform their annual service contracting (Consortium, 2018). These plans were to be developed collaboratively with community partners and identify their joint work priorities for the coming year (Consortium, 2018). The ministry's decision to designate lead agencies with planning responsibilities, but not give them sub-contracting authority over direct service providers, is an interesting and unusual approach that will be referred to as a "modified lead agency" approach. This unique situation provides an opportunity to consider what is happening in Ontario as an *experiment* that has implications for Canada in general as well as the U.S. What happens when lead agencies in a human services contracting system are charged with the tasks of leadership, planning, service delivery coordination and performance measurement but are not provided with the incentives and sanctions associated with sub-contracting authority and financial management? Given this unique context, a relevant research question is whether a modified lead agency approach without sub-contracting authority is a viable alternative to the traditional lead agency approach?

This chapter will focus on how the modified lead agency approach is working in Ontario, illustrated by research findings in three CYMH agencies, and provincial government reports. This research study follows an earlier study on the lead agency application process, and agency leaders' strategic and innovative adaptations to this ministry directive (Vito, 2017). The historical context of ministry funding and directions in CYMH services, and the purpose of shifting to lead agencies will be explained. This will be followed by an overview of the methodology for the research study. The findings from this study will then be presented, integrated with relevant reports. Topics include: the shift to a modified lead agency approach; implementation areas, strengths and challenges; funding model opportunities, insufficiencies and uncertainties; performance indicators and standardized data management tools; government response and lessons learned. The chapter will end with a summary and conclusion, and key points. This chapter ultimately aims to ensure that leaders in human service organizations benefit from learning about the viability of implementing a modified lead agency approach sector-wide, as a unique example of human services contracting.

HISTORICAL CONTEXT OF CHILDREN AND YOUTH MENTAL HEALTH (CYMH) SERVICES IN ONTARIO, CANADA

The Ontario Ministry of Children and Youth Services (MCYS) was created in 2003. Their mandate is to work directly with government and community partners to establish policies, programs, and a service system to strengthen families and assist vulnerable children and youth; and to lead across government on common issues (MCYS, 2014). The ministry's role includes accountability for the delivery and/or oversight of clinical and community-based children and youth mental health (CYMH) services as transfer payment agencies (MCYS, 2014). These CYMH agencies are the focus of this current chapter.

According to Children's Mental Health Ontario (CMHO), the provincial association representing Ontario's publicly funded CYMH services, these agencies have been chronically underfunded, with a modest 8% increase to base budget since 1992 (CMHO, 2013). This lack of financial investment has negatively impacted the maintenance of core services, administration, clinical supervision, quality assurance and evaluation, staff retention and professional development (CMHO, 2013). Moreover, CYMH agencies have reported a 10% annual increase in service demand for several years without increases to core funding, resulting in long waitlists, reduced service capacity, and program closures in some cases. Hospital emergency visits and inpatient admissions for children and youth have also increased over 50% in the past 8 years (Auditor General, 2016). Recently, MCYS (2016) has invested new funding for staff in direct client services, for an overall total of more than $444 million since 2011. CMHO (2015a) acknowledges the benefits of these investments, in terms of reducing client wait times for brief and short-term services; however, they assert that investment in agencies' base funding and longer-term services is lacking, despite increased service demand. They are advocating for further funding to strengthen client service access and quality and to retain staff through higher salaries (CMHO, 2016).

Along with funding challenges, children, youth, and families have experienced struggles trying to access timely and appropriate mental health support and treatment, with a confusing and fragmented service system (MCYS, 2013). In response to these issues, in November 2012 MCYS developed a "Moving on Mental Health" (MOMH) action plan, as part of the Ontario government's mental health and addiction strategy (MCYS, 2012). The goal of this plan was to create a coordinated, responsive system to improve the access, accountability, evidence-base and coordination of children's mental health services (MCYS, 2013). The ministry established multiple objectives to achieve this goal: creating and supporting clear pathways to care; defining core mental health services for every community; establishing community lead agencies responsible for planning and service delivery; creating a new funding model; and building a legislative and regulatory (accountability) framework (MCYS, 2013). However, CMHO (2015b) cautioned that while this initiative strives to improve client services and collaboration across sectors, lead agencies will require further human, technology and training resources to achieve this goal. To understand how the modified lead agency approach is currently being implemented, a research study was conducted with three CYMH agencies, as detailed next.

METHODOLOGY

The purpose of this research project was to explore the implementation of a modified lead agency approach in children's mental health organizations in Ontario. A qualitative research approach was used, which is an interpretive, emergent approach that focuses on the meanings participants give to their experiences in natural settings (Denzin & Lincoln, 2005). A focus group was conducted with the leaders (executive and senior directors) of three lead agencies, and a written guide of prepared questions was developed. The research question focused on the viability of a modified lead agency approach. Specifically, this included: historical context and purpose; impact of this change (e.g. agency funding, service delivery, relationships with service partners); implementation steps taken, opportunities and challenges; financial and human costs of this change; performance outcomes; government response to implementation and evaluation efforts; and lessons learned.

This study was approved by the Research Ethics Review Committee at the author's university. Agencies were selected through purposive sampling (Rubin & Babbie, 2011). A detailed email with an attached "Letter of Information" was prepared, explaining the research study and inviting interested agency directors to participate. This email was sent to the researcher's contact at one children's mental health agency, who forwarded the email to the co-chairs of the "Lead Agency Consortium," which consists of the 31 executive directors for the lead agencies across Ontario. The second email was sent to the Director of Research at the Ontario Centre of Excellence for Child and Youth Mental Health (The Centre), who agreed to forward the email to the co-chairs of the "Community of Practice," which consists of the senior directors in each agency who are responsible for lead agency implementation. Three executive directors and two senior directors responded, indicating their interest in participating in this study. The directors were then sent the "written guide" of prepared questions for the focus group, an informed consent statement to review and sign, and an agency/participant demographics form to complete. A summary of the agency/participant demographics is listed in Table 8.1.

Due to the relatively small numbers and geographical distance of participants, the focus group was conducted by video conference (arranged through this author's university). The video conference was audiotaped and transcribed, and the transcript was analyzed following the phases of thematic analysis to organize the data according to emerging themes (Braun & Clark, 2006; Lapadat, 2010). The emerging key themes were sent to the directors for review and feedback as part of member checking (Rubin & Babbie, 2011). A coding system was developed to help maintain continuity in reporting (Corden & Sainsbury, 2006), which specified each participant in numerical sequence (e.g., pp. 1, 2, 3). The themes reported in the following sections represent implementation efforts on a regional level by these individual agencies. They provide good practice

Table 8.1

Agency and Participant Demographics

Number and type of agencies	Three childrens' mental health agencies
Mandate/services	Comprehensive child and youth mental health services; some developmental services, youth addictions/justice
Funding/budget	MCYS annual funding for CYMH ranges from 2.6 to 7 million dollars
Population	Urban cities (90,000+) and rural geography; some diversity (Indigenous, new immigrants)
Service partners	Range CYMH/core agencies (0–11); multiple cross-sector organizations (up to 25)
Staffing	Range 32 to 175 interdisciplinary staff (e.g. child and youth workers, social workers, psychologists, nurses, developmental service workers)
Clients served	Range 1500–2500 infants, children, youth (ages 0–18), parents/caregivers, families served per year
Participants	Three executive directors, two service directors; age range 49–65 (average 57); gender three males, two females; years in current position most four to six years, one more than 30 years.

examples, but the generalizability of these findings is limited by the small sample size and low response rate (Rubin & Babbie, 2011).

To supplement these themes and provide more comprehensive data from a broader provincial perspective, key findings from two additional reports will be included in the following sections. The first report is *"Lead Agency Provincial Priorities Report" (2018)*, prepared by the Lead Agency Consortium. This report is based on a survey of all executive directors/CEOs of lead agencies across the province conducted by the Consortium. The focus of the report was to provide updates regarding progress on the Consortium's previous recommendations and lead agencies' implementation efforts in local service areas, and provide future recommendations on addressing barriers and advancing opportunities (Consortium, 2018). The second report is *"Child and Youth Mental Health" (2016)*, prepared by the Auditor General of Ontario. This report is based on interviews and procedural review with staff in four CYMH lead agencies, four MCYS regional offices, and representatives from CMHO and The Centre, parent and youth groups. The purpose of this report was twofold: to assess MCYS' policies and procedures to ensure appropriate and timely CYMH services in alignment with program requirements; and to assess whether MCYS funding provided to agencies matches value of provided services (Auditor General, 2016).

FINDINGS

Key findings will be presented, integrating themes from the focus group, the Consortium (2018) report, and the Auditor General's (2016) report where applicable.

Shift to Modified Lead Agency Approach

CYMH agencies applied to become lead agencies in a phased process in 2014–15, with the first lead agencies planning their local services in 2014, continuing into 2016 (Consortium, 2018). Participants stated that the final two lead agencies are less than two months old, having been decided in April 2018. As previously noted, the five core functions of lead agencies originally set out by the ministry were: leadership, planning, service delivery/alignment, performance measurement, and financial management including sub-contracting with core service providers (Consortium, 2018). Participants confirmed the *original purpose* of lead agencies was to improve service delivery, by "creating better partnerships" (p2), "improving . . . or creating a (service) pathway" (p3) and "creating a more aligned service . . . really client-focused" (p1) removing barriers to service access. One participant confirmed their original understanding was the "full meal deal" covering the five areas as lead agencies, assuming much of the ministry role with local responsibility, "in a much more effective and cost-efficient way" (p2). Participants suggested the *underlying purpose* for lead agencies was to consolidate and monitor agency contracts, "the ministry wanted to eliminate the number of payment contracts it had" (p2); and to address funding usage, "there were questions about the nature of the use of funds, so lead agencies are vested with the responsibility" (p3).

However, the ministry decision to hold the contracts and funding decisions with core service providers was a *significant unanticipated change*: "they started to retract some responsibilities . . . we became more of a planning agency and a partner with the ministry versus having more full authority" (p2). One participant noted that Consortium members were "surprised . . . even shocked" (p3) by this shift in their responsibilities. Another commented, "for the Consortium, it was a really major concern, take away a share without [authority]" (p1). Lead agencies are working with multiple core service providers, and with the removal of their authority over funding and contracting, they are concerned about how they would address agency performance problems, "how far can we go actually making a change if performance is a problem?" (p3). One agency is starting to get their "feet under us" with core service providers, using the "power of their recommendations" (p3). They have a "core service leadership council" with multiple agencies that operates on a consensual model to make system changes. Although this has been challenging, they have maintained engagement with their service partners. Another participant (p1), who is a sole core service provider and has no authority over others, wonders about their impact over other agencies; with planning as the primary focus, they anticipate tension with the ministry. A third participant, suggested they retain "some power and authority" through planning, which "drives the contracting and funding" (p2). They perceived benefits, by having less risk and responsibility for core service providers and funding. Instead, they are focusing on planning and resources: "pulling together your community and trying to figure out how you can use your resources but when push comes to shove, it's really the Ministry that holds the final decision-making and the contract" (p2).

Implementation Areas, Strengths and Challenges

There were several themes arising regarding areas of lead agency implementation. These areas pertain to the primary lead agency functions and include planning opportunities, challenges, and shared processes; service coordination, systems-level lens and building relationships across sectors; and service standardization and pathways, caregiver/family and youth engagement. Each of these areas is detailed in the following sections.

Planning Opportunities, Challenges and Shared Processes

Participants in all three agencies discussed *planning opportunities* with other core CYMH services in their region. One director had developed a "lead agency council" to plan with multiple other service providers. Their *challenges* were updating all partners and priority setting, "trying to figure out how to really identify gaps and priorities because there just is so many to choose from" (p3). For their first year, they prioritized serving an influx of Syrian refugees, along with intake/access with a "walk and talk" brief service, and intensive residential services, requiring a long-term plan. They also initiated conversations with community partners regarding funding French language and Indigenous services. Another director was implementing a full mental health and addiction plan county-wide. Their planning table identified 17 priority areas, and three were selected: intake/access, with a "connecting everyone to the right door approach" with a "warm handover" of clients to other services (p. 1); pathways to care, with common templates and hard targets for wait times, crisis, walk-in and overall services; and crisis services, developing an efficient and effective adult system for hospital emergencies, and managing children and youth in crisis with decision trees and a common risk assessment. A third director noted *challenges in planning and creating service equity* given their rural location, large geography, small communities and difficulties with staff recruitment, "the truth is people don't want to live in those communities, so you can't get professionals up there" (p2). The majority of their population resided in an urban area, which was an advantage for service delivery. They also had a higher Indigenous population, with multiple provincial territory organizations, which posed challenges with maintaining relationships and services, "constantly trying to figure out how to have relationships that are both part of the healing and Truth and Reconciliation process, while concurrently try to move your own agenda forward" (p2). Their planning goals were "aspirational" and included improving the flow of services, building a residential system, and reducing systemic racism.

On a provincial level, the majority (87%) of lead agencies agreed that MOMH *planning mechanisms are effective* for their service area, especially with other CYMH core service providers and English-language school boards (90%), hospitals and early years organizations (87%). However, there were *challenges integrating stakeholders from other sectors*, including French-language school boards (43%), developmental services (autism) 42% and health services (primary care) 35%. The *greatest challenges for planning* CYMH services were: competing cross-sectoral priorities (84%), internal competing priorities (55%), partner/lead agency finance and infrastructure limitations (48% and 42%) and geographic/distance barriers (30%) in remote areas. Although not a top priority, developing planning processes was rated important by some (13%) lead agencies for the coming year (Consortium, 2018).

The directors were also asked about their *shared planning processes* with each other. One director noted that there is not a formalized process, and agencies coordinate on a provincial level with the ministry, "it's really looking at the big systems pieces as opposed to what's happening on the ground, regionally or locally" (p. 1). There is also a "Community of Practice," where senior directors can share planning efforts at the ground level. The provincial planning is achieved through the Consortium, who have a presence with the ministry at a partnership table. One participant reported "significant movement in the last three years . . . a real relationship had formed" (p1); however, they were concerned about the impact of a new conservative government "now different people, government, so who knows how that will take shape" (p. 1).

Service Coordination, Systems-Level Lens, Building Relationships Across Sectors

Participants in all three agencies discussed *coordinating across sectors* and assuming *a systems-level lens* to build the children's mental health system. This included working across the health (LHINS) and education sectors to build relationships and develop a core services plan and broader community mental health plan, "when you come to the table for a common purpose and try to figure out what's going on in your child and youth mental health system . . . they had some intent to look beyond our own world, which was a really strong point for this particular initiative" (p2). This also included bringing together multiple cross-sectors to collaborate on a systems level, "at the local level . . . it really has crossed sectors, it has crossed disciplines . . . we have now 19 sectors around the table and we're looking at both children and adults and addiction" (p. 1). As well, this included having honest conversations with the LHIN and local agencies about service pathways between hospitals and community services: "To have them now join our table and have really honest discussions about things like the pathways that have been created from the emergency department to the community without any funding" (p. 3).

Participants also emphasized the importance of *building relationships across sectors* to move initiatives forward. They shared insights regarding the time and effort required to implement these relationships and that they depend on the people involved, "if you have the right person in that relationship . . . I'm way more likely to move planning forward" (p. 2). They also noted that parent and youth voice can impact the process to be more effective and positive. One agency indicated their guiding principles are based on relationships, "our whole movement forward is relationship-based . . . taking the principles of the consortium to our local planning table" (p. 1). They required all agencies involved in planning to sign an agreement that they are representing their sector and bringing a system focus, rather than an individual agency focus, with the majority of participants invested.

They also discussed some of the *challenges with service integration* with other sectors. For example, one director (p. 2) spoke about working with agencies in the adult system, who are not similarly compensated for their system work, and often the same staff are taking on this additional work. Another director agreed, "we have (multiple) reps sitting around the table . . . they're not getting paid for it, they're making system changes . . . that's probably to me the biggest Achilles heel of this systems management process" (p. 1). Directors also explained that in the health sector, LHINs are mandated to work with lead agencies and have been collaborative, whereas Boards of Education are not mandated, and these connections are "always dependent on goodwill and relationships" (p. 2)). All three directors confirmed a working relationship with the English-language boards of education, but more challenges with the French-language boards. These challenges may be due to French-language boards covering "large geographical areas . . . difficult to engage key representatives" and "limited engagement strategies . . . with French communities as whole" (p4), including translation services, recruiting bilingual staff, etc.

Similarly, on a provincial level, lead agencies rated *service coordination highest* with English-language education (91%), child welfare and other CYMH core service providers (83% and 81%), and moderate with early years and special needs (71% and 58%), hospitals and youth justice (66% and 64%), adult/youth mental health and addictions

(53%). Service coordination was considered *least effective* with French language education and services (45% and 29%), children's rehabilitation and autism (33% and 29%), health planning and primary care (26% and 19%), and Indigenous services (20%) (Consortium, 2018).

Service Standardization and Pathways, Caregiver/Family and Youth Engagement

One participant acknowledged service duplication and gaps in their region, stating that core service areas are improving, although not yet defined. They emphasized *service standardization*, "we're creating some standardization so that there's equity across the province in terms of core services that are available" (p1). Also, for common elements regarding service access and pathways "there are great discussions both regionally and provincially around models and methodologies" (p1). This participant also noted planning mental health services with multiple other agency providers, trying to align services that are client focused and accessible, rather than planning in isolation. This is a significant shift, in terms of creating a standard for equitable core service access across the province, led by the Consortium.

On a provincial level, about half (53%) of lead agencies agreed that pathways into and through service are clear; however, few (23%) agreed that pathways out of service (i.e. transition to adult services) are clear. Several community partners were perceived to have a common understanding of pathways into service, including the education sector (87%), CYMH core services (71%), and cross-sectors (52%); whereas families and the health sector had considerably less (39% and 35%). Lead agencies had introduced initiatives to improve service pathways with partners, and many rated coordinated access to pathways as one of their greatest achievements. However, there remained multiple barriers, and service care pathways were rated a top priority (52%) by lead agencies for the coming year.

Regarding caregiver and youth engagement, all the directors agreed that this was a goal. One senior director emphasized, "family and youth voice is a key component to system change . . . without their voice, system change is incomplete" (p. 4). One agency had a "huge engagement process with youth, caregivers and care service providers to understand what they saw as the current system" (p. 1) and they developed a planning table for youth engagement, receiving good feedback. This director recommended "going to where the youth are" (p. 1) to increase engagement, such as high schools and drop-in centers. Engaging caregivers was a larger gap, and they were finding creative ways to accomplish this, as focus groups were not adequately representative. Another agency (p. 3) was partnering with youth serving organizations but recognized they needed dedicated staff to focus on youth strategies and mental health. They were also working on family engagement with a parent coordinator and needed someone dedicated. The third director also noted progress in this area, "one of the things my agency has worked on is client engagement" (p. 2).

On a provincial level, the majority (68%) of lead agencies agreed that service providers in their area share a common understanding of meaningful stakeholder engagement in service planning. Most reported *strong engagement* (94%) with community partners but only *mild engagement* (58% and 61%) with caregivers/families, and children/youth. Interestingly, many (58%) lead agencies rated engagement as one of their greatest achievements, yet family engagement was still rated as one of their top priorities (29%), and youth engagement to a lesser degree (16%) for the coming year (Consortium, 2018).

Funding Model Opportunities, Insufficiencies and Uncertainties

In terms of funding opportunities for the lead agency initiative, all three agencies received some *system management funding*. One director noted, "the systems management funding was critical in terms of making it work . . . it actually helped a much larger version for the agency in terms of moving forward" (p. 1). In terms of human resources, this funding allowed agencies to increase and restructure their management complement. One agency received $400,000, which allowed them to hire a 'full-time system coordinator position" (p. 3), as the director had been "trying to do all that work myself with help from the senior team and a couple of consultants in the community" (p. 3), along with a director of quality improvement, which was an important element. The other two agencies, with less core service providers, received between $200,000 and $250,000, which they used to restructure their senior management team, "we did hire another senior manager . . . being a lead agency helped us restructure some of our management services" (p. 2) and invest in required services, "we could invest more in our French language service responsibilities so now we've made headway" (p. 1).

Despite this investment, all three directors spoke about *insufficient funding to implement* lead agencies. One agency with multiple core service providers received significantly less funding than their budgeted requirements ($600,000). As a result, they had to scale back their plans, as the costs for lead agency meetings, travel, preparation, human resources, and finance exceeded their funding received. This resulted in a deficit position due to costs, requiring them to draw from their base budget, meaning that "the actual mechanics of being a lead agency are fairly costly here" (p. 3). Similarly, another director spoke of the gains in funding outstripping the required work for their agency, such that management felt overworked and were having to prioritize what projects to follow through on versus letting go, "you start parking projects that you just can't get off the ground because your work has outstripped your resources at the management level" (p. 2). The third director agreed that "there is never enough (funding), you do what you can, you figure it out" (p. 1), noting that if there was greater funding, they would be further along, "if I had the ability to hire one more position, we could have moved double faster . . . we would be well into implementation right now" (p. 1).

These funding inadequacies also resulted in *role conflicts and resource allocation issues*. For example, in one agency, the executive director was required to assume more of an external focus rather than internal agency business and delegated responsibilities to directors, which impacted the senior management team. This dual role was not sustainable, and a "system coordinator" was subsequently hired. As well, hiring a director of quality improvement while also having to cut direct service positions resulted in a "great divide" (p. 3), and impacted their dynamic with the union, who had questions about this situation. Another director (p. 1) also acknowledged being pulled away from internal operations to attend external meetings with the other core service providers, although they expressed appreciation for the ministry funding provided, without which implementation would have been more difficult and slow. However, this director lamented *the lack of resource allocation* for core service agencies to participate in this process, "there was not consideration of how we help out those agencies that are having extra time, planning time, infrastructure time" (p. 1). Another director also acknowledged the limited resources, "we all recognize our resources are limited so that we are really trying to work with our partners to be more effective in delivering a good service" (p. 4).

These directors also emphasized that the *lack of funding investment in core services* (0% increase over many years), had reduced their service capacity (fewer staff and programs) and increased client risk, "the big issue with funding levels overall for us is that capacity has been over with zero percent for many, many years. Our capacity is at huge risk" (p. 1). In one agency, these service gaps conflicted with their role as lead agency trying to address regional service gaps, resulting in "an interesting dance . . . being both a core service provider and a lead agency, we've actually run into ourselves a few times where we've had to deal with our own funding inadequacy as a core service agency" (p. 3). This director concluded, "we're pretty well experts at planning and scarcity" (p. 3). Another director agreed that the lead agency initiative is a *cost-effective way* for MCYS to conduct planning and move their agenda forward, "I bet you, dollar-for-dollar, the lead agencies have gone further with planning than the LHINs ever did" (p. 2). However, they noted such planning requires a long-term "10-year runway" (p. 2), which is interrupted by government changes, "at a systems level, so much is dependent on the four-year increment of provincial government" (p. 2).

The need for funding investment in core CYMH services is a realistic concern. According to the Auditor General's (2016) report, MCYS spent $438 million in 2015/16 transfer payments to approximately 400 agencies to deliver CYMH programs, serving 120,000 children and youth. However, this agency funding continues to be provided based on historical spending patterns, and the Auditor General (2016) recommended that MCYS allocate funding to CYMH agencies according to the mental health needs of children and youth served. The Consortium (2018) also upheld that MCYS investments in base funding and service expansion were required to ensure sufficient capacity and quality of CYMH services. MCYS agreed with this recommendation, and during 2017 they had been finalizing a "needs-based funding allocation model" (Consortium, 2018, p. 6), which would be based on community needs, allocating funds to geographic service areas, with implementation scheduled for 2018/19 (Auditor General, 2016).

However, there is now *uncertainty regarding this new funding model*, with the recent shift to a Conservative provincial government. Directors expressed concerns about this new funding model being "a dream that never took hold" (p. 1). This director explained that the previous Liberal government had committed funding for CYMH services, "there is earmarked dollars that the funding formula was going to be utilized. So, agencies across the province, core service providers would have been receiving some increases, fairly substantial" (p1); however, this funding is now in question. Another director explained they had negotiated a "funding investment model" where no agency would lose funding, which was important for small agencies with large geographical regions who were overfunded per capita: "That was the beauty of the lead agency model in action, where they negotiated how best to do this" (p2). This was an equity-based solution designed to not destabilize the service system and was considered a fair solution offered by the ministry, although also now in question. More broadly, the status of the MOMH/lead agency initiative and ministry representatives with this new government is unknown, leading to frustration and concern.

Performance Indicators and Standardized Data Management Tools

The need for *effective data management tools* to measure CYMH agencies' performance is an important consideration. The Auditor General (2016) recommended identifying and implementing consistent and appropriate performance indicators and data requirements, including measurement of long-term client outcomes; and setting targets, collecting data, following up and publicly reporting on agencies' performance. The Consortium (2018) also recommended that the ministry "ensure clear and consistent definitions for its key performance indicators (KPIs)" (p. 19). The ministry planned to strengthen program, service and oversight tools to improve monitoring of agencies' performance and client outcomes, and they were working collaboratively to develop performance indicators and data collection, including caseloads, costs, clients served, and long-term outcomes (Auditor General, 2016). These efforts included a "*Business Intelligence Solution*" (BIS) to streamline and standardize system-wide data collection processes, and further refinement of performance indicators and data collection standards (Consortium, 2018, p. 6).

Directors confirmed the ministry's efforts to have "proper data governance in place . . . there's been a lot of work on that but it's really slow-going" (p5); and agencies are "invested in making better clinical and organizational decisions that are more data informed" (p2). However, the directors were critical in their feedback of the planned *data collection system being ineffective and uncertain.* One director labelled the Business Intelligence Solution (BIS) a "big garbage collector" that gathers data and "spits out" (p2). They explained that, in theory, the BIS gathers all data from the lead agency and core service providers to the ministry, who use it to form local and provincial plans. However, the ministry has not mandated using the BIS as one system across the sector. As well, whereas this tool is considered acceptable and agencies have laid the groundwork for it and are ready to move forward, it may be discontinued by the new provincial government, "the problem will be if it just gets dumped away" (p2).

The directors were also *critical of the ministry's key performance indicators (KPIs).* The definitions were unclear, "because that work with definitions is really just in its beginning stages, I share the concern that people will look at it and well say this isn't helping us right now, although there's been a huge amount of work done to get us here" (p5). As well, although the KPIs have aggregate value on the ministry level, they have *limited clinical value*, "they really made a mistake in not building a system that both had clinical value, program value, agencies, service delivery, ministry value" (p2). Directors were concerned that the data being produced would be useless as it was not considered in context. Another director agreed that whereas the ministry had identified KPIs, they were not always present or make sense in their clinical work, begging the question of how to operationalize KPI definitions. One agency was implementing these, "we are . . . looking at how to understand outcomes and client trends and where we're doing well and not doing well," (p1) and trying to mitigate weaknesses, although they noted this would not help with service excellence at a provincial level because context was not being considered. Another director suggested that staff literacy regarding data collection was needed, "helping staff understand the importance of collecting data and functions, so there's a lot of work to be done in this area" (p5).

Participants also discussed the need to choose a *standardized data measurement tool*, "it's really hard to know where you are going if you don't quite know where you are and measuring that accurately . . . There's been a lot of work put into the idea of data and data processing and trying to create some standardization" (p1). Two agencies had shifted to using "interRAI" a standardized international clinical tool that provides a needs assessment of symptoms on a system level, with a steering committee to coordinate implementation in one region. One participant identified this tool as providing new opportunities, "to get some common definitions and to start collecting data systematically and collated in one system" (p5). Another tool all three agencies had implemented for case management purposes was "EMHWare" (electronic mental health) clinical record. Directors were discussing it with regional groups and focused internally on implementation within their agencies. One director had received funding for both new databases, and spoke very favorably of both tools, in terms of efficiency and reducing staff workload, "the systems management money helped us to do that shift and so we have EMHWare and interRAI. It's well integrated and working extremely efficiently" (p1). Another director also spoke highly of EMHWare, using it on a regional level across multiple service delivery areas, and would consider implementing interRAI if this was adopted on a province-wide basis. They noted that conversations were happening, "we're all trying to lay the seeds of the foundation" (p2); however, this director was concerned about these foundations being "ripped apart" by the new provincial government, "it's going to suck if the government wipes all this out because lots of us have just got the groundwork" (p2).

On a provincial level, the vast majority (90%) of lead agencies had begun initiatives to *improve their data usage* in service planning, and many had the capacity to use data on client service usage (61%), client experiences (48%), and client outcomes (43%). However, very few (15%) rated data usage as effective in informing service delivery. The most *significant barriers* to data usage for quality and performance improvement were: poor data quality (87%), lack of time/resources (84%), lack of consistency in defining data elements and collecting data (81% and 74%), lack of information technology (IT) infrastructure and financial resources (42% and 35%), and lack of expertise

(35%). Moreover, whereas some (29%) lead agencies rated quality, performance measurement, and data use as one of their greatest achievements, others (19%) rated data access to inform service planning and data integrity within service areas as top priorities for the coming year (Consortium, 2018).

Mixed Government Responses

Directors spoke about their *improved relationship with the ministry*. They noted a marked difference with the lead agency initiative, "having a relationship between the Consortium at the partnership table and corporate (ministry) . . . It was a matter of you know 'we need to decide for you' as opposed to 'we need to plan together" (p1). There were examples of positive interactions: one director received concrete feedback from the ministry that they were observed "doing a good job of engaging people" (p3); another enjoyed it "I just thought it was a fun part of the job . . . have them help you look at your services and be part of the development" (p2).

There were also examples of *negative interactions around advocacy efforts*. One director experienced differing agendas initially, having presented a service plan including all ages and sectors in their region, which the ministry tried to narrow to CYMH services. This expanded plan required advocacy from their program supervisor before the ministry accepted it. Another director reported the ministry "pushing back" when they engaged in system advocacy efforts that were viewed as "political advocacy . . . which you can't do with public funds" (p3). This director managed system advocacy by separating the work between paid staff and the Board of directors as "unpaid volunteers" (p3). A third director reported getting their "wrist slapped" (p2) when parents and youth assumed advocacy roles, as "the government . . . they want you to engage and have relationships with families . . . as long as they do it within the rules" (p2). This director noted, "if you really engaged with families then and they're equal partners and you share power, that's a very different relationship than just asking them their opinion."

LESSONS LEARNED

The directors spoke on both philosophical and practical levels regarding lessons learned. On a philosophical level, one director (p2) highlighted the "*long-term game of change*", noting there were partnerships at a systems level, improved relationships with the government, and directors and senior managers were focused on getting some things done, but there was "always the next piece" to accomplish. The other two directors shared their *commitment to continuing this priority work*, noting that even if the MOMH strategy was discarded by the new provincial government, they would carry on, "we're actually still going to do it and we have a commitment to making this work" (p1). They felt lead agencies had been a positive initiative, "this is brilliant and it's working" (p1), with a healthy process between the ministry and agencies, "you actually felt it was trying to be constructed together and work in partnership" (p2). Everyone was involved and focused on working together to create a better system, with a planning table to make things work and consider what changes were needed.

The directors also provided some *practical insights*. One director cautioned that organizational cultures are different and may "crash together" (p2), as not everyone approaches problem-solving in a similar way. These issues need to be mitigated, and providing food during meetings is a practical way to build relationships and forge a shared culture. This director also recommended including children, youth and families, as equal voices in service improvements. Another director emphasized *consensus building at the planning table* and when points are pushed, to "go where there is agreement" or "the greatest consensus," as "small steps breed success" (p1). The third director suggested the need for *engagement of new leaders*, as there will be multiple new leaders due to upcoming retirements, and the sector will need to "get people fired up about the same vision . . . how do you maintain the momentum?" (p3).

SUMMARY

The research question for this study was whether a modified lead agency approach to human service contracting is a viable alternative to a traditional approach. The findings highlighted some key areas regarding this viability that will be summarized later in the chapter, along with future directions. The Consortium (2018) has also developed several foundational recommendations, which include system-wide and cross-sector initiatives. Whereas a detailed review is beyond the scope of this chapter, several of these recommendations relate to the key areas and may prove fruitful to realizing these objectives, and they are also summarized in this chapter.

Viability of a Modified Lead Agency Approach

The ministry's shift to a modified lead agency approach is a significant change. With the removal of their sub-contracting and funding authority over core service providers, lead agencies are now primarily responsible for a planning function, to develop regional service delivery plans with partners. They are relying on the strength of their relationships and the power of their recommendations to plan services with core service providers. One agency has developed an effective structure known as the "core leadership council" to engage community partners. However, other directors anticipate tension with some core service providers, and they acknowledge the ministry retains final decision-making power and authority over contracts. Thus, whereas lead agencies retain some influence through their planning and resource functions, their decision-making and funding authority have been removed, potentially reducing the future viability of a modified lead agency approach.

Progress Planning With Core Service Providers/Ministry

Both the provincial reports and the directors indicated good progress with core service providers and other service providers (hospitals, English-language school boards) in developing regional service plans and priorities. However, there were challenges collaborating with other sectors (primary health care, French-language school boards).

Directors cited multiple examples of service priorities established, such as intake/access, pathways to care, crisis services, and serving refugee and minority populations, although some noted challenges with small rural communities and large geographical regions. They also highlighted a stronger partnership with the ministry regarding planning. This progress in planning and service coordination is a hopeful sign for the children's mental health sector on a systemic level, although this may shift with the new provincial government. In terms of future directions, the Consortium plans to strengthen formal linkages between CYMH and other child and youth services by defining a provincial standard for inclusive service system planning and developing relationships to promote integrated planning, which they suggest MCYS can further support on a provincial policy level.

Variable Service Coordination Across Sectors

Directors emphasized the importance of collaboration and building relationships across the health and education sectors, and assuming a broad systems perspective, with some success collaborating across multiple sectors. This included parent and youth voices as key stakeholders. Still, having only partial mandated collaboration with other sectors is proving to be more challenging for lead agencies in their modified role. Service coordination was rated highest with core service providers and English-language education, and least effective with French-language education, primary care and Indigenous services, which pose several challenges for lead agencies to coordinate. Being mandated to collaborate, such as with LHINs, seemed to be more effective than relying on relationships and goodwill, such as with education. In terms of future directions, the Consortium (2018) plans to strengthen engagement and integrated planning with health and education sectors through joint mapping and service planning with the LHINS and establishing formal linkages with the provincial education school system. MCYS has already been working on an integrated planning mechanism with key partners in health and education.

Progress With Service Standards/Access and Caregiver/Family/Youth Engagement

Directors acknowledged service duplication and gaps, and the need to define core service areas as a future priority. They highlighted progress in establishing provincial standards regarding equitable service access. Provincially, service pathways were clear for most service partners, although less clear for families and health services. Whereas lead agencies are working to strengthen service pathways, multiple service barriers remain suggesting that further cross-sector collaboration is required. Lead agencies also reported strong engagement with service partners, but challenges with meaningful engagement of caregivers and youth. Directors were making efforts to engage these stakeholders, and they recognized the benefits, emphasizing that family and youth voice is a key component to system change. However, some highlighted the need for dedicated staffing, which signals the need for ministry funding. In terms of future directions, the Consortium (2018) plans to increase meaningful child/youth and family engagement in system transformation by defining this concept and establishing a provincial standard of measurement, and there are several initiatives already underway to support this plan.

Insufficient/Uncertain Funding and Political/Government Impacts

MCYS has provided some funding to lead agencies for system change, which has facilitated some management restructuring, broader agency initiatives and the hiring of a "system coordinator" to accommodate additional workload. However, this funding was insufficient, curtailing planned projects and further reducing base funding, as lead agencies were forced to draw from their base budget to cover operating costs, which created further service gaps and internal agency conflicts. As well, there were role conflicts and resource allocation issues, as executive directors' attention was directed more to external issues, and senior management teams were overworked, resulting in some priorities being discarded. On a broader scale, significant funding issues remain, with long-standing 0% increases to base budget, resulting in compromised service delivery and staff capacity. Whereas the ministry has committed to developing a new "needs-based funding allocation model," the status of this initiative is now uncertain with the recent change to a Conservative provincial government. The directors successfully negotiated a "funding investment model" based on equitable services across regions. Without this required investment in base funding, lead agencies and core service providers will have continued difficulty closing the widening service gaps. This finding highlights the political nature and instability of government initiatives, which are costly for human service organizations. Although the directors are committed to this process, and understand the long-term nature of planning, their efforts may be shortchanged by disruptive external political and government forces.

New Standard Data Management Tools & Ineffective Performance Indicators

On a provincial level, lead agencies have committed to improving data usage, and they have made progress in using client data to inform their service planning. The ministry has also implemented a performance measurement tool, the 'Business Intelligence Solution' (BIS), and some lead agencies have adopted new standardized data measurement tools (interRAI and EMHWare). These new tools were efficient and expected to address current data issues, although they were not yet adopted province-wide. This is important given lead agencies' responsibility for reporting regional data to the ministry. However, there were multiple barriers to lead agencies using data for quality and performance improvement, including poor data quality and definition of terms, lack of time and consistency in data collection, and lack of infrastructure resources and expertise. These issues need to be addressed, and more support at the regional and ministry levels is warranted. As, well the directors were critical of the new BIS tool and key performance indicators established by the ministry, as they had limited clinical utility and data produced were not meaningful to service planning. These multiple issues suggest the need for the ministry to further refine the selected tools to ensure utility before promoting them sector-wide. However, with the change in provincial government, this may not be feasible, and lead agencies may be forced to contend with compromised data management and performance measurement tools. On a positive note, in terms of future directions, the Consortium (2018) plans to use data to map the current funded capacity of core services in Ontario, provide advice to MCYS on core service definitions, and establish collaborative governance with MCYS on a new data strategy.

Positive Ministry Partnerships and Long-Term Commitment

The directors emphasized the unique opportunity to engage in a true partnership approach with the ministry in planning a more coordinated service delivery system, which was a departure from previous approaches, although this was now tentative with new ministry representatives pending. Whereas some had reported positive reinforcement, others had experienced negative interactions with MCYS especially regarding advocacy efforts, which were considered 'too political.' Still, directors highlighted the positive system partnerships developed and signaled their long-term commitment to continue this priority work despite anticipated government changes. They offered some helpful practical suggestions regarding engaging stakeholders, building consensus, and supporting new leaders in this important work. In terms of future directions, through their 'Partnership Table,' the Consortium (2018) plans to collaborate with MCYS on key messages regarding *Moving on Mental Health* goals, and how to achieve these through lead agencies and integrated planning within and across sectors. The success of this venture remains unclear, as one executive director confirmed that children's mental health will now be under the Ministry of Health and Long-Term Care (MoHLTC), as per the new Conservative provincial government.

CONCLUSION

This chapter has reviewed the viability of a modified lead agency approach in children's mental health services in Ontario, Canada as a unique example of human services contracting. Key findings from directors in three CYMH agencies, along with selected findings in provincial reports from the Consortium and Auditor General, have been included. Most significant, lead agencies' responsibilities have shifted from sub-contracting and funding authority to a primary planning function. There has been some good progress with this initiative, in terms of planning with core service providers and ministry partnerships. There has also been variable progress with service coordination across sectors, service pathways and stakeholder engagement, with multiple barriers noted. Pressing funding issues have been identified, and the reality of a promised funding model is now uncertain given disruptive government changes. Data management tools are promising but key performance indicators are problematic and will require further refinement. On a positive note, the directors interviewed here are committed to continuing this priority work, and the ministry and Consortium members have committed to collaborating and bringing the key components of this initiative forward together. There is strength in this partnership, and it is hoped their efforts will continue, with or without the support of the new government. It remains to be seen how the future unfolds, and further evaluation of the lead agency progress is recommended in future research.

KEY POINTS

- The modified lead agency approach is a significant change, limiting lead agencies' decision-making authority and potential future viability.
- Progress was achieved in planning with core service providers and the ministry, although challenges remain with some health and education sectors.
- Building collaborative relationships across sectors and assuming a broad systems-level lens is critical to effective service planning and coordination.
- Provincial standardization of equitable services/access and creative engagement of caregivers/family and youth is progressing, although barriers remain.
- Ministry funding is partial and insufficient, and further funding is uncertain due to provincial government changes and political instability.
- Standardized data management tools are efficient, but ministry performance indicators are ineffective and not provincially mandated.
- Positive ministry partnerships and directors' long-term commitment have been forged, although these are at risk with a new provincial government/ministry.

REFERENCES

Auditor General of Ontario. (2016). Child and youth mental health. *Annual Report*, *1*(3), 111–147. Retrieved from www.auditor.on.ca/en/content/annualreports/arreports/en16/v1_301en16.pdf

Braun, V., & Clark, V. (2006). Using thematic analysis in psychology. *Qualitative Research in Psychology*, *3*(33), 77–101.

Child and Youth Mental Health Lead Agency Consortium. (2018). *Lead agency provincial priorities report*. Prepared with the Ontario Centre of Excellence for Child and Youth Mental Health (provided by the Consortium with permission).

Children's Mental Health Ontario. (2013, May). *A CMHO position statement. Towards a sustainable future: Working together to transform Ontario's child and youth mental health system, part 1*. Retrieved from www.kidsmentalhealth.ca/documents/res-towards-sustainable-future.pdf

Children's Mental Health Ontario. (2015a). *Pre-budget submission 2015*. Retrieved from www.kidsmentalhealth.ca/documents/CMHO-PreBudget-Submission-2015-16.pdf

Children's Mental Health Ontario. (2015b). *2015 report card: Child and youth mental health moving towards a fully functioning system*. Retrieved from www.kidsmentalhealth.ca/documents/cmho-report-card-2015-english.pdf

Children's Mental Health Ontario. (2016). *Improving mental health outcomes for Ontario's children and youth: 2016 pre-budget submission*. Retrieved from http://files.ctctcdn.com/314f3f09501/9d2c194a-05ea-471e-aa4f570f651e8327.pdf?ver=1454535550000

Corden, A., & Sainsbury, R. (2006). *Using verbatim quotations in reporting qualitative social research: Researcher's views*. York: University of York Social Policy Research Unit. Retrieved from www.york.ac.uk/inst/spru/pubs/pdf/verbquotresearch.pdf

Denzin, N. K., & Lincoln, Y. S. (2005). *The sage handbook of qualitative research* (3rd ed.). Thousand Oaks, CA: Sage Publications.

Lapadat, J. (2010). Thematic analysis. In A. Mills, G. Durepos, & E. Weibe (Eds.), *Encyclopedia of case study research* (pp. 926–928). Thousand Oaks, CA: Sage Publications.

Ministry of Children and Youth Services. (2012, November). *Moving on mental health: A system that makes sense for children and youth*. Retrieved from www.children.gov.on.ca/htdocs/English/professionals/specialneeds/momh/momh.aspx

Ministry of Children and Youth Services. (2013). *Draft child and youth mental health service framework*. Retrieved from www.children.gov.on.ca/htdocs/English/documents/specialneeds/mentalhealth/ServiceFramework.pdf

Ministry of Children and Youth Services. (2014). *Growing together: 2013–2018 strategic plan*. Retrieved from www.children.gov.on.ca/htdocs/English/documents/about/stratplan13-18.pdf

Ministry of Children and Youth Services. (2016, January 22). *News release: Ontario hiring more mental health workers for children and youth*. Retrieved from https://news.ontario.ca/mcys/en/2016/01/ontario-hiring-more-mentalhealth-workers-forchildren-and-youth.html?_ga=1.205380432.1510804380.1458233369

Rubin, A., & Babbie, E. (2011). *Research methods for social work* (7th ed.). Belmont, CA: Brooks, Cole.

Vito, R. (2017). The impact of service system transformation on human service agencies: Competing ministry directives and strategic innovative leadership adaptations. *Human Service Organizations: Management, Leadership & Governance*, *41*(5), 477–491.

9

Results-Based Funding for Youth Care in the Netherlands

From Conditions and Challenges to the Outlines of a System[1]

M. S. de Vries

INTRODUCTION

Since January 2015, the Dutch youth care system has been under construction. By adopting and implementing the Youth Act, the Dutch parliament decentralized all administrative and financial responsibilities related to youth care from the national and regional governments to the country's 393 municipalities. The new youth care system should be more efficient, coherent and cost-effective by focusing on prevention, on the capacities of youths and parents, on customized care and on better cooperation between youth care professionals. At this moment, most Dutch municipalities are, separately or jointly in regional youth care alliances, struggling with the development and implementation of some form of results-based funding. A wide array of terms is used to address the same concept as results-based funding, for example, performance-based contracting, results-based financing, payment-by-results and pay-for-performance. In this chapter, results-based funding refers to a type of funding in which payment is based on achieved results and the relationship between payment and results is pre-defined.

This chapter explores the conditions and challenges of results-based funding from the perspective of municipalities as well as youth care providers and sketches the outlines of a system of results-based funding in youth care. The chapter is based on the results of two empirical studies (Brouwer, Brouwer, Denekamp, Huiskamp, Kok, & De Wit, 2017; De Vries & Wolters-Ravoo, 2016) that were recently conducted by the Research Institute *Youth*, which is part of the *Health Care and Social Work* Research Centre of Windesheim University of Applied Sciences in the Netherlands. Over the course of these studies, literature was reviewed and documents were analyzed. Furthermore, a questionnaire was completed by representatives of 13 regional youth care alliances and interviews were held with representatives of the regional youth care alliance IJsselland and three municipalities. Subsequently, managers and professionals of nine youth care organizations were interviewed on the opportunities and constraints of results-based funding in youth care.

WHY CHANGE WAS NEEDED IN THE DUTCH YOUTH CARE SYSTEM

Before 2015, the Dutch youth care system consisted of universal, preventive and specialized services that were the responsibility of, and funded by, a variety of organizations. *Universal services* aimed to facilitate the normal development of children and to prevent minor problems experienced by children and families from turning into severe problems. These universal services were funded by various agencies, but were ultimately the responsibility of the municipalities. Examples of these universal services include youth work, daycare and schools. *Preventive services* included child health care, general social work and parenting support. Preventive services aimed to detect and intervene in problems at an early stage, to coordinate support and to refer children and families to the provincial youth care services. Like the universal services, preventive services were funded by various agencies, but the municipalities were primarily responsible for facilitating suitable offers of preventive services and for coordinating cooperation between these services in youth and family centers. Both the regional and national governments were responsible for the *specialized services* for youth and families. In the Netherlands, 12 provinces and three large urban areas were responsible for the so-called youth care agencies and the youth care services. The provincial youth care agencies functioned as access points for the provincial youth care services. These independent agencies assessed the needs and the situations of children and families with serious development and/or parenting problems and referred them to these services. The provincial youth care agencies were also responsible for the coordination of care, youth protection and youth probation. In contrast, the provincial youth care services provided specialized care, coordination of care and aftercare. Their services included intensive ambulatory support and specialized pedagogical support at home for multi-problem families, as well as semi-residential care, residential care, foster care and secure care (Hilverdink, Daamen, & Vink, 2015; Bosscher, 2012).

The Dutch youth care system has historically faced many problems (e.g., Hilverdink et al., 2015; Clarijs, 2014; Bosscher, 2012). In 2014, more than 600,000 children in the Netherlands received some kind of institutionalized care. The demand for specialized care increased by approximately 10% every year. According to epidemiologists, this increase cannot be explained simply by an increase in problems. Instead, there was a growing imbalance between attention to normal development and the development of risks. Specialized services received more funding in proportion to universal and preventive services. Further, with many different specialized services, one organization often could not meet all of the needs of the children and adolescents requiring services and their families could not be supported by a single organization. They were therefore referred to different organizations. The admission procedures for these organizations were complicated and took much time. This prevented children and families from receiving the care they needed quickly. Children and families were also referred to specialized services too easily and deviant behavior was treated with medication too often. Increased use of specialized care led to increased expenditures and every seven to eight years, the budget needed for youth care doubled. Furthermore, the Dutch youth care system was problem-oriented and administration-centered instead of opportunity-focused and youth-centered.

Moving forward, more attention should be paid to acquiring skills and competences and the role of youth work in supporting the normal development of children. Youth participation in their own care as well as in the policy processes should also increase. In the past, Dutch youth care policies were accused of having a patronizing tone in their thinking. Additionally, the Dutch youth care system was fragmented—many different organizations funded by different authorities were involved in the care and support of children with physical, mental and behavioral problems. There was insufficient coordination between organizations and municipalities. Additionally, there was no integral approach to problems and there was inadequate response to danger signs. In such a fragmented system, the implementation of innovations was difficult. In summary, the Dutch youth care system was inefficient and ineffective, sometimes with dire consequences for the children involved. It was time for this to change.

MAJOR CHANGES IN THE DUTCH YOUTH CARE SYSTEM: TRANSITION AND TRANSFORMATION

As of January 2015, a new Youth Act took effect in the Netherlands. The main goals of this act include integrating policies, creating well-coordinated care that meets local and individual situations and needs and reducing costs. The Youth Act requires both transitions and transformations in the youth care system.

Transition

The new Youth Act applies to all the tasks and monetary means related to the youth care system. It also replaces parts of other laws that previously regulated issues like child and youth mental health care and care for mentally disabled children and youth. Since the law went into effect, all administrative and financial responsibilities related to youth care shifted from national and regional governments to local governments. The transition of the youth care system is part of a wider process of transition within the social service sector, which aims to make Dutch municipalities responsible for most services in the social domain in addition to youth care participation, social support and suitable education. These changes are intended to provide municipalities with opportunities for more integrated approaches to support and guidance from a variety of disciplines and policies. Within the new youth care system, it is the duty of local governments to offer services to children, parents and professionals. The goal of this transition is to allow children to grow up safely and healthily, to become independent and to participate socially in accordance with their age and developmental stage. Each municipality now decides which services are available for all children and families and which are available only for children and families with specific needs. Municipalities must contract youth care providers and give shape and substance to the relationships among families and these (often private) organizations. Most municipalities introduced multidisciplinary neighborhood teams consisting of professionals from various health and welfare organizations. The target groups and the extent of the care provided by these neighborhood teams depend on the focus of the municipality. Municipalities cooperate in regional youth alliances in order to organize specific care programs including residential care, foster care, child protection measures, youth probation and certain types of specialized care.

At the same time the Youth Act was enacted, a single funding system for all youth care was introduced. Municipalities receive the means for providing youth care services from the central government according to a cost-allocation key. In addition to a basic amount per child, the degree to which risk factors occur, such as single parent households, poverty, social benefit situation and psychological problems of parents, is also taken into consideration. Protective factors, such as the ability of a young person to solve his own problems, affect the level of the budget as well. In the cost allocation key, the risk and protective factors are given a weighting factor on the basis of which municipalities receive more or less extra budget on top of the basic amount. The means that are available for youth care are not earmarked, in other words, municipalities make their own agreements with youth care providers and are allowed to combine (part of) the budgets at the regional level for the regional procurement of certain types of youth care. Youth care budget cuts are projected to rise from 3% in 2015 to 15% in 2018.

Transformation

The changes in the Dutch youth care system not only reflect a change in responsibilities, but also require a change in processes. Currently, youth care is focused on activating, restoring and strengthening the capacities of children, youth, parents and their social environments to solve problems. It is also focused on improving parenting capacities and the social environments of parents. The underlying principle of the transformation of youth care is: "One family, one plan, one coordinator." Youth care providers should thus aim to offer timely, suitable and made-to-measure care that is close to home and focused on prevention, early detection and early support. Effective and efficient multidisciplinary cooperation regarding families should be pursued. This change in the system and proposed reduction of costs has provoked a paradigm shift with regard to the approaches for working with parents, children and young people. New approaches should be more demand-driven and tailor-made in collaboration with clients. This demands a different way of working and a different kind of collaboration among agencies and workers (Hilverdink, 2013).

A SOFT LANDING: PRELIMINARY CHOICES IN FINANCING YOUTH CARE

The transition and transformation of the Dutch youth care system have been accompanied by major changes in the funding of youth care. In 2015, when the Youth Act came into force, most municipalities continued all existing contractual relationships in order to achieve a "soft landing". Maintaining continuity of care for young people and their parents was an important aim of the municipalities. As a result, many municipalities have contractual relationships with hundreds of care providers. Most youth care providers are funded by Fee-for-Services (FFS): they receive payments for specific tasks or procedures. The youth care provider is responsible for purchasing inputs, and now faces a financial incentive to deliver as many services as possible as long as the fee exceeds the costs of delivery (Musgrove, 2011). Outputs are intended to yield outcomes that benefit young people and their parents. In practice, it appears that there are hardly any agreements between municipalities and youth care providers with regard to quality and accountability.

At this moment, most municipalities are struggling both separately and jointly in regional youth care alliances with the development and implementation of some form of results-based funding. This type of financing is based not only on output, but on outcome as well. For example, the 11 municipalities that co-operate in the regional youth care alliance IJsselland—a region in the northeastern part of the Netherlands—pay for the time that is spent on providing care to the client by the provider. Payment is made on the basis of hourly and half-day rates and sometimes rates for the treatment program as a whole. Trust in youth care providers turns out to be very important in this system, because there is hardly any insight into, or control of, the effectiveness and efficiency of the care that is actually provided. This causes a good deal of discussion between municipalities and youth care providers about costs and the care that should be provided under certain circumstances. Some of the contracts with youth care providers are accompanied by budget ceilings. This means that a maximum amount of money has been established that can be spent on the process of care. The budget ceilings are set to reduce costs. However, these spending limits results in disagreement between municipalities and youth care providers. Sometimes, youth care providers do not comply with the agreements that were made, thus creating more costs than the ceiling allows. Runover is allowed with timely reporting and in consultation with the youth care alliance. However, this doesn't happen in many cases and, as a result, the youth care alliance does not finance cost surpluses. The downside of this system is that it conflicts with the freedom of choice for the clients—an important principle of the new Youth Act. The regional youth care alliance in IJsselland assumes that the introduction of a system of results-based funding in 2018 will solve the aforementioned problems (Brouwer et al., 2017).

THE ADVANTAGES AND CHALLENGES OF RESULTS-BASED FUNDING IN PUBLIC SERVICE ORGANIZATIONS

In the context of the so-called New Public Management (NPM) movement, business economic organization and control models and methods have gained an increasingly prominent role in organizations in the Dutch public sector in the past three decades (Visser & Den Bakker, 2018). NPM has led to a high level of contractual and financial management control in the public sector, whereby the central political and administrative authorities set general policy goals and then translate these into detailed targets for implementing organizations and human service providers. These targets are in turn concretized into performance contracts with a large number of performance measurements, performance indicators and target figures, which the implementers and service providers have to perform and administer to make clear in what way and to what extent they have achieved the underlying objectives. All this has led to a clear preference for management control "by the numbers" with a strong emphasis on quantitative measurements, indicators and targets in most Dutch human service organizations, for example in the fields of health care, education, safety and security and youth care. The introduction of a system of results-based funding is in line with this preference.

But what is results-based funding? And what advantages can be expected when implementing such a funding system in youth care? According to Musgrove (2011), results-based funding for health can be defined as: "*a cash or non-monetary transfer made to a national or sub-national government, manager, provider, payer or consumer of health services after predefined results have been attained and verified. Payment is conditional on measurable actions being undertaken*" (2011, p. 1). Witter et al. summarize the core features of results-based funding as currently practiced in health care systems using the following criteria (2013, p. 2):

- They take a supply-side approach, meaning performance-based incentives are earned by service providers.
- Payments are targeted at individual health facilities and administrations, often with trickle-down to health workers.
- There is most often some split of functions between regulation, purchasing, fund-holding, verification and service delivery, although the practices vary by context.
- Payments are linked to outputs and are modified by quality indicators.

Results-based funding is supposed to lead to a better quality of care. As Musgrove (2011) argues, "*Clearly an output can be defined without regard to quality, but the outcome for the patient generally does depend on quality. This leads to efforts to build into the method of payment an incentive for good quality and therefore requires something more than just FFS*" (p. 2). But results-based funding may also result in better quality of policy and decision-making processes in public service organizations. The information that is obtained by measuring the performances of professionals can help policymakers and managers make better-founded policy and better-informed decisions (De Bruijn, 2001). In addition to good quality, results-based funding has other advantages such as stimulating entrepreneurship and innovation in organizations (Witter et al., 2013; Musgrove, 2011; De Bruijn, 2001). According to Witter et al., the core concept of results-based funding is to promote a results-oriented focus and to encourage entrepreneurial behavior by staff and managers: "*This is done by establishing a set of more explicit contractual arrangements between different players. Payments do not reflect real service production costs, but aim at investing in front line services and modifying behavior, while leveraging existing resources in the health system*" (p. 3). Furthermore, performance measurement leads to transparency. When an organization formulates goals and activities and then measures performance, transparency and corresponding incentives to organizational innovation occur. As De Bruijn (2001) has demonstrated, "*What gets measured, gets done. [. . .] When an organization can show its achievements, there are goals to focus on. This is often taken as an incentive to improve organizational performance*" (p. 18).

However, the implementation of results-based funding may have some disadvantages as well. One of these disadvantages is that results or effects are often difficult to measure in practice and/or are affected by other factors that cannot be influenced by the provider of care. When results are affected by other factors, there is hardly a direct link between the activities and efforts of a provider and the results or social effects that are achieved. Another disadvantage is that the implementation of such a system takes time and perseverance. As Mayne (2007) has demonstrated, "*Evidence shows at least four to five years of consistent effort—and many organizations have been working towards it for much longer. The problem is that key people move on, governance structures change, priorities shift. [. . .] To quote a cliché, integrating performance information into managing and budgeting is a journey, not a destination*" (p. 89). Duration of the agreements between principals and providers is also of interest; results-based funding calls for arrangements in the longer term to make it possible for providers to actually achieve the intended results (Eijkenaar & Schut, 2015; Ministry of Security, Ministry of Health, & VNG, 2013). Another disadvantage is that developing and using performance information costs time and money—time and money that an already—harassed public or non-profit organization often does not have. Mayne explains: "*The general point is that if the challenge is seen mainly as one of measuring, or as an initiative that can be completed in a year of hard work, or that it can be carried out using existing resources—since after all, it is just part of good management!—then progress will likely be slow, spotty and not lasting*" (2007, p. 89).

As a result, when implementing results-based funding in public service organizations, several challenges occur. Among these are technical challenges including the ways in which results will be measured and questions about how to make clear the extent to which and in which ways activities have contributed to results. De Bruijn (2001) describes several conditions that facilitate or impede the introduction of performance measurement, which is the basis of results-based funding. He claims that performance management is possible when an organization produces single and uniform products and is product-oriented, when the production is autonomous and quality can be defined by performance indicators, when causalities are known and when the environment is stable. The downside of performance management is that it is problematic when an organization fulfills duties and is strongly value-oriented, when it produces multiple intertwined products or a variety of products and when it is process oriented. Performance management is also problematic when products are produced in interaction with other organizations (co-production), when causalities are unknown and when quality cannot be defined by performance indicators. Finally, a dynamic environment impedes the implementation of performance measurement and, with that, results-based funding as well.

In addition to these technical challenges, there are also organizational challenges that are just as—or maybe even more—important in realizing the successful implementation of results-based funding. Mayne (2007) states: "*The challenges are more than technical ones dealing with, for example, various measurement problems. Rather, the main challenges are often organizational and behavioral in nature, whereby organizations and the people in them need to change how they do or see things*" (p. 90). Organizational challenges include avoiding distorting behavior, the extent to which there is support within the organizations for the system and the commitment to the results that should be achieved, but also a sense of mutual trust between municipalities in their role as principal and healthcare providers as contractor (e.g. Eijkenaar & Schut, 2015).

According to Mayne (2007), integrating performance information into management and budgeting is not easy. It is doable, but the challenges are formidable. An important first step is to recognize the various challenges and consider how to deal with them. In the next section, several of the challenges—technical as well as organizational—which occur when implementing results-based funding in youth care, will be identified. Subsequently, the possible outlines of a system of results-based funding for youth care will be sketched from the perspective of these challenges.

THE MAIN CHALLENGES IN YOUTH CARE

As one youth care provider noted, "*Results-based funding, no one can be against it.*" However, both municipalities and youth care providers were critical of this funding system when it was first introduced, especially regarding the scope and relativity of performance indicators, the risk of strategic behavior by youth care providers and the intended time frame for the implementation of the new system.

The Youth Care "Product"

As described previously, municipalities have become administratively as well as financially responsible for *all* types of youth care. These services range from universal services such as youth work and daycare to preventive services like child health care and parenting support to specialized services such as residential and foster care. In other words, the term youth care refers to a variety of services that have come about in co-production among children, youth, parents, their social environments, municipalities and youth care providers. In research by De Vries and Wolters-Ravoo (2016), several youth care providers indicated that when making choices regarding the funding system, municipalities and youth care providers should work to ensure that clients have influence when choosing providers who meet their support needs. The desired co-production, in conjunction with the integrated approach in the social domain and multidisciplinary cooperation regarding families which are contemplated by the Youth Act, results in multiple and intertwined services for children, youth and their parents.

Furthermore, with regard to youth care, causalities are often unknown and results can only partially be defined by performance indicators. For instance, the Youth Act focuses on prevention, early detection and early support. But how can we measure the results achieved by preventive activities that were undertaken by, for example, youth workers? And how can we be sure that the results are accurately measured? For example, can a decrease in the number of children that are referred to specialized care or a decrease in antisocial behavior be attributed to preventive activities? And how can we be sure that the results were not affected by other factors that cannot be influenced by youth workers alone? The scope and the relativity of performance indicators for youth care are of concern for municipalities as well as youth care providers. Both groups consider client satisfaction to be an important and useful indicator for the results obtained through youth care. However, client satisfaction does not say it all. As one youth care provider put it: "*If you ask the parents, really not all parents are happy with us. Because we always put our finger on the sore spot. What kind of picture do you get? If you just had a hearty talk with us and you have to fill out a form, then I'm sure you're not optimistic about us. And what does that say?*" Another youth care provider said: "*A good development from the perspective of a therapist can be perceived as particularly burdensome by the parents and vice versa.*" Other indicators that are mentioned by municipalities and youth care providers are the decline in long-term care to specific groups, the contribution to the empowerment of clients, care content, reporting and satisfaction, absenteeism and the capacity of staff. Municipalities and youth care providers disagree on the question of whether indicators should be formulated at the level of individual clients, groups of clients or society as a whole. One of the municipalities indicated that focus should be placed on achieving social outcomes: "*Not one client is interesting, but the neighborhood as a whole is*" (De Vries & Wolters-Ravoo, 2016).

MUTUAL TRUST VERSUS DISTORTING BEHAVIOR

Research by De Vries and Wolters-Ravoo (2016) shows that the trust between communities and youth care providers, which is essential in a system of results-based funding, leaves much to be desired. In part, distrust between municipalities and youth care providers is the result of the relatively short duration of the contracts signed with providers. As a representative of a municipality remarked, "*The current duration of contracts is two years. This results in much uncertainty for providers; if I do not perform, they kick me out. What you should do is join forces and create multi-year contracts . . . I would involve fifteen large or innovative providers in the policy process and give shape to the transformation in the coming years, and I would close long-term contracts of five or seven years.*" According to this respondent, municipalities and youth care providers should cooperate on the policy level in order to create support and trust. Youth care providers make critical statements about their relationship with municipalities as well. One of them noted in this respect: "*Is there really no money left or do municipalities have some money hidden elsewhere? That's absolutely invisible for us.*" Another youth care provider indicated that youth care providers have the same goal as municipalities.

However, it feels as if professionalism has been reduced and bureaucracy has grown with the increased emphasis placed on accountability and tighter framing, while at the same time the original goal was lost. One respondent of a municipality recognized this and concluded: "*Everyone hates bureaucracy, but at the same time we want to monitor everything*". Another youth care provider recognized that the trust of municipalities in providers still needs to grow, but expected that this trust building would take time: "*Trust does not just happen at once. We may long for that, but it will not happen. You have to have that much confidence in each other that you know that when an organization is asked to provide care, it does that conscientiously, without abusing money. That's always tricky. And I get it, although. But when money and people get together . . . distrust remains.*" That the distrust between youth care providers and municipalities has a financial background was also experienced by a youth care provider who was accused by a municipality of problematizing issues in order to bring in more money for his organization. Respondents agree that multi-year contracts with (perhaps) less youth care providers would increase trust between municipalities and youth care providers.

Both municipalities and youth care providers indicate that results-based funding may result in strategic behavior by youth care providers (De Vries & Wolters-Ravoo, 2016; Brouwer et al., 2017). Youth care providers may focus on the feasibility of care and may refer complex cases in which results are difficult to establish to other youth care providers. Financing results then brings a risk to the security of clients. As one youth care provider noted: "*It could happen that youth care providers search for a quick win, just like insurance companies.*" It is also conceivable that this type of results-driven system focuses on easily-achievable goals rather than on goals that actually solve the real problems of children, youth and parents. Data can be manipulated, and money will likely become a leading factor instead of treatment outcomes. An obligation to accept clients could be included in contracts to mitigate the risk of distorting behavior by youth care providers.

TIME FRAME

Both municipalities and youth care providers mention that the introduction of results-based funding should not occur too quickly. One youth care provider explained: "*The previous transition from national to provincial government took seven years. Everything went smoothly in the end. It takes time to establish the right work relations and confidences. It is not to be expected that decentralization can be realized within two years because results-based funding should be implemented by then. Actually, there should be a plan to determine where you want to be in five years.*" Another youth care provider thinks that 2018 is too early to move to a system of results-based funding; at least one additional year would be necessary. He outlines two possible scenarios for the longer term: First, youth care providers will be placed under pressure and the field will be thinned out so far that we might question whether results-based funding still makes sense. In this scenario, the available capacity will be just enough to serve the clients.

Second, youth care providers will find a way to deal with the changes that have been deployed over the past two years and will capture the financial collapses, thus allowing for a successful transition to a system of results-based funding.

FROM CONDITIONS AND CHALLENGES TO THE OUTLINES OF A SYSTEM

With the aforementioned challenges in mind, the outlines of a system of results-based funding for youth care can be described.

Principle 1: Distinguish Between Basic Funding and Performance-Related Pay

In the study by Eijkenaar and Schut (2015) quoted earlier in this paper, the researchers made a distinction between basic funding and rewards for performance. Their starting point is: *An essential building block of good results-based funding is adequate basic funding. This is necessary because it is not possible for all relevant outcomes of care (e.g. with regard to the quality of care) to properly measure and assess to what extent they are due to certain treatments and/or care providers.* (p. ii). This basic funding could be supplemented with performance-related pay in order to incorporate explicit incentives for quality and cost. With regard to youth care, this leads to the premise that it is desirable to make a distinction between the basic funding and performance-related pay for care; this reflects the desires of municipalities as well as youth care providers. Basic funding could follow the client; the individual care plan could then provide the basis for funding. This form of funding aims at custom-made care, gives more freedom of choice to the client and leads to more accurate funding from the municipalities to the care providers. The performance related-pay can be connected to indicators for results that relate to children, young people and their parents on the one hand and care providers on the other. This correspondence will be elaborated in the third principle.

Principle 2: Utilize Client Profiles and Self-Reliance Matrices as a Starting Point for Basic Funding

In 2012, the Dutch Youth Institute (NJI) disclosed client profiles for youths. Client profiles are descriptions of the characteristics and care needs of specific audiences. To provide truly effective care, specific audiences with specific problems should be targeted. The client profiles provide a framework for the measurement of (a part of) the results in several youth care regions in the Netherlands—for example, the youth care region of IJsselland. A proposal has been made to combine client profiles with self-reliance matrices. In practice, several municipalities in the Netherlands are already working with these matrices. The degree of self-reliance and the development therein can be used as indicators in a measuring system for financing results.

Principle 3: Formulate and Measure Results on Different Levels and From Different Perspectives

The desire of youth care regions to introduce a system of results-based funding fits within the broader development of a system of financing in which results are taken as the basis for funding human services. But what are the results of youth care? Several authors venture into a description of possible results that concern individual clients; youth care providers and/or society as a whole (e.g. Kruiter & Kruiter, 2013; Van Yperen, De Wilde, & Keuzenkamp, 2014; Eijkenaar & Schut, 2015). A third principle for a system of results-based funding in youth care is: "When formulating and measuring outcomes of youth care, make a distinction in results that concern (groups of) children, young people and their parents and results that concern youth care organizations." The following performance areas and (general) indicators can serve as starting points:

Quality of Care

1. Goal achievement
2. Satisfaction of children, adolescents and their parents
3. Failure/range

Cost-Conscious Behaviors of Youth Care Providers

1. Duration of treatment
2. Decreased use of specialized care
3. Deployment of innovative and cost-effective treatment methods (e.g. online services)
4. Cost of care

Multidisciplinary Cooperation and Coordination of Aid

1. Formalization of (structural) cooperative agreements
2. Presence of common ICT infrastructure

Effective Prevention

1. Decreased need for assistance at the population level

Principle 4: Embedding Results-Based Funding in a Performance Management System

Eijkenaar and Schut (2015) have stated that "*The practical design of outcome funding will have to balance partly conflicting conditions. What the right balance is, however, is often unclear in advance, and moreover context-dependent. It is therefore important to gradually implement new forms of funding and carefully monitor and evaluate them*"

(p. iii). Performance management—for example, the Deming circle (PDCA)—is a valuable tool that can be used to monitor, evaluate and steer developments. Performance management implies a long-term implementation process, a fourth principle for results-based funding of youth care.

Principle 5: Long-Term Planning and Appointments

When implementing results-based funding, a multi-year implementation process should be the starting point. Starting small and expanding gradually as preconditions are fulfilled is desirable. The importance of this process became evident from the literature review as well as from our interviews with local authorities and youth care providers. In the beginning, both technical and organizational conditions should be addressed, including technical implementation issues, the creation of mutual trust, the implementation of a (preferably jointly and uniform) ICT system and the registration and delivery of indicators. Research shows that in projects with annual contracts, conflicts of interest and a lack of mutual trust have continuously undermined the implementation of results-based funding (Eijkenaar & Schut, 2015). Mutual trust between communities and youth care providers—a cause for concern, as our research showed—would be better served if municipalities would create multiannual contracts with youth care providers. The establishment of longer-term contracts demonstrates confidence and would give youth care providers the time to recoup investments. When writing contracts, municipalities should reconsider the number of providers being contracted; both municipalities and providers themselves indicate that a situation with fewer contracted providers is preferable. To prevent youth care providers from strategically selecting and helping clients, open enrollment and a duty of care may be included in the contracts. This would also contribute to the mutual understanding and trust among providers—another point of consideration revealed by our research.

KEY POINTS

- Dutch municipalities are struggling to develop some form of results-based funding.
- The struggles include: the character of the youth care "product", the need for mutual trust versus distorting behavior and the intended time frame.
- A system of results-based funding for youth care should distinguish between basic funding and performance-related pay.
- A distinction should be made in results that concern (groups of) children, young people and their parents and results that concern youth care organizations.
- Results-based funding should be embedded in a performance management system and should include long-term planning and appointments.
- Results-based funding should start small and expand gradually and establish and secure longer-term contracts.

NOTE

1. This chapter is based on a paper presented at the annual conference of the International Research Society for Public Management, Budapest, Hungary, April 19–21, 2017.

REFERENCES

Bosscher, N. (2012). *The decentralization and transformation of the Dutch youth care system*. Utrecht: NJI.

Brouwer, N., Denekamp, M., Huiskamp, N., Kok, J., & De Wit, L. (2017). *Transformatie Jeugdzorg Regio IJsselland*. Zwolle: Windesheim.

Bruijn, H. de (2001). *Prestatiemeting in de publieke sector: Tussen professie en verantwoording*. Utrecht: Lemma.

Clarijs, R. (2014). *Jeugdhulp en jeugdbeleid: Lokale zorg voor kinderen na 2015*. Amsterdam: Uitgeverij SWP.

Eijkenaar, F., & Schut, E. (2015). *Uitkomstbekostiging in de zorg: een (on)begaanbare weg?* Rotterdam: Erasmus Universiteit.

Hilverdink, P. (2013). *Generalist working with youth and families in the Netherlands*. Utrecht: NJI.

Hilverdink, P., Daamen, W., & Vink, C. (2015). *Children and youth support and care in the Netherlands*. Utrecht: NJI.

Kruiter, A. J., & Kruiter, H. (2013). *De praktijk als landingsbaan*. Den Haag: Ministerie van VWS.

Mayne, J. (2007). Challenges and lessons in implementing results-based management. *Evaluation, 13*(1), 87–109.

Ministry of Security, Ministry of Health, & VNG. (2013). *Stelselwijziging Jeugd. Eerste inventarisatie Bekostigingsmodellen*. Den Haag: Ministry of Security, Ministry of Health, & VNG.

Musgrove, P. (2011). *Financial and other rewards for good performance or results: A guided tour of concepts and terms and a short glossary*. The World Bank.

Van Yperen, T., de Wilde, E. J., & Keuzenkamp, S. (2014). *Outcome in zicht: Werken met prestatie-indicatoren in de jeugdhulp*. Utrecht: NJI.

Visser, M., & Bakker, J. D. (2018). Management control in de zorg: Een kritisch essay. *Maandblad voor Accountancy en Bedrijfseconomie, 92*(1–2), 47–52.

Vries, M. S. de, & Wolters-Ravoo, J. (2016). Resultaatfinanciering in de jeugdhulp: van praktische uitdagingen naar concrete uitgangspunten. *Jeugdbeleid, 10*, 213–220.

Witter, S., Toonen, J., Meessen, B., Kagubare, J., Fritsche, G., & Vaughan, K. (2013). Performance-based financing as a health system reform: Mapping the key dimensions for monitoring and evaluation. *BMC Health Services Research, 13*(1), 367.

Part 4

The Future of Human Services Contracting

10

Where Has Human Services Contracting Been and Where Is It Going?

Robert A. Shick and Lawrence L. Martin

The first part of this chapter follows-up on the key issues in human service contracting identified in the preceding chapters. The key areas identified are: (1) the growth of human service contracting, (2) changes in the way human service contractors are compensated, (3) the financial risks human service contracting create for small to medium sized nonprofit agencies, (4) how governments manage their human service contracts and the effects on their contractors, and (5) changes in the human service contracting process itself.

The second part of the chapter speculates on the future of human service contracting. As part of this discussion, the argument is made that the basic financial relationships between governments and their human service contractors are still in the process of being sorted out. How successful this sorting out process is will largely determine the number of potential contractors available and capable of providing services, the presence or absence of competition in human service contracting and the extent to which governments and their contractors can develop collaborative approaches to human service contracting policies and procedures.

GROWTH OF HUMAN SERVICE CONTRACTING

Human service contracting had its beginning with the federal legislation of the 1960s. This legislation resulted in uniting the public and private human service systems through the mechanism of contracting. Many government human service agencies lacked the internal capacity to address expanding human service needs and consequently turned to contracting. The private sector (primarily nonprofit organizations) had experience in providing the required human services and had the added advantage of knowing their local communities.

A contributing factor to the overall growth of human service contracting was the New Public Management (NPM) movement of the 1980s. NPM sought to increase contracting by governments at all levels. Osborne and Gaebler's (1993) book *Reinventing Government* was another contributing factor. The book encouraged governments to be more entrepreneurial and to explore options to direct government service delivery including contracting. The human services were influenced by these movements and contracting continued to expand.

The expansion of human service contracting continues to the present day as governments confront the evermore complex service delivery needs of: children, the elderly, persons with physical and mental disabilities, the homeless and other populations.

Government data on human service contracting are difficult to obtain and in some instances are non-existent. Various reasons exist for this situation including the failure to collect, maintain, publish and evaluate data on the extent of human service contracting and the types of contracts used. Nevertheless, a picture of human service contracting can be pieced together from various studies of government contracting in general and human service contracting in particular. Data from the Congressional Budget Office provide a limited view of federal government contracting (both human service and non-human service). Overall federal contracting increased 87% from 2000 to 2012. Total federal contracting was $518 billion in 2012, which represented 15% of all federal government expenditures. Data on state and local government contracting (human service and non-human service) has increased 33% from 2007 to 2014. Total annual state and local government contracting is estimated at $2 trillion (Ginter, 2015).

The Urban Institute (2018) estimates that nationally state and local government contracting for human services totals some $100 billion annually. Human service contracting by New York City amounted to $6.9 billion in fiscal year 2018 and represented 36% of all New York City's contract dollars. Human service contracting constituted 8.1% of the city's $85.3 billion budget in that year (The New York City Mayors Office of Contract Services and The City of New York Adopted Budget, Fiscal Year, 2018). Suffice it to say, that human service contracting today is "big business" and is getting bigger each year.

FROM COST-REIMBURSEMENT TO PAY-FOR-SUCCESS

In Chapters 1 and 2, Shick and Martin traced the history of human service contracting and pointed out the importance of contractor compensation approaches. Human service contracting began using cost-reimbursement contracts. Human service contractors were reimbursed for their costs in accordance with mutually agreed upon budgets. Contractors submitted detailed invoices documenting the costs incurred in providing services. Governments reimbursed their contractors up to the dollar amounts of the contracts. Cost-reimbursement contracts focused on the inputs (e.g., personnel, rent, etc.) of human services. Financial accountability was the primary concern; contractor performance was of little concern.

The next step in the evolution of human service contracting was a change in focus to the amounts of services provided by contractors (outputs) and their attendant costs. Efficiency became the major focus. Governments placed increasing emphasis on the amounts of services provided by their contractors (using unit-of-service definitions) and the costs of those services (e.g., the cost of a family visit in child welfare services, the cost of a counseling session in mental health, and the cost to train an individual in work force development programs).

Performance Based Contracting (PCB) was the next evolutionary step (Chapter 2). PBC began holding human service contractors accountable for performance. PBC defined performance in terms of outputs (efficiency) and outcomes (effectiveness). Reimbursement was replaced by payments tied to performance. This change was not well understood by human service contractors. With payment mechanisms tied to performance, no performance meant no payment. PBC represented an entirely new approach to accountability in human service contracting that for the first time placed contractors at financial risk for failure to perform.

In Chapter 3, Dimitrijevska-Markovski and Martin discussed various extensions of the PBC approach including: pay-for-success, pay-for-results, outcome funding, results-based funding and social impact bonds (SIBs). These approaches attempted to more clearly define the obligations of human service contractors to focus on performance. SIBs in some ways are similar to PBC and different in other respects (Urban Institute, 2019). PBC focuses on the effects of human service delivery, whereas SIBs focus on promoting evidence-based learning. Contractor risk with PBC is moderate to high; with SIBs contractor risk is low to non-existent.

Collins-Camargo and McBeath (Chapter 4) described two studies (Meezan & McBeath, 2008; Taylor & Shaver, 2010) that demonstrated the effectiveness of PBC in child welfare services. These two studies showed that with PBC, children were more likely to be adopted compared to other service delivery approaches. However, Collins-Camargo and McBeath also expressed concerns about the use of economic incentives and disincentives and their influence on attempts to create productive partnerships between governments and their human service contractors. The Meezan and McBeath study cautioned that PBC had the potential to incentivize the pursuit of more expedient permanency goals rather than the goals most appropriate to the individual child.

Hirschi and Bachman (Chapter 5) cited literature suggesting that performance measures are difficult to define, particularly outcome performance measures. Hirschi and Bachman also cite (Korda & Eldridge, 2011), whose research suggests the absence of consensus about the both design of human service interventions, such as contracting, as well as their effectiveness.

In workforce development (Chapter 6), Barnow and Spaulding pointed out that although competition may improve efficiency in some instances of human service contracting, a lack of evidence exists suggesting that productivity and efficiency has occurred in employment and training services. In addition, Barnow and Spaulding note that little evidence exists to suggest that PBC and other pay-for-performance contracting approaches improve the performance of human service programs. These observations raise fundamental questions about the ability of PBC and pay-for-performance approaches to achieve their intended results.

In summary, human service contracting perhaps can be described best as an on-going attempt to understand and develop the relationships between governments and their contractors. Accountability in human service contracting has evolved from primarily a financial focus to a dual financial/performance focus. Human service contracting today is increasingly characterized by performance approaches that tie contractor compensation to performance. However, issues remain concerning the selection of the best performance measures and what percentage of contractor compensation (all or some proportion) should be tied to performance.

FINANCIAL RISKS FOR NONPROFIT HUMAN SERVICE CONTRACTORS

Nonprofit agencies constitute the majority of human service contractors. The financial risk associated with human service contracting can be a significant problem for small to medium sized nonprofits. Some nonprofits are heavily, if not totally, dependent on the revenues they receive from human service contracts. The change from cost-reimbursement contracting to PBC and other pay-for-performance approaches has significantly increased the financial risk placed on these agencies.

PBC and other pay-for-performance approaches are affected by the appropriateness of the performance measures (particularly outcomes) used in contracts. For some human services (e.g., workforce development), performance measures are more easily developed. For other human services (e.g., child welfare and mental health) developing performance measures is a more difficult task. Cranochan, Samples, Meyers and Austin (2014) found that efforts to develop outcome performance measures can be challenging due to the complexity of human change processes and variation among individual clients. This situation presents challenges and financial risk for small to medium sized nonprofit human service contractors in child welfare and mental health services. If human service contracting continues to increase the use of PBC and other pay-for-performance approaches, then a real possibility that some small to medium sized nonprofit contractors may cease to exist and go out of business.

Governments today are seeking approaches to human service contracting that promote performance while also maintaining the financial viability of their nonprofit contractors. New York City (Chapter 7) utilizes an interesting variation of performance-based contracting (PBC) that attempts to address this challenge. Daniel Symon, the Director of the New York City Office of Contract Services, explains that New York City's health and human service contracts may be structured utilizing a performance-based budget or a line-item budget. In the former, payment for services is based on realizing delivery milestones and outcomes, whereas the latter is based on expenses. In both scenarios, the city attempts to ensures accountability through annual performance evaluations. The vast majority of contracts are paid via line-item reimbursement (Symon, 2019) New York City evaluates the performance of its human service contracts, but uses line-item reimbursement, an approach similar to cost reimbursement, to compensate the vast majority of its contractors.

The New York City approach promotes performance by influencing the behavior of contractors. If contractors perform poorly, they face the possibility of not having their contracts renewed. This approach reduces the financial risk for small to medium sized human service contractors by insuring that their basic service basic costs are covered.

HOW GOVERNMENTS MANAGE THEIR HUMAN SERVICE CONTRACTS

How governments go about managing their human service contracts have also changed over time. Previously, governments had direct relationships with all their human service contractors. There was a one-to-one relationship. Human services contract management today involves complex service delivery networks comprised of multiple contractors. These complex network arrangements are often accomplished using a lead agency (a prime contractor) that subcontracts with several other human service agencies. In some instances, governments have the right to approve the subcontractors. In addition to increasing the complexity of service delivery, these network contract arrangements require more coordination and cooperation (contract management) between governments and their lead contractors and subcontractors. John Donahue, a well-known scholar on government contracting has said that "Governing by network is hard, really hard. There are countless ways it can go wrong." (Goldsmith & Eggers, 2004, p. 22). Goldsmith and Eggers also note that governments are designed to operate within a hierarchical model of government, not a networked model of governance (Goldsmith & Eggers, 2004, p. 22).

The challenges presented by human service network contracting are highlighted in Chapters 8 and 9. In Chapter 8, Vito details how a modified lead agency approach being utilized in Canada for children and youth and mental health services has complicated decision-making authority with implications for the entire human service contract network. In Chapter 9, de Vries identified human service network contracting problems that have occurred in the Netherlands' youth care program when service delivery responsibilities were rearranged, from national and regional governments to local governments. In workforce development (Chapter 6), Barnow and Spaulding note that requirements of the Workforce Innovation and Opportunity Act of 2014 lead to human service network contracting systems where oversight responsibilities were shared by a number of entities including employer-majority boards at the state and local levels and mandatory partners in oversight and service provision.

Network contracting in the human services requires a different approach to government management and oversight. Instead of being responsible for one contract, government contract manager oversees a network involving a number of contractors. Effective network management requires different skills than the older one-to-one contracting relationship. These new skills include communication, coordination and negotiations with all the contractors involved in the network. This is a more sophisticated and nuanced approach to human service contract management.

Monitoring and auditing of human service contracts are also important elements of contract management. However, there is little information about how governments actually monitor and audit their human service contracts.

CHANGES IN THE HUMAN SERVICE CONTRACTING PROCESS—FROM PAPER TOP DIGITAL

The human service contracting process itself is undergoing changes. For most of the examples contained in this book, the steps in the human service contract process were accomplished with paper. These steps included using paper to: notice of the availability of human service contracting opportunities, submit responses to requests for proposals (RFPs) and create standard forms contracts and financial records. This paper system required human service contractors to submit duplicate copies of documents for each individual procurement. The paper process was burdensome, lacked transparency and discouraged some small to medium sized nonprofits from participating causing a reduction in competition.

The change from paper to electronic systems is an area where many governments have made significant progress. Governments have developed electronic systems, which provide real time lists of available human service contract opportunities. Interested potential contractors can submit procurement documents electronically. Contractor reimbursement and payments can also be tracked electronically.

THE FUTURE OF HUMAN SERVICE CONTRACTING

In the future, human services contracting will be characterized by continued growth, the need for improved government/contractor relationships, the increased use of technology and more research into best practices.

Continued Growth

Human services contracting will continue to grow as it is now an integral part of the way governments delivers human services. The growth of human service contracting will also be affected by expanding human service needs. As new human service needs are identified, governments will again be confronted with the same decisions they have faced over the last 50 years, should the service be provided in house or contracted?

Several factors mitigate against a decline in human service contracting. Governments are dependent on their human service contractors; government simply cannot meet their human service delivery responsibilities today without their cadre of contractors. Nonprofit human service contractors have coalesced and now represent important stakeholders in the planning and delivery of human services. Governments are unlikely to take the steps required (more government workers, increased costs and organizational structure changes) to assume more direct human service delivery responsibilities.

Government and Contractor Relationships

As important and consequential issue for the success and effectiveness of human service contracting in the future will be the types of relationships forged between governments and contractors. In the future, individual governments will be faced a clear choice: do they want to promote short-term competition between contractors or promote long-term partnership relationships? How governments answer this fundamental question may ultimately determine the efficiency and effectiveness of their human service contracting systems.

Technology

Additional opportunities will exist for the use of technology in human service contracting. The increased use of technology holds the potential to reduce contracting timeframes, increase efficiency and improve data reliability. The increased use of technology may also lead to more transparency in human services contracting.

Research

Accepting the premise that human service contracting is here to stay, more research is needed on best practice methods of managing this mode of service delivery. More research is needed to better understand human service contracting in general and which contracting approaches (e.g., PBC, pay-for-success, etc.) are most successful in achieving performance outcomes.

More research is also needed on the impact of various compensation approaches (cost reimbursement, PBC and pay-for-performance). How do these different compensation approaches affect human service contractors? Do they promote or retard the achievement of human service contracting outcomes? Additional research into human service contracting may also shed light on the overall efficiency and effectiveness of human service programs.

REFERENCES

The City of New York Adopted Budget Fiscal Year. (2018). Retrieved from https://www1.nyc.gov/assets/omb/downloads/pdf/erc6-17.pdf

City of New York, NYC Nonprofits, "Nonprofit Resiliency Committee," 2017, 2018, 2019. Retrieved from https://www1.nyc.gov/site/nonprofits/funded-providers/nonprofit-resiliency-committee.page

The Urban Institute (2015). *Nonprofit-government contract and grants: Findings from the 2013 national survey.* Washington, DC: Author. Retrieved from https://www.urban.org/sites/default/files/publication/24231/412962-Nonprofit-Government-Contracts-and-Grants-Findings-from-the-National-Survey.PDF.

Congress of the United States, Congressional Budget Office, Letter to the Honorable Chris Van Hollen, Federal Contracts and the Contracted Workforce. (2015, March). Retrieved from www.cbo.gov/sites/default/files/114th-congress-2015-2016/reports/49931-FederalContracts.pdf and The White House, Office of Management and Budget Historical Tables, Table 14.2. www.whitehouse.gov/omb/historical-tables/

Cranochan, S., Samples, M., Meyers, M., & Austin, M. J. (2014). Performance measurement challenges in nonprofit human services agencies. *Nonprofit and Voluntary Sector Quarterly*, *43*(6), 1014–1032.

Ginter, D. T. (2015). *Contracting in state and local governments, chapter in government contracting* (R. A. Shick, Ed.). London: Routledge.
Goldsmith, S., & William, E. (2004). *Government by network: The new shape of the public sector* (p. 22). Brookings Institution Press.
Korda, H., & Eldridge, G. N. (2011). How can we bend the cost curve? Payment incentives and integrated care delivery: Levers for health system reform and cost containment. *Inquiry*, *48*, 277–287.
Meezan, W., & McBeath, B. (2008). Market-based disparities in foster care outcomes. *Children and Youth Services Review*, *30*(4), 388–406.
New York State Comptroller Thomas P. DiNapoli, *Prompt Contracting Annual Report*, 2011, 2015.
New York City Comptroller Scott M. Stringer. (2018, May). *Running late: An analysis of NYC agency contracts*.
New York City Mayors Office of Contract Services. Retrieved from https://www1.nyc.gov/site/mocs/reporting/citywide-indicators/procurement-by-industry.page
Osborne, D., & Gaebler, T. (1993). *Reinventing government: How the entrepreneurial spirit is transforming the public sector*. New York: Addison-Wesley Publishers.
Samar Khurshid, *Gotham Gazette*, Citizens Union Foundation, 2016, 2017.
Symon, D. (2019, June 13). New York City mayor's office of contract services, Director, personal communication (email).
Taylor, K., & Shaver, M. (2010). Performance based contracting: Aligning incentives with outcomes to produce results. In M. Testa & J. Poertner (Eds.), *Accountability: Using evidence to guide and improve child welfare policy*. Oxford: Oxford University Press.
Urban Institute. (2019). *Incentivizing results: Contracting for outcomes in social service delivery*. Washington, DC: Urban Institute. Retrieved from www.urban.org/sites/default/files/publication/100450/incentivizing_results_contracting_for_outcomes_in_social_service_delivery_0.pdf

About the Editors and Contributors

Sara S. Bachman, Ph.D., is Dean of the School of Social Policy and Practice at the University of Pennsylvania. Formerly, she was the Paul Farmer Professor at the Boston University School of Social Work; Research Professor in the Department of Health Law, Policy and Management at the Boston University School of Public Health; and Director of the Boston University School of Social Work's Center for Innovation in Social Work & Health. Dr. Bachman is an expert in health care financing and organization, focusing on alternative payment strategies. She has more than 20 years of experience with health policy research and program evaluation, especially in the areas of health care finance, health reform, social work, and state health policy for individuals with disabilities or complex health and social conditions, including children with special health care needs. She has published on state approaches to the issue of contracting for mental health services. Dr. Bachman received her MS in Epidemiology from the University of Massachusetts School of Public Health, and her Ph.D. in Health Policy from the Florence Heller School at Brandeis University where she was a Pew Health Policy Fellow.

Burt S. Barnow, Ph.D., is the Amsterdam Professor of Public Service and Economics at The George Washington University. Prior to joining George Washington University, Dr. Barnow was Associate Director for Research at Johns Hopkins University's Institute for Policy Studies, where he worked for 18 years. Prior to that, he worked for eight years at the Lewin Group and nearly nine years at the U.S. Department of Labor, including four years as Director of the Office of Research and Evaluation in the Employment and Training Administration (ETA), a Senior Executive Service (SES) position. He has conducted many studies of Department of Labor programs, including studies of how the programs are being implemented and how effective they have been. He is currently co-principal investigator of the study of performance measures for employer services under the Workforce Innovation and Opportunity Act, director of the outcome study for the American Apprenticeship Initiative, and a senior researcher on the evaluation of the Reemployment and Eligibility Assessment evaluation. He has served on 11 National Academy of Sciences committees and one NAS board, and he is currently Consulting Editor for *Evaluation Review* and Methods Section Editor for the *Journal of Policy Analysis and Management*. Dr. Barnow is an elected member of the National Academy of Social Insurance and an elected fellow of the National Academy of Public

Administration. Dr. Barnow received a B.S. in Economics from Massachusetts Institute of Technology and M.S. and Ph.D. degrees in Economics from the University of Wisconsin at Madison.

Crystal Collins-Camargo MSW, Ph.D. is a professor and Associate Dean for Research at the University of Louisville Kent School of Social Work, where she teaches macro theory in the doctoral program. Her research focuses primarily on organizational interventions to promote system improvement in child welfare. This includes interorganizational dynamics and processes such as public-private contracting, collaboration and partnership; organizational supports for evidence-informed practice and data-informed decision-making; trauma-informed organizational initiatives, including standardized universal screening and assessment for trauma and behavioral health needs; and, intersystem integration to promote positive child and family outcomes. She directed the National Quality Improvement Center on the Privatization of Child Welfare Services, a Children's Bureau-funded initiative. The Quality Improvement Center conducted multisite research on public-private partnership and the use of performance-based contracting and quality improvement processes to promote child welfare outcomes. She also directed the Southern Regional Quality Improvement Center on Child Protection, which studied the implementation of clinical supervision in four state child welfare systems. She has a Master's degree and Ph.D. from the University of Kentucky College of Social Work.

M. S. de Vries Since 2012, Marsha de Vries has worked as a freelance lecturer and researcher for local governments and human service organizations. She graduated in Public Administration at the University of Twente (MSc, 1998) and received her doctorate from the same university in 2001. Until 2007, she subsequently worked as a senior researcher for IPIT Institute for Social Safety Studies and for the Dutch National Crime Squad. Marsha was an assistant professor in Public Administration at the Behavioral, Management and Social Sciences Department of the University of Twente from 2007 until 2012. From 2014 until 2018, Marsha worked as an associate professor at Windesheim University of Applied Sciences in the Netherlands, where she studied, wrote and lectured on the transition and transformation of youth care in the Netherlands. Her current research interests include transformation in leadership, performance management and interorganizational cooperation in the social domain.

Tamara Dimitrijevska-Markoski is an assistant professor of public administration in the Department of Political Science and Public Administration at Mississippi State University. She earned her Ph.D. in Public Affairs at the University of Central Florida where she was a recipient of the Graduate Dean's Fellowship. Her research focuses on performance measurement and management issues, local governments and pay-for-performance contracting. She authored several peer-review academic articles, policy briefs and book chapters. She has presented at a number of international and national conferences, including the American Society for Public Administration (ASPA), Association for Public Policy Analysis and Management (APPAM) and Public Management Research Conference (PMRC). Currently, Dr. Dimitrijevska-Markoski is collaborating with the Stennis Institute of Government on a project that focuses on the state of strategic planning and performance measurement and management among municipalities in Mississippi.

Melissa Hirschi, Ph.D., LCSW, is an assistant professor at the School of Social Work at the University of Memphis. Her research focuses on the intersection of first responders and individuals living with mental illness, including their role as frontline mental health workers. She is also interested in better understanding power, including the role of power in racism, oppression and stigma. In addition, she does work with individuals living with HIV and children with special health care needs, focusing on improving access, health outcomes and social justice for these individuals. Dr. Hirschi is also very interested in integrated health care and is doing work with the Wellness & Stress Clinic in Memphis, Tennessee, with The Healing Center Baptist Church. She has extensive practice experience working with members of disadvantaged and marginalized communities, such as formerly homeless women and as a clinical caseworker with the Division of Health and Family Services in Utah. She received her MSW from Boston University in 2007 and her joint sociology and social work Ph.D. from Boston University in 2017.

James A. (Jack) Krauskopf came to Baruch College (City University of New York) in 2004. He has been Director, Center for Nonprofit Strategy and Management, and Distinguished Lecturer in the Austin W. Marxe School of Public and International Affairs. As Chief Program Officer of the 9/11 United Services Group, he coordinated social services organizations assisting people affected by the September 11 World Trade Center attack. He was Commissioner of the New York City Human Resources Administration under Mayor Ed Koch. His other government positions were as Deputy Secretary of Wisconsin's Department of Health and Social Services, head of Cleveland's Department of Human Resources and Economic Development under Mayor Carl Stokes, and Director of the Rutgers University's Office of Newark Studies to assist Mayor Kenneth Gibson. In academic administration, he was Senior Vice President for Administration and Finance at The New School (formerly New School for Social Research) and Dean of the Robert J. Milano Graduate School of Management and Urban Policy. He has taught urban policy, human services, emergency management and other graduate and undergraduate courses at Baruch, The New School, Rutgers, Princeton and the University of Wisconsin. He was President of the Corporation for Supportive Housing, and was Senior Fellow at the Aspen Institute in New York. He is on boards of the Center for Urban Community Services, United Neighborhood Houses, Citizens' Committee for Children, Brotherhood-SisterSol and Cultural Institutions Retirement System. His degrees include a B.A. in Government, Harvard, and Master in Public Affairs, Woodrow Wilson School of Public and International Affairs, Princeton.

Lawrence L. Martin (Ph.D., MSW, MBA) is Professor of Public Affairs at the University of Central Florida in Orlando. Dr. Martin also taught at the Columbia University School of Social Work (New York City) where he directed the specialization in social work administration. He has published 42 books and major monographs and more than 100 professional articles and book chapters. His areas of expertise include social work administration; state and local government, government contracting and public-private partnerships. His works have been translated and reprinted in Chinese, French, Korean, Mongolian, Portuguese and Russian. Dr. Martin has consulted with and provided training to numerous government and nonprofit organizations both domestically and internationally.

Bowen McBeath is a professor in the School of Social Work and Hatfield School of Government Division of Public Administration at Portland State University. He has held scientific appointments and visiting professorships with the University of California-Berkeley, the Oregon Social Learning Center and Beijing Normal University. He received his MSW and Ph.D. in Social Work and Political Science from the University of Michigan. Dr. McBeath is broadly interested in three areas of inquiry: the institutional and organizational context of human service delivery, human service model development and prevention science, and evidence-informed organizational and management practice. Current research interests concern the organization and financing of human services, including performance-based contracting and relational contracting; organizational and managerial factors informing work practices and outcomes; and the development of learning organizational cultures promoting innovative, community-based and service user-centered care. He is also involved in NIH-funded and W.T. Grant Foundation-funded intervention studies evaluating sibling, parent and peer relationship skill development for at-risk populations. A Fellow of the Society for Social Work and Research, Dr. McBeath has served the organization in many leadership positions. He has received national awards and honors for his scholarship and research; serves on the editorial boards of numerous social work research journals; and consults with national, state, and local human service organizations. He is the editor in chief of the journal *Human Service Organizations: Management, Leadership, and Governance*.

Robert A. Shick, Ph.D., is an adjunct assistant professor at John Jay College for Criminal Justice and an affiliated faculty member at Rutgers-Newark School of Public Affairs and Administration (SPAA). He was formerly on the faculty of SPAA and Long Island University. At SPAA, Dr. Shick was the Director of the Executive Master in Public Administration Program and pursued academic partnerships with institutions in the Republic of Korea and China. Dr. Shick is the editor of *Government Contracting*, Routledge. He has given numerous presentations at conferences in the U.S. and other countries. Dr. Shick has extensive experience in the public sector as a senior administrator in New York City government, working in contracting-out of government services, financial and budget management, policy analysis, and intergovernmental and community relations. His research is in the contracting-out of government services and nonprofit management. Dr. Shick served on the editorial board of the *Journal for Health and Human Services Administration* for 15 years, until December 31, 2018. He is active in the American Society for Public Administration, being an officer in the International Chapter, the Section on Procurement and Contract Management, and the Section on

Public Management Practice. Dr. Shick received a B.S. in Economics from The City College of New York, an M.A. in Economics from Indiana University, and a Ph.D. in Public Administration from New York University.

Shayne Spaulding is a senior fellow in the Income and Benefits Policy Center at the Urban Institute, where her work focuses on the evaluation of workforce development and postsecondary education programs. She has spent more than 20 years in the workforce development field as an evaluator, technical assistance provider and program manager. Her research has examined the public workforce system; community college innovations; employer engagement in workforce programs; services to parents, youth, noncustodial fathers, individuals with criminal records, performance measurement in workforce programs; and other topics. Ms. Spaulding co-leads several Urban Institute projects and initiatives, including Building America's Workforce, which brings together workforce development research from across the Urban Institute; Bridging the Gap, which centers on the intersection of child care and workforce development for low-income parents; and the U.S. Department of Labor's Analysis of Employer Performance Measurement Approaches, for which she serves as principal investigator and project director. Before joining Urban, Ms. Spaulding was the university director of Workforce Development for the City University of New York (CUNY), the nation's largest public urban university system, where she oversaw workforce and continuing education programs in CUNY's 24 colleges and professional schools. From 2001 to 2009, she worked for Public/Private Ventures as a researcher and technical assistance provider. Ms. Spaulding holds a Master's of Arts degree in Public Policy from Johns Hopkins University and Bachelor of Arts degree in American Government from Wesleyan University. She resides in Swampscott, Massachusetts, with her husband Josh and sons Wiley and Kieran.

Rosemary Vito, Ph.D., MSW, RSW, is an assistant professor in the School of Social Work, King's University College, London, Ontario, Canada. Her teaching and research interests include participatory leadership and organizational culture and change in human service organizations, reflective supervision, mental health policy and practice, and supervision of field practice. Her multiple case study dissertation research focused on leadership practice and organizational culture during service system transformation in children's mental health and child welfare agencies. Rosemary has more than 20 years of social work experience in community/children's mental health services, including direct practice, clinical supervision, administration and leadership, service development, external consultation, community development, diversity initiatives and board membership. Her extensive experience informs her teaching and research interests.

Index

Page numbers in *italics* indicate figures and in **bold** indicate tables on the corresponding pages.

Index

Page numbers in *italics* indicate figures and in **bold** indicate tables on the corresponding pages.